THE EVOLUTION OF THE
ENGLISH HYMN

THE ALLELUIA RELIEF
Luca Della Robbia

THE EVOLUTION OF
THE ENGLISH HYMN

AN HISTORICAL SURVEY OF THE ORIGINS
AND DEVELOPMENT OF THE HYMNS
OF THE CHRISTIAN CHURCH

BY

FREDERICK JOHN GILLMAN

WITH A FOREWORD
BY
Sir H. WALFORD DAVIES

ILLUSTRATED

NEW YORK

THE MACMILLAN COMPANY

1927

All rights reserved

Let everything that hath breath praise the Lord.
Praise ye the Lord.

PSALM CL. 6

FOREWORD

I COUNT it a joy to be asked to write a Foreword for such a book as this, and I also count it a privilege to be associated with our author. For he is our proper and, as I believe, our most ready and most genial companion for such a journey through Hymnody as we must take with him if we read this book.

First, gentle reader, I venture to suggest that you should read the bare titles of the chapters slowly through, giving a thought to each—just as you might stand on an eminence in the centre of England and gaze upon the "coloured counties" one by one, giving a thought to each of them. Then plunge into your journey with Mr. Gillman. Be, as he is, both careful student and care-free enthusiast. Hold the golden thread that he holds. Keep in hand the purpose and motive of Hymnody. For in it we may surely expect that music works, not so much as an adornment of life; not as a mere friendly aid to worship, or a disposing influence to prepare us for worship; but as a vehicle for the very spirit of worship itself. Melody is in any case the language of a mind that is both orderly and at liberty. In Hymnody it is the actual carrier of wonderment and devotion. Beauty and fitness together make it a most wholesome means to this glorious end.

WALFORD DAVIES.

PREFACE

THE theme upon which I have essayed to write seems to me to be of primary importance to the Christian Church. Next only to the Bible, the Hymnody of Christendom is probably the most influential medium of religious culture we possess. In public worship it directly affects millions of people every week ; awakening, educating, and sustaining their spiritual life, and guiding them, quite as effectually as sermon or prayer, to an understanding of Christian truth ; whilst its influence upon the individuals who turn to it in privacy for the nurture of their inner life is no less pronounced.

The literary and musical critics are inclined to scoff at the subject, and to conclude that the artistic content of our hymnals is not worthy of notice ; so they turn aside to bestow their attention on folk-songs, old ballads, Christmas carols and negro " spirituals " ; not always mindful of the incomparably greater part which the simple hymn and hymn tune have played in the history of the race.

Leaders of religious thought, and particularly clergymen and ministers upon whom the responsibility for the conduct of public worship rests, might be supposed to make a serious study of the contents of their hymn books, but experience teaches me that this is frequently not the case.

Although a few good books and pamphlets dealing with hymnology, alike from the historical, doctrinal and musical standpoint, are to be found among current literature, yet I have been forced to the conclusion that the need has by no means been fully met, and that a more widespread effort is called for to provoke thought upon a subject which so closely concerns the whole theory and practice of worship. I suggest that the time is overripe for the regular historical and critical study of Christian hymnody in our theological colleges (as is sometimes done in America), and by all who are concerned for the right ordering of religious thought and emotion.

I do not possess the necessary qualifications to write for the learned, nor is there any need to do so, for they already know the facts; but I hope my story will enlist the interest of the ordinary reader and provoke in his mind a desire to know more; and I shall indeed be thankful if in any degree this books helps to impart a deeper spirit of reverence to the worship-song of our time.

I gratefully acknowledge my indebtedness to many who have assisted me in my delightful task; nor can I forget the special debt I owe, in common with all students of hymnology, to the patient investigators who are no longer here among us, but who, being dead, yet speak to us through their writings. Dr. Julian's *Dictionary of Hymnology* has been my indispensable companion, and I have valued the opportunity, kindly accorded me by the Corporation of the Church House, to consult his comprehensive Library, now housed at Westminster. The Rev. A. H. Walker has also kindly permitted me to consult the Library of Hymnology at the Central Hall, Manchester. The list of other authorities that I have drawn upon is far too long to be enumerated here, but some I have been able to acknowledge in the footnotes that follow. Conspicuously valuable has been Dr. Benson's admirable treatise on *The English Hymn*. It was written for the American public, but is as indispensable as Julian to the English student.

I could not have ventured upon my researches but for the honour extended me by the Woodbrooke Council in awarding me an Edward Cadbury Research Fellowship. During my residence at Woodbrooke I have enjoyed the leisure and the opportunity to study and collate the necessary information; and Mr. H. G. Wood, Mr. W. E. Wilson and other members of the Staff of the Selly Oak Colleges have greatly helped me by their sympathy, by reading my manuscript, and in many other ways. My friends Mr. Norman Penney, the Rev. Henry

Bett, and Mr. J. T. Lightwood have also read the manuscripts respectively of Chapters X, XII and XV.

A word must be said about the title. My story is international in its compass, but its aim has been to show how the hymns of many lands and many ages have contributed to the treasury of worship-song enshrined in our present-day English hymnals.

Some readers may think that an undue amount of space has been devoted (in Chapter X) to the Society of Friends, but I am convinced that important issues are involved in the attitude of the Society to public worship, which deserve earnest consideration by all who are concerned for the future of the religious life of this country. The almost complete absence of any record of Quaker hymnody in Julian also makes it seem desirable to put some of the facts on record here.

With Robert Louis Stevenson, I confess " I have a small idea of the degree of accuracy possible to man, and I feel sure these studies teem with error." I have done my best to be accurate, and where I have failed I ask pardon.

Whate'er the end, this thought will joy afford,
My lips have sung the praises of my Lord.

FREDERICK J. GILLMAN.

ACKNOWLEDGMENTS

I HAVE gratefully to thank the following Authors, Translators, Publishers, and other copyright-holders for kind permission to include reprints from their works :—

Miss Eleanor J. Alexander for Mrs. Alexander's hymn, "On the dark hill's western side "; The Association for Promoting Christian Knowledge, Dublin, for Mrs. Alexander's translation of "St. Patrick's Breastplate "; Mrs. Theodore Beck for her translations from Jacopone da Todi ; Mr. Robert Bridges for two hymns ; Mrs. Grace Chatfield for the hymn " Lord Jesus, think on me," by the late Mr. A. W. Chatfield ; Messrs. J. M. Dent & Sons, Ltd., for translations by Dr. D. Martin Pope of Prudentius's verses, and for the lines from Countess Cesaresco's *Study of Folk Songs* ; Messrs. J. M. Dent & Sons, Ltd., and the Executors of the late Mr. Wm. Canton, for the lines from *The Invisible Playmate* ; The Publishers of *The Friends' Quarterly Examiner* for permission to reprint parts of my article on " Christmas Carols "; Dr. J. Rendel Harris for his translation and metrical paraphrase of the 26th *Ode of Solomon* ; The Industrial Christian Fellowship for the Rev. G. A. Studdert-Kennedy's hymn ; Messrs. Longmans, Green & Co., Ltd., for selections from Miss Winkworth's *Lyra Germanica* and from J. H. Newman's *Lyra Apostolica* ; Mr. Wilfrid Meynell for the lines from Francis Thompson ; Mr. Lionel Moorsom for selections from the late Dr. R. M. Moorsom's *Renderings of Church Hymns* ; Mr. John Murray for Mr. W. A. Phillips's two translations from Walter Von der Wogelweide ; The National Adult School Union for permission to reprint parts of my pamphlet, *The Music of Fellowship* ; Messrs. Jas. Nisbet & Co., Ltd., for Mrs. Bevan's translation from Tauler, and for various quotations from Mrs. Rundle-Charles's *Voice of Christian Life in Song* ; Messrs. Oliphants, Ltd., for two selections from Dr. Brownlie's *Hymns of the Greek Church* ; The Oxford University Press for " C. B.'s " translation of the hymn " Creator of the earth and sky," and for the verse by Mr. Laurence Housman, " To George our Saint," Nos. 49 and 219 in *The English Hymnal* ; The Oxford University Press and Mr. Laurence Housman for the hymn " The Maker of the Sun and Moon," from *Songs of Praise* ; Mr. J. H. Pafford, for his adaptation of an early English Marian poem ; Messrs. Sampson Low, Marston & Co., Ltd., for C. J. Abbey's rendering of the thirteenth-century poem, " Summer is

Come " ; The Society for Promoting Christian Knowledge, London, for two poems by Miss Rossetti ; The Rev. Geo. Ratcliffe Woodward, M.A., Mus.Doc., Editor of the *Cowley Carol Book*, *Songs of Syon*, etc., for his verses " I know a Rose," and for his translation of Gerhardt's " Nun ruhen alle Wälder " (" Now Woods and Wolds are sleeping "), from *Songs of Syon*. The rhythmic passages from the Sermon on the Mount are from Dr. Briggs's articles in *The Expository Times*, Vols. 8 and 9, published by Messrs. T. & T. Clarke.

Great, too, is my debt—our common debt—to the many singers no longer with us in the flesh, but whose songs we may still count among our most precious spiritual treasures.

I am especially grateful to my friend Sir H. Walford Davies for his valuable Introductory words.

The photograph of Calvin's Auditoire has most kindly been specially taken for me by Mr. August Hirsiger of Geneva ; Dr. Julian's portrait is reproduced from that by W. Rosemount in the Church House, Westminster, through the courtesy of Sir Lewis T. Dibdin ; Father Faber's portrait is inserted by kind permission of the Oratorians, The Oratory, South Kensington.

CONTENTS

ILLUSTRATIONS

B

THE EVOLUTION OF
THE ENGLISH HYMN

CHAPTER I

MUSIC AND RELIGION

BEAUTY is a form of Divine speech : it reveals God to man.
Writing amid the cloudless peace of the snows of Chamonix,
John Ruskin, in a memorable passage, declared

> that the knowledge of what is beautiful leads on, and is
> the first step, to the knowledge of the things that are
> lovely and of good report ; and that the laws, the life, and
> the joy of beauty in the material world of God, are as
> eternal and sacred parts of His creation as, in the world
> of spirits, virtue ; and in the world of angels, praise.[1]

Nor is God seen alone in the beauty of the natural world,
in cloud and mountain, snow and vapour, green forest and
spacious sea. Every artist in words or colour or sound reveals
something of His wisdom and power. The preacher and the
theologian may reveal Him, too, though sometimes they
obscure and pervert His likeness. His ministers are not a
close corporation of ordained clergy. Raphael is amongst
them, and Millet and Burne-Jones. Not David only, but
Palestrina and Beethoven and Elgar sound His praises. Alike
every builder of our stately cathedrals, and every humble
workman who with heart and hand creates as best he can the
meanest vessel that ministers to man's daily needs, are His
artists and fellow-workmen.

Among the many creative artists whose work bears the
marks of the Divine credentials, the poet and the musician

[1] The Epilogue, *Modern Painters*.

take high place. All great literature is essentially religious ; that is to say, it is concerned not so much with the imparting of facts as with the education of the spirit. It includes within its ambit such transcendental qualities as imagination, awe, sympathy, aspiration, passion, love ; its final purpose is the complete development of man's powers of spiritual discernment. Especially does poetry serve such high ends. Poetry " troubles the waters of the spirit." It invites us to the throne of the heavenly grace. Its province is to appeal to those basal instincts of our being which we feel to be essential to our truest life. " Good poetry," Matthew Arnold wrote in his 1880 Report on Elementary Schools, " does undoubtedly tend to form the soul and character ; it tends to beget a love of beauty and of truth in alliance together ; it suggests, however indirectly, high and noble principles of action, and it inspires the emotion so helpful in making principles operative."

. There are some " practical " people who look with impatience upon the study of poetry in our schools, unless it is strictly related to industry. There is no time, they say, in this workaday world to wander off into these fairy-lands. But there is a spirit within man which tells him that he does not live by bread alone. The word as well as the loaf is his by natural right. And so instinctively he throws open mind and heart in order that the spirit of beauty, which is the spirit of God, may come down upon him—

> As dew in Aprille
> That falleth on the grass.[1]

Side by side with the poet stands the musician. These two are heavenly twins, and for centuries they have been found wandering about the world together. The one sister comes to the other and says, " Take my gift of sound and use it to carry your words to the heart of men." Even alone music can speak with power to our deeper natures. Some of

---

[1] For a helpful treatment of this subject see *The Teaching of English in England* : a Report by a Departmental Committee of the Board of Education, 1921.

Mendelssohn's Songs are " without words," and yet there is no sense of incompleteness in them. Such music, the literature of sound, goes beyond speech and is the language of feeling. That is why men have so highly exalted it.

> When Jubal struck the corded shell,
> His listening brethren stood around,
>   And, wondering, on their faces fell
> To worship that celestial sound :
> Less than a god they thought there could not dwell
>   Within the hollow of that shell,
>   That spoke so sweetly and so well.
> *What passion cannot music raise and quell ?*

Dryden, in that closing line, hints at both the positive and negative powers of music in its relation to emotion. It can excite deep feelings : it can also guide and control them. It can minister to anger, lust and pride ; and it can also soothe and purify and awaken a sense of beauty, until an inner melody responds to the outward one. It is a suggestive fact that both in times of joy and of sorrow music brings relief. It has dark tones and light ones. When a child is happy, he sings, and his song is infectious. How joyously it is caught up by the mother ; love answering to love, as voice to voice. The world is positively a happier place because birds and children sing. Who can listen without a thrill of joy as the lark raises its morning Te Deum high in the blue dome of Nature's great cathedral ?

In times of sorrow, too, men find solace in song. That simple fact is deeply engraven on the pages of history.

Consider the relation of music to health. Here we enter upon an uncharted sea, still awaiting patient exploration. Without enlarging upon such interesting topics as the use by the ancients of musical incantations to combat the diseases of animals and men, we need only think of the introduction of " wireless " music into hospitals, to realize that the whole subject calls for scientific thought. It may be that we are on the eve of important discoveries in this field of research.

The theory, advanced with much force by Dr. Agnes Saville,[1] Dr. C. W. Saleeby and others, is that music affects the subconscious self through the medium of the nervous system, and that rhythm and harmony and discord produce actual physical effects. Experiments made in mental hospitals seem to show that certain types of music can induce sleep and dull the perception of pain and fatigue and anxiety. Burney, a hundred and fifty years ago, quoted a statement of a doctor who testified to its value in cases of sciatica, and who believed not only that it distracted attention from the pain, but actually " occasioned vibrations of the nerves " which " gave motion to the humours and removed the obstructions which occasioned the disorder." Ages before Burney, when Saul was possessed of an evil spirit, " David took an harp, and played with his hand ; and so Saul was refreshed, and was well, and the evil spirit departed from him." Even animals are well known to yield to music's spell. A dog howling beside a piano is a familiar domestic experience. One thinks of Orpheus charming ferocious beasts, and of the Hebridean seals, that, according to Mrs. Kennedy Fraser, echo back the folk-songs of the fisher-folk. History and mythology can produce you quite an array of pied pipers, besides the hero of Hamelin's town in Brunswick on the Weser.

Some recent educationists are suggesting that music might be much more widely used in the schoolroom to subdue the disorder that comes from fatigue. Where admonition and scolding merely aggravate the teacher's difficulties, music, it is urged, if of the right kind, will relieve the over-tension which weariness creates.[2] So sailors sing their jolly chanties to lighten their work, and every soldier knows that a regimental band is worth an extra mile or two in a day's march.

On the other hand, music may prove positively injurious to health. Loud percussion sounds, or irritating " jazz " music, may set the nerves on edge and do the patient actual harm.

[1] See her *Music, Health and Character.*
[2] O'Shea's *Dynamic Factor in Education.*

The very terms used in music suggest its power to create moods. Certain chords, or sequences of chords, induce their corresponding mental states : " allegro " stands for cheerfulness, " languido " for weariness, " dolente " for sorrow, " vivace " for liveliness, and so forth. Thus we see the musician side by side with the doctor and the psychologist ministering to the minds and bodies of men, if haply they can win for them that richest of all gifts, *mens sana in corpore sano*.

Sensitiveness to emotion is most acute in youth, before the senses grow dull and

> Shades of the prison house begin to close
> Upon the growing boy.

Hence the importance of music in education—an importance which the Greeks fully realized. Did not Plato declare that it makes the soul graceful ? And are not many of the old gods and goddesses—Orpheus and Apollo, Olympus and Pan and the Sirens—still potent names in the musical world ? And did not the Greeks restrict the use of the word " music " (a word which has the same root as " the Muses ") to those sounds that " educate the soul in virtue " ?

In our own land, great thinkers like Milton and Ruskin have advocated the fuller use of music in schools. In a well-known passage in his tract *Of Education*, Milton says that before meat boy scholars are to be—

> recreating and composing their travailed spirits with the solemn and divine harmonies of music heard or learnt ; either while the skilful organist plies his grave and fancied descant, in lofty fugues, or the whole Symphony with artful and unimaginable touches adorn and grace the well-studied chords of some choice composer, sometimes the lute, or soft organ stop waiting on elegant voices, either to religious, martial, or civil ditties ; which, if wise men and prophets be not extremely out, have a great power over dispositions and manners, to smooth and make them gentle from rustick harshness and distemper'd passions.

Happily, successive Ministers of Education within recent years have done something to encourage music teaching in schools, and considerable advance has taken place in certain places. But much awaits to be done before music takes its rightful place in our school curricula. Can we not at least recognize that the power to appreciate a Beethoven Sonata is quite as necessary to our youth as the capacity to name the capitals of the English counties and the dates of great battles ?

But the emotional life, strongest no doubt in youth, remains a life-long element of personality, and especially of the religious personality. Feeling is not merely " an integral part of religious experience " : it is central, vital, its inmost core. William James speaks of it as " the deeper source of religion," and says that philosophical and theological formulas come below it in importance. It is the dynamic factor in the religious life. When it is absent, religion degenerates into mere formalism or barren intellectualism. The elusiveness of music thus makes it in a special sense the natural channel for the expression of religious emotion. Its very indefiniteness establishes its place in worship. It expresses, in a degree more satisfying than its sister-arts of painting and sculpture, man's craving for the unknown. It can convey a sense of awe and devotion. Speech breaks down under the stress of intense spiritual experience ; the very springs and sources of the soul's life, craving for expression and unable to find it in words, discover in music a truly liberating force.

And there is yet another debt which religion owes to music. It is independent of sects and creeds and tongues. The historic Christian creeds, intended in their inception " to remove all grounds of difference and to wind up by laws of peace every link of controversy," [1] have, as a matter of history, placed stumbling-blocks in the way of the very cause they were meant to serve. They are divisive, but music is unifying. Like the firmament, in declaring the glory of God, its voice

---

[1] The quotation is from the Emperor Constantine's speech at the opening of the Council of Nicæa. See Stanley's *Eastern Church*, Lecture IV.

sounds on through every land, and to the ends of the world, its speech.[1] It is true that we sometimes speak of " Catholic music " and " Nonconformist music," but these are unreal distinctions. Good music belongs to no one Church, but to all. It is a universal language. And for that reason it is preeminently the people's art—an art, too, of which the people are " not hearers only, but doers also." For few can become painters or sculptors or architects, while nearly all can sing.

It is therefore in accordance with the fitness of things that our greatest musical compositions are religious. " The art as we know it spent a serene and prosperous childhood in the care of the Church. It was virtuously and Christianly brought up." [2] So much is this the case, indeed, that the student of Church history is constantly confronted with the fact that Christianity marches to music, and nearly every great advance has been accompanied by a new outburst of song. It has been truly remarked that it may be possible to study religion in the abstract without allowing a place for music, but historically no such task can be achieved.

The close connection, then, between religion on the one hand and poetry and music on the other, is determined for us in the natural order of things. The three are found next to each other in Nature's table of consanguinity.

Dr. Johnson held the theory that devotion cannot be aided by poetry. The ideas of Christian theology, he held, are too majestic for such ornamentation. To the worshipper, he said, versification is worse than a superfluity ; and faith has no need to be invested by fancy with such decorations ; " repentance, trembling in the presence of the Judge, is not at leisure for cadences." But history contradicts the Doctor. That poetry and music can minister, and through many generations have ministered, to worship, is a fact too deeply embedded in history to be open to dispute.[3]

[1] Wellhausen's *Book of Psalms*, translated by H. H. Furness.
[2] Sir Henry Walford Davies's *Music and Christian Worship*.
[3] For an interesting treatment of this subject see " The Archbishops' Committee of Enquiry's Report on the Worship of the Church."

" But," the reader will be asking, " what has all this to do with the theme of this book ?. Surely you do not suggest that either music or poetry are to be looked for inside the covers of a modern hymnal ? " Such criticism, in some degree justifiable, is widely popular to-day. The case may perhaps be summed up in the words of a recent writer (who, however, it must be added, was not referring particularly to hymnology) : " The artist's function has little or nothing to do with the intellect, for it presents not ideas but images, that produce in us a definite state of feeling, but have no meaning that can be expressed in intellectual conceptions." [1]

If that definition is true, it is obvious that the artist, as such, is out of place in the realm of hymnody. He will avoid it, as a rich man avoids his poor relations. But generalizations of this kind are not always helpful. It may at once be conceded that our hymn books yield scarcely any literary or musical masterpieces. They do here and there introduce us to the art both of the poet and the musician in miniature form, and in most gracious and simple garb ; and for good or ill such poetry and music as are found there affect a larger number of people, and affect them more continuously and on a more susceptible plane than any other form of those sister-arts throughout the world. So do not let us despise the humble hymn, and let us in all fairness apply reasonable standards of criticism to it. Obviously the purely artistic standard is unsuited to the case. " Secular verse covers many provinces : sacred verse scarcely goes beyond its own limited sphere. To expect masterpieces," F. T. Palgrave says, " in this field approximately numerous as those in the secular lyric is unreasonable. But even more unreasonable is it, when of this single province (i.e. sacred verse) a district only is chosen out for censure, and treated as a whole domain. Hymns, wellnigh limited to the functions of prayer and of praise, are precisely that region in which a practical aim is naturally, almost inevitably predominant. The writers (not to dwell upon the imperfect training of many

[1] *Rudiments of Criticism*, by E. A. G. Lamborn.

among them) have hence far too frequently and easily made the sacrifice of pleasure to usefulness, of beauty to edification." [1] Happy indeed is a hymn-writer if the loftiness of his theme can be matched by the beauty of his language, and that sometimes this result has been achieved, it is hoped the following pages may testify. And even where this is not the case, the sheer earnestness and sincerity of purpose which have animated hymn-writers such as Cennick and Olivers will often be felt to atone for mere literary shortcomings.[2] We do not look to such writers for artistry : we come to them for spiritual help, and we do not come in vain.

For what, after all, is a hymn ? Augustine's definition— " a song of praise to God "—has long since been recognized as inadequate. Particularly has it been pointed out that Augustine seems to have forgotten St. Paul's definition of the purpose of song-worship in the primitive Church—" teaching and admonishing one another." A hymn, that is to say, has a teaching office, and an office of mutual encouragement and edification, as well as an office of prayer and praise, as indeed is abundantly clear to anyone who examines the contents of a typical modern collection. The potentialities of the hymn as a means of propagating Christian ideals calls for careful consideration on the part of the leaders of religious thought in this country.

In these pages our studies will again and again be found to conduct us to the borderland dividing the hymn proper from devotional verse. No sharp line of demarcation can be drawn between the two. Schaff's definition of a hymn as " a spiritual meditation in rhythmical prose or verse " has one foot in both territories. But one thing is clear—a hymn must be suitable for congregational singing. Ideally, it must pass a double test—Does it read well ? and Does it sing well ? If it does

---

[1] Introduction to Palgrave's *Treasury of Sacred Song*.
[2] Cennick's best-known hymn is " Children of the Heavenly King " ; he also wrote the well-known Grace " Be present at our table, Lord." Olivers is the author of " The God of Abraham praise " ; his other hymns are not of great merit.

the one and not the other, it is not a good hymn. Yet if it does both and lacks *life*, it profits nothing.

The art of hymn-writing is still in its infancy. The English hymn, as we understand the term, is a product of quite recent times. The first considerable English hymn-writer, George Wither, published his *Hymns and Songs of the Church* in 1623, but it was not until some time after the appearance, in 1707, of Watts's *Hymns and Spiritual Songs* that hymn-writing in this country made serious headway.

Ellerton, writing in 1864, reckoned that not more than a hundred hymns of the pre-Watts period were still in use. The rest lacked the vitality necessary to keep them alive. Of the tens of thousands with which our land has since been flooded, a large proportion date from the middle decades of the nineteenth century. Few of them are of such a quality that we need wish them to survive.

With this rapid development of the English hymn, a new factor of first-class importance has been introduced into public worship. In the Nonconformist Churches especially, where there is no Prayer Book to aid devotion, the hymn exerts an incalculable influence upon religious thought and feeling. Once a mere rivulet, this stream of sacred song has gone on widening and widening, until now it irrigates the vast territories over which the Christian gospel holds sway, and it is a moot point whether the great hymns, such as " Abide with me " and " Jesu, Lover of my soul," have not been as potent in keeping the soul of the people alive as the greatest creations of literature and art.[1]

No one, perhaps, has realized the importance of the hymn as a popular instrument of religious instruction more clearly than John Wesley. In well-known words, he claimed that his famous collection of 1780 constituted in effect " a little body of experimental and practical divinity," and contained " all the important truths of our most holy religion." Next to the

[1] See an article by Dr. Alington in the *Evening Standard*, November 12, 1925 (reprinted in pamphlet form).

Bible, the common hymn book of Christendom has perhaps done more than any other factor to restore the sôul, to rejoice the heart, to enlighten the eyes, and to sustain the faith and love of Christian men and women throughout the world. Here is a shrine of quietude and peace, and of gracious, healing influences, amid the turmoil and confusion of a restless and noisy world.

Reference has already been made to the contribution which the hymn makes to the cause of Christian reunion. In its poetry the Church discovers a unity which reaches down below its creedal differences. The creeds are like the troubled waves on the surface of the waters : the love of which the poets sing is like the undivided ocean below. It is indeed refreshing, as we study our hymnals, to realize that here we can turn aside from controversy, and, forgetting our differences, can attain a true unity of the spirit in a glad fraternity of praise. And this unity overlaps national as well as ecclesiastical barriers. Through the medium of the music and of the translations which skilful hands and loving hearts have made, we can commune with our fellow-Christians of many lands, even though we cannot speak their tongue. Above the tumult of hatreds and wars, these songs rise from many lips to Him who is the Father of us all.

And, finally, a peculiarly tender value attaches to these familiar strains, because of the subtle power of association. Here again the literary critic must be patient and generous in his judgments. The associations which cluster round our best-known hymns invest them with a value out of all proportion to their literary or musical worth. The hymns of childhood ! How sweetly they sounded on the gentle lips of our mothers ! Ah ! happy days, when, in holy innocence, we knelt and lisped—

> Gentle Jesus, meek and mild,
> Look upon a little child.

Sweet memories ! Sacred pictures ! Days for ever gone ! Who is there that can recall them without emotion ?

The key to the intelligent understanding of the contents of a modern hymn book is the historical one, and unfortunately it is a key which is not often used. Until it is used, the tendency towards " gramophone " singing, the singing of the hymns in church as a mere act of physical enjoyment, will continue. The proper place to begin such a study is in our theological colleges, as is already done in some cases in the United States. It is a reproach to us that our clergy and ministers and leaders of religious thought pass through their training without being given any serious insight into those treasures of devotion which are to companion them upon the duties of their sacred office. And further, desirable as it is to include a serious study of hymnology in colleges, it is much to be hoped that a wider general interest will soon be evoked in a subject so fascinating in itself, and so fraught with vital issues for the religious world of to-day and to-morrow.

Such a study brings with it a rich reward, for it introduces us to some of the greatest and saintliest men of Christian times, and shows the history of our religion in its most alluring aspect—its soul, its " anima," its inner life, rather than its outward forms.

To get behind the hymn book to the men and women who wrote its contents, and to the events, whether personal or public, out of which it sprang and which it so graciously mirrors, is to enter into a world palpitating with human interest. For a hymn book is a transcript from real life, a poetical accompaniment to real events and real experiences. Like all literature that counts, it rises directly out of life. Percy in his *Reliques* holds that the heart of a nation is written in its songs. Even so the heart of the Christian Church is revealed in its hymns ; and if we will take the trouble to relate them to the circumstances that gave them birth, we shall find that they light up with a new meaning and have fresh power to help us in our daily lives. For their writers were men of flesh and blood like ourselves, experiencing the same temptations, the same aspirations, the same faith. Singing the songs they have bequeathed to us, we know ourselves to be participants in an inheritance more precious than gold. As their songs strike at our hearts we realize that our spiritual friendships have multiplied to the enlargement of our hearts. " This," said William Penn, " is the comfort of friends, that though they may be said to die, yet their friendship and society are, in the best sense, ever present, because immortal." We have never seen these singers of Divine Love, but their hymns come floating down the centuries like sweet bells across the fields, like fragrance in the summer air ; and as our hearts go out to theirs, and across these dim tracts of time deep calls unto deep, we realize that the children of God are one family through every generation.

CHAPTER II

THE BEGINNINGS OF CHRISTIAN SONG

BEARING our theory ever in mind—a theory which has been verified by experience through the ages, and is as wide in its application as humanity itself—that song is a divinely appointed channel for the expression of emotion, let us turn to enquire into its place in the history of the Christian Church.

It is surprising at the outset to find that apparently in the wonderful scenes which marked our Lord's ministry in the open air, song had no place. One would have imagined that, as the crowds gathered round Him, saw His wonderful works, and listened spellbound to His matchless eloquence as He played upon all the chords of the human heart, the people would almost instinctively have broken into songs of gratitude and joy. It was so in later Christian history, when the Flagellants raised their laude in the villages of Umbria ; when Francis and brother Pacifico, with impassioned zeal, told of the love of Jesus to the peasantry of Italy and of France ; when Savonarola sought to counteract the obscene ballads that defiled the lips of the young nobles of Florence ; when Luther, purging Christ's Church, " sang the people into Protestantism " ; and when the Wesleys, in a perfect rapture of praise, preached the all-embracing and all-conquering love of God to the people of England.

But it is not so recorded of the Master. The children, it is true, on one memorable day welcomed Him to the city of His tears with glad Hosannas ; and when the shadows of the last tragedy lengthened we know that He and His disciples, before going out to the Mount of Olives, " sang a hymn " together. Nor have we any reason to doubt that on many occasions, when He visited the synagogues, He joined in the singing of the Hebrew Psalms. His own words are marked by rhythmic beauty, such as we should expect from His poetic soul.

This book is not primarily concerned with the structure of verse, nor with what Poe speaks of as the philosophy of composition ; but some reference must be made to the artistic beauty and freshness of many of the sayings of Jesus.[1] In Matthew's Gospel (chap. xxiii. 8–11) Jesus is recorded to have spoken on this wise :

> Be not ye called Rabbi :
> For One is your Rabbi ;
> And all ye are brethren.

> Call ye no one Father :
> For One is your Father ;
> He which is in Heaven.

> Be not ye called Master :
> For One is your Master ;
> The greatest among you is your servant.

Dr. Briggs, commenting on this utterance, says, " Jesus put His wisdom in this poetic form for the reason that wisdom had been given in the artistic form of Gnomic poetry for centuries, and was so used in His time. If He was to use such wisdom, He must use its forms. Jesus uses its stereotyped forms, and uses them with such extraordinary freshness, fertility and vigour, that His wisdom transcends all others in its artistic expression."

The following passage, based on Luke vi. 20–26, is cast in the form of a pentastich, that is, a five-line verse. Each line in the second verse will be seen to be antithetical to the corresponding line in the first verse, the four " woes " being contrasted with the four " blessings." Dr. Briggs's version has been shorn of what he speaks of as " other homogeneous material," inserted by Luke " from a much later period in

---

[1] The references and quotations that follow are taken from a series of articles by Professor Briggs in the *Expository Times*, vols. viii and ix. See also Moffatt's Preface to the First Edition of his *Historical New Testament*.

C

the teaching of Jesus," thus making the inverted relationship of each verse much clearer :—

I

Blessed are ye poor, for yours is the Kingdom of God ;
Blessed are ye that hunger, for ye shall be filled ;
Blessed are ye that weep, for ye shall laugh ;
Blessed are ye when all men shall hate you,
    For in the same manner did their fathers unto the prophets.

II

Woe unto you rich, for ye have received your consolation ;
Woe unto you that are full, for ye shall hunger ;
Woe unto you that laugh, for ye shall (mourn and) weep ;
Woe, when all men shall speak well of you,
    For in the same manner did their fathers to the false prophets.

Dr. Burney believes that such prominent sayings as the Lord's Prayer, the Beatitudes and the parable of the Good Shepherd, in their Galilæan Aramaic rendering, exhibit both rhythm and rhyme ; and that these traits were intended by our Lord as an aid to memory.[1]

Many further illustrations could be given, but perhaps enough has been said to show that Jesus, or the Evangelist who edited His sayings, spoke in terms of artistic design. And this, let it be repeated, is what we should expect to happen, for the " style is the man." Words of grace proceeded out of His mouth, because His life was full of it.

The hymn book of the primitive Church was undoubtedly the Book of Psalms. That great collection was " to the early Christians what the national epic and the sacred lyric had been to the other races of antiquity. The Church succeeded to the splendid inheritance of the Hebrew temple and synagogue." [2] Oesterley quotes a statement that in the synagogues the Psalms were chanted responsively by the precentor and the congregation, " Hallelujah " being the word with which the people were invited to take part in the chanting. Beyond the Psalter, the infant Church had no special hymnal of its own : in the nature of things that was inevitable. One had

---

[1] *The Poetry of Our Lord*, by C. F. Burney.
[2] Milman's *History of Christianity*.

to be created, and the need of it was quickly felt. The first
reference to a hymn in the New Testament is in Mark's
Gospel (xiv. 26), where Jesus and His disciples are recorded
as having sung one together. One of the Hallel or Passover
Psalms—Ps. cxiv—has for many centuries been believed to
be the one used on that supreme occasion. An interesting,
but entirely unsubstantiated, tradition is preserved in the
Apocryphal Acts of St. John that the Master and His apostles
danced as they sang. The narrative says :—

> He commanded us to make as it were a ring, holding
> one another's hands, and Himself standing in the middle.
> He said, Respond Amen to me. He began then to sing
> a hymn, and to say,
>
> Glory to Thee, Father !
>
> And we going about in a ring said Amen.
>
> *   *   *   *   *
>
> So, then, my beloved, after this dance with us, the
> Lord went out : and we as men gone astray or awakened
> out of sleep fled all ways.

In Luke we see the beginnings of a distinctly Christian
hymnody. First of all comes the Gloria—the angels, the
choir ; the theme, goodwill and peace ; the audience, rude
shepherds on a lawn ; the setting round about them, " the
glory of the Lord."

> The helmed Cherubim
> And sworded Seraphim
> Are seen in glittering ranks with wings displayed,
> Harping in loud and solemn quire
> With inexpressive [1] notes, to Heaven's new-born Heir,
> Such music (as 'tis said)
> Before was never made
> But when of old the sons of morning sung,
> While the Creator great
> His constellations set
> And the well-balanced earth on hinges hung.

[1] Inexpressible.

Then follows that splendid triad of hymns, morning songs of a glorious dawn, first notes of an unending melody, the " Magnificat," the " Benedictus " and the " Nunc Dimittis," all incorporated by Luke in his story of the Saviour's infancy. Certain lyrical passages from the Old Testament, such as the Songs of Moses and of Hannah, and the " Benedicite " or Song of the Three Holy Children, from the Apocryphal version of Daniel, were also probably used in worship.

Some passages in Paul's epistles suggest that new Christian hymns soon began to be produced.[1] Paul gives quotations from these new hymns, such as the passage in 1 Tim. iii. 16 :—

> Manifested in the flesh,
> Justified in the Spirit,
> Seen of Angels ;
> Preached unto the Gentiles,
> Believed on in the world,
> Received up into glory :

which obviously forms a part of some strophes " on our Lord's Incarnation and Triumph " ; but Leigh Bennett (in an article in Julian's Dictionary) points out that it has not been shown whether such passages were used in the worship of the Church.[2] He thinks it more probable that they were reserved for private reading and social gatherings.

Other evidence is available, besides that already referred to, to show that the Christians at an early date began to write original psalms and hymns. In his *History*, Eusebius, the third-century Bishop of Cæsarea, says, " How many psalms and hymns, *written by the faithful brethren from the beginning*, celebrate Christ the Word of God, speaking of Him as Divine." The same writer, a little later in his book, gives a vivid account of the trial of a certain Bishop of Antioch, one Paul of Samosata, for heresy and corruption of life. After picturing this Paul as a haughty, tyrannical person, who " struts in the market-place, makes himself a lofty throne in Church assemblies, and

[1] Eph. v. 19, 20 ; Col. iii. 16, 17 ; 1 Cor. xiv. 26.
[2] For other rhythmic passages, see Eph. v. 14 ; 2 Tim. ii. 11-13 ; Titus iii. 4-7 ; Rev. v. 13.

strikes his thigh with his hands and stamps with his feet,
and rebukes and insults those who do not applaud him," he
says that amongst other offences the bishop " stops the singing
of the psalms to our Lord Jesus Christ, *as being the modern
productions of modern men*, and trains women to sing psalms
to himself in the midst of the Church on the great day of the
Passover, which anyone might shudder to hear."

But an earlier witness than Eusebius is Pliny the Younger,
who was the Roman governor of Bithynia in the opening
decades of the second century. In the course of his official
duties Pliny reported to the Emperor Trajan the proceedings
of the Christians at their morning meetings, and asked for
instructions how to deal with them, feeling himself in perplexity about it. His report gives the interesting information that the Christians sang hymns, antiphonally, to Christ
as God.

Another writer of the second century, Clement of Alexandria,
records that the Christian communities sang at meal-times,
though he again gives no hint of the character of their
" graces."

The record of the Acts (chap. ii. 46-47) shows the disciples
not only breaking bread at home and meeting daily in the
temple, but also praising God. Again, however, there is
nothing to tell us the nature of their praises : nor do we
know what the hymns or psalms were which the prisoners
heard Paul and Silas singing at midnight at Philippi. It is
conjectured that, as far as public worship was concerned, the
Psalms and New Testament hymns remained practically the
only sources of praise until the fourth century, except perhaps
at Antioch.

If, as some believe, original hymns were produced and sung
under the influence of the Spirit, Antioch was probably a
very early centre for their use. The Odes of Solomon are
believed by J. Rendel Harris to emanate from Antioch, and
to have been first sung there. The story of the discovery of
these Odes reads like a romance. At the time that he made the

discovery, in 1909, Dr. Harris was the Director of Studies at Woodbrooke, the Quaker Centre at Selly Oak. The manuscript, he says, " had been lying with a heap of other stray leaves of manuscript on the shelves of my library without awakening any suspicion that it contained a lost hymn book of the early Church of the apostolic times, or at the very latest of the sub-apostolic times ; that is to say, a document contemporary, or almost so, with the New Testament itself." [1] The manuscript is in the Syriac language.   Harnack thinks the Odes are Jewish-Christian, that is to say a Jewish hymn book, edited and enlarged by a Palestinian Christian.   Bernard believes them to be Christian baptismal hymns, dating . in their present form from between A.D. 150 and 190.   Other experts regard them as Gnostic.   But the learned discoverer remains convinced of their very early Christian origin, and that they were first sung in the Church at Antioch, probably with a " Hallelujah " refrain, thus taking us back to early Christianity in its poetical, musical, metrical and simple forms. The Odes are decidedly rhapsodical in character.   Their distinguishing note is one of joy.   They reflect the sense of triumph and boundless life which filled the hearts of the first believers.   " They are utterly radiant," Rendel Harris says, " with faith and love ; shot through and through with what the New Testament calls the joy of the Lord."

A great day has shined upon us (says one of them) ; marvellous is He who has given us of His glory.   Let us, therefore, all of us unite together in the name of the Lord, and let us honour Him in His goodness, and let us meditate in His love by night and by day.

They contain many references to singing, as though the abounding joy of the heart must perforce become lyrical. " Open to me," the singer cries, " the harp of Thy Holy Spirit, that with all its notes I may praise Thee, O Lord ! "

[1] *Rylands Bulletin*, vol. ii.

Here is Ode XXVI, with its metrical paraphrase by Dr. Harris :—

THE ODE

I poured out praise to the Lord ;
For I am His :
And I will speak His holy song,
For my heart is with Him.
For His Harp is in my hands,
And the Odes of His Rest shall not be silent.
I will cry unto Him from my whole heart ;
I will praise and exalt Him with all my members.
For from the East and even to the West
Is His praise :
And from the South and even to the North
Is His confession :
And from the top of the hills to their utmost bound
Is His perfection.

Oh ! that one could write the Odes of the Lord,
Or that one could read them !
Oh ! that one could train his soul for life,
That his soul might be saved !
Oh ! that one could rest on the Most High,
That from His mouth he might speak !
Oh ! that one could interpret the wonders of the Lord !
For he who interprets would be dissolved,
And that which is interpreted would remain.
For it suffices to know and to rest ;
For in the rest the singers stand ;
Like a river which has an abundant fountain,
And flows to the help of them that seek it.
       Hallelujah !

THE PARAPHRASE

Fountain-head of endless bliss,
He is mine and I am His ;
Let me music's call obey,
Rise and tune a heavenly lay.

In my hands His holy Lyre,
On my lips His sacred Fire,
Music heavenly in my breast,
Songs of peace and songs of rest.

Heaven to earth for music calls ;
Sing His praise, ye ransomed thralls ;
Rescued from the galling chain,
Sing His praise and sing again.

Sound it forth from East to West,
Sing again the songs of rest ;
South is warbling to the North,
Warble thou His work, His worth.

Far beyond horizon's bound,
Hill to hill takes up the sound ;
Echoes back the furthest zone ;
Join and make His praise thy own.

Oh ! that one could join the strain,
Mingle with that glad refrain ;
Capture angel-songs for earth,
Dower of the second birth.

Oh ! that Jesus from on high
Gave me heav'n's minstrelsy ;
Set my songful soul to tell
All His wealth unsearchable.

Still when I pursue the chase,
Following Praise from place to place,
Making higher, further flight,
In the depth or in the height,

Fails my spirit in the spheres,
Languishes and disappears ;
Fades from off the heavenly plains,
Passes, while its song remains.

Could I once that music reach,
Once attain that sacred speech,
Once expound that wondrous Love,
Gladly would I then remove ;

Gladly leave my finished quest,
Finding once His songs of rest ;
This the fount of life for me,
This the river, this the sea.

Notable among other very early hymns are the Lamplighting
or Candlelight Hymn, the " Ter Sanctus," and an extended

and beautiful form of the " Gloria in Excelsis " of Luke's narrative. These are all in the Greek tongue.

The practice of singing at the bringing in of the lamps at supper-time is very ancient. Tertullian, writing c. 198, says that among the Christians of his day, after their common meal, " each man, according as he is able, is called on, out of the holy Scriptures or of his own mind, to sing publicly to God." " Hence it is proved," he adds, " in what degree he hath drunken " : by which he almost certainly is defending the Christians from the charge of gluttony and drunkenness which was from time to time brought against them In effect he says, " They could not sing publicly as they do, if the charge were true." The date and origin of the surviving Candlelight hymn are unknown, beyond that it was quoted by Basil in the fourth century as even then widely known. The best modern translations are Keble's, " Hail, gladdening Light," and Longfellow's, " O Gladsome Light." Here is a third, by Mrs. Charles :—

> Joyful light of holy glory,
> Of the immortal Heavenly Father,
> Holy, blessed
> Jesu Christ !
> We, coming at the setting of the sun,
> Beholding the evening light,
> Praise Father and Son
> And Holy Spirit, God ;
> Thee it is meet
> At all hours to praise
> With sacred voices ; Son of God,
> Thou who givest life ;
> Therefore the world glorifies Thee.

This hymn is affecting in its simplicity ; there is no straining after effect, no sentimentalism : just a pure, reverent word of thanksgiving to God for the gift of Him who is the Light of the world.

The " Gloria in Excelsis," as stated, is an extended version of the Angels' Song at Bethlehem. It appears in the

Apostolic Constitutions (fourth century) among the daily prayers :

> Glory be to God in the highest, and upon earth peace, goodwill among men. We praise Thee, we sing hymns to Thee, we bless Thee, we glorify Thee, we worship Thee by Thy great High Priest ; Thee who art the true God, who art the One Unbegotten, the only inaccessible Being. For Thy great glory, O Lord and heavenly King, O God the Father Almighty, O Lord God, the Father of Christ the immaculate Lamb, who taketh away the sin of the world, receive our prayer, Thou that sittest upon the cherubim. For Thou only art holy, Thou only art the Lord Jesus ; the Christ of the God of all created nature, and our King, by whom glory, honour and worship be to Thee.[1]

The " Ter Sanctus " is equally direct and lofty in tone. It is included in the earliest Christian liturgies that have come down to us, having doubtless been brought over from the Jewish liturgical books.[2] Like the " Gloria," it is to be found in the *Apostolic Constitutions*, where, in dealing with the liturgical services, the writer soars in imagination to where cherubim and seraphim, angels and archangels, with loud voices hymn it before God, all the people being called to join the heavenly choir :—

> Holy, holy, holy, Lord of hosts,
> Heaven and earth are full of His glory :
> Be Thou blessed for ever.
>   Amen.[3]

In addition to these and other more or less formal hymns, the early congregations joined in certain brief responses and refrains, such as the " Kyrie Eleison " (O Lord, have mercy upon us), the " Amen " and the " Gloria Patri." The earliest

---

[1] *Apostolic Constitutions*, Book VII, 47. Another version will be found in the English Prayer Book, near the end of the Communion Service.
[2] Oesterley's *Jewish Background to the Christian Liturgy*.
[3] *Apostolic Constitutions*, Book VIII, 12 ; also Isa. vi. 3 ; Rom. i. 25.

version of the " Gloria " simply ran, " Glory be to the Father and to the Son and to the Holy Ghost, world without end. Amen." But when the Arian controversy waxed high, the orthodox parties, eager to emphasize at every point the " consubstantiality " of the Father and the Son, inserted the further phrase, " As it was in the beginning, is now, and ever shall be " ; and this extended form was in due course ordered to be used instead of the earlier one.

A greater hymn than any we have been considering is the " Te Deum." It obviously comes from the period when the Hebrew Psalm was still the model for Christian praise. It is generally assigned to Niceta of Remesiana, but the issue is one for the specialists to decide. Niceta lived during the Arian controversy, and was a personal friend of some of the chief disputants, no doubt himself desiring, amid the intellectual complexities and moral chaos of the times, to play his part in maintaining and propagating the pure faith. In his truly great hymn (if, indeed, he is its author), the creeds take wing and soar into a heaven of praise.[1] For more than fifteen centuries it has formed a part of the public worship of the Western Churches, and its noble thought and stately language have given it a place in the affections of Christian people next only to the Bible itself.

The earliest known Christian hymn still in general use in this country is almost certainly from the pen of Clement of Alexandria. It dates from about the year 170. It is necessary to say " almost certainly " because at this dim distance of time the ascription of authorship is almost inevitably conjectural. With this hymn, therefore, begins our study, fascinating in its human interest, of the actual men and women, and their lives and interests, who through the centuries have built up the goodly structure of Christian song. No one can read Clement's *Pedagogus* (or Schoolmaster), with its homely rules for daily living, without feeling himself to be in the

[1] For a full treatment of the " Te Deum " see Julian's *Dictionary of Hymnology* and A. E. Burn's *Niceta of Remesiana*.

company of a charming and lovable personality. The book has well been described as " a manual of good breeding." It presents a portrait of a true *gentleman*, who in the simple walks of daily life, in dress and furniture and food, in speech and exercise, in laughter and anxiety, in the home and the shop, lives his life in the benignity and sweetness and wisdom of the spirit of Christ. It " views all life as sacramental, all days as holy, every hour meet for praise." [1] Clement had studied many systems of philosophy, and had come from them unsatisfied, until at length in Jesus he found the living water for which his soul thirsted. " Jesus," he said, " has made truth simple." From his chair at the Catechetical School at Alexandria he showed his young pupils (of whom Origen was one) that the perfect life is not to be found in a series of clever answers to speculative theories, but in the practice of goodness, uprightness and love in life's ordinary relationships and duties. His hymn, which comes at the end of the *Pedagogus*, and which commences in our present-day hymnals sometimes with the words, " Shepherd of tender youth," and sometimes with " Curb of the stubborn steed," contains an interesting reference to Christ as a Fisherman. This was a favourite simile with the early Christians, the fish, along with the dove and the lamb, figuring conspicuously in Christian sculptures and paintings. So Jesus, the Master Fisherman, catches men for life, not death :—

> Fisher of men whom Thou to life dost bring,
>   From evil sea of sin,
>   And from the billowy strife,
>   Gathering pure fishes in,
>   Caught with the sweet bait of life.[2]

While Clement, with so much charm, was leading his scholars to Jesus, a man who is pictured to us as of a very different type was writing " heretical " verses at Edessa, in Syria. Bardesanes, as his name was, a shadowy, insubstantial

[1] *Clement of Alexandria*, by Rufus M. Jones.
[2] Dr. Alexander's translation in the *Nicene and Post-Nicene Fathers*.

figure, is reported to have used the allurements of popular music to subvert the minds of the young men and women of Edessa.

> In the resorts of Bardesanes
> There are songs and melodies :
> For, seeing that young persons
> Loved sweet music,
> By the harmony of his songs
> He corrupted their minds.

We need not trouble ourselves over the heresies of Bardesanes. It is not at all likely that he was as black as his opponents painted him. The significance of his songs is to be found in the reaction which they are said to have provoked in the mind of Ephrem, who, in the fourth century, a hundred and fifty years or so after the days of Bardesanes, was a teacher at Edessa, at a time when that city was a centre of culture and religious enquiry. Following the example of his rival, whose hymns he described as " poisoned sweetness," Ephrem called in the aid of music to defend the faith. He established, apparently from among his young converts, a class of " the daughters of the Convent " and taught them " odes and scales and responses." Every day they met in the churches of Edessa, and their good teacher, " like a spiritual harper, stood in their midst and taught them simple hymns and antiphons of Christ, the saints and martyrs, until his adversaries were put to shame." Most of his hymns are said to be theological doggerel,[1] but they have undoubtedly influenced history ; for with them began the controversial use of the hymn as a weapon in the hands of the theologians which continued through many generations.

To wade to-day through those endless pages of controversial orations and verses is a task as tedious as it is depressing. One cannot keep pace with these fine distinctions between Gnosticism, Valentinianism, Arianism, Apollinarianism, Manicheism, and all the rest of the Isms. It would be a mistake,

[1] R. A. Aytoun's *City Centres of Early Christianity*, chap. vii.

however, to assume that the disputants were engaged in a mere game of hair-splitting, " a battle about a diphthong "— to quote a well-known phrase. They were for the most part in deadly earnest. They were determined, even to death, to maintain the purity of the faith as they conceived it. They feared, and they had reason to fear, a revival of paganism, which to them was as some poisonous miasma, carrying death not to the bodies, but to the souls of men. And two facts, at least, must be remembered before we condemn them : they lived on the very edge of an era of terrible persecution, and at a time when the principle of religious toleration had scarcely dawned upon the world. But it was all very pathetic, and it shows how easy it is, in the heat of debating about the faith, to forget that the orthodoxy that really matters is a life of love. Ephrem himself felt this, and in a poem " On the Mystery of the Trinity " he laments that men give themselves to such endless attempts to analyse the faith : he is weary to death of this mania for argumentation :—

> Captious enquiry hath now begun :
> Disputation hath entered :
> War is commenced :
> And the truth is fled away !
>
> It is preferable
> In a time of thirst
> To drink of the waters
> Than, instead of drinking,
> We shall measure the fountain !

And so he ends with the prayer :—

> Increase in me, O Lord !
> Both silence and the gift of speech,
> That by them I may be saved,
> As I put away enquiry respecting Thee,
> And utter Thy praises.

One more quotation is worth recalling. It is from a touching poem on the death of his little son ; the translation is by

Mrs. Charles, who says that it used to be sung at children's
funerals :—

Thy voice, thy childish singing,
Soundeth ever in my ears ;
And I listen and remember,
Till mine eyes will gather tears,
Thinking of thy pretty prattling
And thy childish words of love :
But when I begin to murmur,
Then my spirit looks above,
Listens to the songs of spirits—
Listens longing, wondering,
To the ceaseless glad hosannas
Angels at thy bridal sing.

In such lines the controversialist is forgotten, and we feel we
are listening to the voice of a father, as he seeks the con-
solations of the gospel of life in the hour of bereavement.
The hymns ascribed to Ephrem are important as directing
the mind of the infant Church to the educational value of
hymnody in building up the believer of his holy faith.

In the fourth century the storm of the Arian controversy
broke in all its fury over the heads of the leaders of Christian
life and thought. Its leader, Arius, is pictured by Stanley
as a giant of a man, ungainly and fanatical, but extraordinarily
captivating to those who came across him. He propounded
a theory of the relations of the three Persons of the Trinity,
which the orthodox party believed to constitute an infringe-
ment of the Divinity of Christ. " Christ," he said, " is not
equal, no, nor one in substance with God." These " blasphemies," as Athanasius described them, he drew up in the
form of hymns, known as *Thalia*, and set them to base,
licentious song melodies, such as only those used " who sing
songs over their wine, with noise and revel." This caused
great offence to the orthodox, especially when they heard the
common people singing them at their work.[1]

[1] See *The Treatises of Athanasius*, where a hymn by Arius is given.

Readers of Kingsley's *Hypatia* will be able to form some conception of the turmoil which swept over such great centres of learning and intellectual curiosity as Alexandria, Athens and Constantinople. At Constantinople, Chrysostom, annoyed by the persistence of the Arians in holding meetings and singing insulting hymns outside the walls of the churches and in public places, caused orthodox hymns to be sung in procession, with lighted torches and silver crosses, until at length feeling ran so high that even the Christians lost control of themselves, clamouring and gesticulating in the excitement of anger, and calling down the rebukes of Chrysostom for converting the churches into mere theatres.[1]

At Alexandria there was the famous Lecture-School, over which, in earlier days, as we have seen, Clement presided, where culture could be met on its own ground and the many problems of " controversial divinity " could be discussed. In the year 379 Gregory of Nazianzus was called to the city to stem the tide of heterodoxy. On his arrival, he found the place in an uproar, for, as Paul found at Athens, the people " spent their time in nothing else, but either to tell, or to hear, some new thing." He has himself given us an account of the state of affairs. " Every corner and nook of the city," he says, " is full of men who discuss incomprehensible subjects—the streets, the markets, the people who sell old clothes, those who sit at the tables of the money-changers, those who deal in provisions. . . . Enquire the price of bread, you are answered ' The Father is greater than the Son, and the Son subordinate to the Father.' Ask if the bath is ready, and you are answered, ' The Son of God was created from nothing.' " No wonder Gregory again and again sought retirement with his friend Basil in the solitude of the mountains, where together they planted vines and felled trees, leading, as Mrs. Charles charmingly describes it, " a happy Robinson Crusoe life " until the needs of the hour called them back again to

---

[1] Hawkins's *History of Music.*

help to guide and quell the unseemly strife.[1]   The strain and
anxiety amid which so much of his life was spent led him at
length to withdraw to the home of his childhood, where, in
quiet retirement, he penned those hymns and poems which
have given him fame.   His " Evening Hymn " shows the old
man glancing backward with regret over his stormy past.   The
translation is by Dr. Brownlie :—

> O Word of Truth ! in devious paths
>   My wayward feet have trod,
> I have not kept the day serene
>   I gave at morn to God.
>
> And now 'tis night, and night within,
>   O God, the light hath fled !
> I have not kept the vow I made
>   When morn its glories shed.
>
> For clouds of gloom from nether world
>   Obscured my upward way ;
> O Christ the Light, Thy light bestow
>   And turn my night to day !

Synesius was another of the Greek hymn-writers to be
caught in the toils of the Arian controversy.   To have
attracted in modern times the notice of Gibbon and Coleridge,
Kingsley and Mrs. Browning, bespeaks him a man of unusual
qualities.   As a pupil and friend of Hypatia, he is known
to a wide circle of English-speaking people, who have no
acquaintance with his hymns.   In the novel he appears as
a " squire-bishop," a lover of gardens and bees, of dogs and
horses ;   philosopher, ecclesiastic and poet.   Some of his
poems show him to have been a tender-hearted parent,
bitterly stricken by the early deaths of three of his children.
Once, when one of the boys recovered for a while from
threatened death, he penned this affecting hymn of prayer
and thanksgiving :—

[1] See Mrs. Charles's *Christian Life in Song* ;   also the references to
Gregory in the article on " Hymns " in Hastings's *Encyclopædia of
Religion*.

On that darling son of mine
May Thy protecting mercy shine,
Whom, just when passing gate of death,
Thou didst restore to vital breath.
O Lord of life, 'twas Thou didst wrench
From death's firm grasp his prey, and quench
My burning grief in floods of joy ;
For Thou didst give me back my boy !

When, afterwards, his son died, he poured out his grief in
a letter to Hypatia, crying, " May I cease either to live or
to remember my boy's grave ! " A free paraphrase of one
of his hymns, by Chatfield, " Lord Jesus, think on me," has
a secure place in recent hymnals. It has the strength of
simplicity :—

Lord Jesus, think on me,
And purge away my sin ;
From earthborn passions set me free,
And make me pure within.

Lord Jesus, think on me,
With care and woe opprest ;
Let me Thy loving servant be,
And taste Thy promised rest.

Lord Jesus, think on me,
Nor let me go astray ;
Through darkness and perplexity
Point Thou the heavenly way.

Lord Jesus, think on me,
When flows the tempest high :
When on doth rush the enemy
O Saviour be Thou nigh.

Lord Jesus, think on me,
That, when the flood is past,
I may the eternal brightness see,
And share Thy joy at last.

Dr. Brownlie is responsible for the following charming canto
from Synesius's third Ode, written to his " own beloved Libya."
Very beautifully and with poetic grace, it may be said to be a

commentary on the Psalmist's words, " The heavens declare the glory of God " :—

> When darkness falls and night is here,
>   My hymns of praise in silence rise—
> This knows *the moon*, whose silver sphere
>   Shines in the star-bespangled skies.
>
> When morning breaks, and glorious day
>   Shines in the dawn and noontide fair—
> This knows *the sun*—a grateful lay
>   Springs from my heart in fervent prayer.
>
> When fails the light at sunset gray,
>   And twilight listens for my song—
> This know *the stars*—in bright array
>   My praises mingle with their throng.[1]

In taking leave for the moment of the early Christian poets of the East, a tribute of gratitude should be paid to such able and patient investigators as Neale and Brownlie, Chatfield and Moultrie and Mrs. Browning, for having rescued their work from the Oriental Service books, and made it accessible to English worshippers. They all speak of the simplicity, directness, and healthy objectiveness which characterize the best of these hymns, the whole body of which, as Brownlie truly says, constitutes a pictorial representation of the history of Redemption—a representation equalled only in its popular influence by the stained-glass pictures of later times.

These men may not be ranked as great poets ; we may distrust them as theologians ; but Mrs. Browning speaks the true word when she says that as we " besom away " their dusty, disputatious folios, and meekly make our way to their hearts, we shall find help to our souls.[2] The fountain of Christian hymnody is pure at its source.

[1] Glover's *Life and Letters in the Fourth Century* contains a chapter on Synesius.
[2] Mrs. Browning's *Essay on the Greek Christian Poets*.

CHAPTER III

DISCORD AND CONCORD

THE Arian controversy spread throughout the Church, and many notable leaders were caught in its toils. For the spirit of theological controversy, once roused, is not easily stilled. The story is unedifying in the extreme, and it is strange to reflect that out of the bitter came forth sweetness, for the controversy undoubtedly continued to furnish the occasion for the writing of many devout hymns. There were, obviously, two ways of combating the dangerous hymnody of the heretical singers : the one was the method adopted by more than one Church Council, and in a later day by Calvin, to forbid the use of all hymns not taken directly from the Scriptures ; and the other was to produce counter-hymns to combat the heresy. This not only the leaders of the Eastern Churches (as already stated), but Hilary of Poictiers, Ambrose of Milan, and some say the great Augustine himself, proceeded to do.

Hilary (fourth century), " the hammer of the Arians," has always been regarded as the father of Latin hymnody, though there is no conclusive evidence that he himself wrote hymns.[1] When an exile in the East he must have witnessed the propagandist use of song by the Arians, and he was a strong advocate of " the public and triumphant raising of our voices in song," which, he said, " gives pleasure to God, and assurance to our hope." It is one of the queer ironies of fate that Hilary is known to most English people to-day, not for his theological writings, which were learned and numerous, but because he has given his name to a term in our Law Courts.

But if Hilary stands first in our story in order of time, it is

[1] E. W. Watson's Introductory Chapter in the *Nicene and Post-Nicene Fathers*, vol. ix.

to Ambrose (b. 340) that we must look as the first great Latin
hymn-writer. He firmly established the custom of hymn
singing in his great church at Milan—the Church to which all
the Western Christians looked for guidance in liturgical affairs.
The story of his election to the famous Italian See throws as
strange a light as the pages of *Hypatia* on the state of religious
life in the fourth century, when the Arian controversy was at
its height. He began life as a lawyer; and at the age of
thirty-four, though only then preparing himself for admission
into the Church, he was called by popular acclamation, or
perhaps we should say by a sure popular insight, to the bishopric
which he adorned. The story says that while the church in
which the election was to take place was filled with an excited
crowd, a child's voice was heard to cry " Ambrose is Bishop,"
and the people, moved by a common impulse, took up the cry
" Ambrose is Bishop " ; and intrigue and opposition died
down at the call of the child.

He had not been in office many years when he found himself
in conflict with the young Emperor Valentinian II. The
Emperor, prompted by his mother, demanded the use of the
principal church in Milan for Arian worship, and sent soldiers
to place hangings on the walls to mark the building as Imperial
property.[1] The whole issue of the relation of Church and
State was focused in that incident. Ambrose refused the
royal demand. " The Emperor," he said, " has his palaces ;
let him leave the churches to the bishop." His supporters,
angered by the interference of the soldiery, set upon the Arians,
and street fighting began. Ambrose, who had no faith in
violence, offered his own neck if that would prevent bloodshed ;
and this action so deeply impressed the soldiers that some of
them joined the Christians, saying they would rather pray than
fight. Ambrose and his followers, among whom was Monica,
the mother of Augustine, locked themselves inside the church,
and while siege was laid to it he encouraged them to sing hymns

---

[1] Two attempts were made to capture the church. For a detailed
account of these events, see B. J. Kidd's *History of the Church to A.D. 461*,
vol. ii.

and psalms until the soldiers withdrew, " lest the people should pine away with the tedium of sorrow." [1]

From that time forward Ambrose developed the song-worship of his people. He wrote hymns for their use, and rejoiced—as he says in one of his sermons—to hear them singing strains of praise and confession to the holy Trinity, " each eager to rival his fellows in confessing, in sacred verses, his faith in Father, Son and Holy Spirit." He also taught them plain and simple tunes, which all could easily learn. He encouraged the whole congregation, probably including the women, to take part in the singing.[2] " Anyone possessed of his five wits," he wrote, " should blush with shame if he did not begin the day with a psalm, since even the tiniest birds open and close the day with sweet songs of devotion." He loved to compare the Church to the sea, as it reverberated to the song of the chanting.

The winnowing of time has robbed Ambrose of the credit of the authorship of many hymns which for long were attributed to him. The number was once nearly a hundred. Later editors have reduced them to twelve, then to four.

The " Ambrosian " hymns, whether from his pen or not, are distinguished by strongly marked characteristics. Travellers to the East on entering a Mohammedan mosque are impressed by its stern simplicity. There is an entire absence of the rich ornamentation which embellishes and sometimes spoils our Western cathedrals : merely an unadorned space where men may worship their God. So the hymns of Ambrose are austere in their rugged grandeur. Here is the hymn that comforted Augustine when alone on his bed he sorrowed for the death of his mother. It is one of the four recognized as written by Ambrose. " I slept," Augustine says, " and woke again, and found my grief not a little softened ;

---

[1] The quotation is from the *Confessions of St. Augustine*, where the incident is described.
[2] Some of the Early Fathers objected to women joining in the singing, and one suggested that the objection might be met if the women would sing softly, so that no one might hear them.

and as I was alone in my bed I remembered those true verses
of Thy Ambrose " :—

> Creator of the earth and sky,
> Ruling the firmament on high,
> Clothing the day with robes of light,
> Blessing with gracious sleep the night,
>
> That rest may comfort weary men,
> And brace to useful toil again,
> And soothe away the harassed mind,
> And sorrow's heavy load unbind :
>
> Day sinks ; we thank Thee for Thy gift ;
> Night comes, and once again we lift
> Our prayers and vows and hymns that we
> Against all ills may shielded be.
>
> Thee let the secret heart acclaim,
> Thee let our tuneful voices name,
> Round Thee our chaste affections cling,
> Thee sober reason own as King :
>
> That when black darkness closes day,
> And shadows thicken round our way,
> Faith may no darkness know, and night
> From faith's clear beam may borrow light.
>
> Rest not, my heaven-born mind and will ;
> Rest, all ye thoughts and deeds of ill ;
> May faith its watch unwearied keep,
> And cool the dreaming warmth of sleep.
>
> From cheats of sense, Lord, keep me free,
> And let my heart's depth dream of Thee ;
> Let not my envious foe draw near,
> To break my rest with any fear.
>
> Pray we the Father and the Son,
> And Holy Ghost ; O Three in One,
> Blest Trinity, whom all obey,
> Guard Thou Thy sheep by night and day.[1]

Augustine was bound by close ties to Ambrose. In the
days of his youth he often went to Milan to hear the bishop
preach, and sometimes would stand in silence at the door of

[1] From *The English Hymnal*, by permission of the Oxford University
Press : No. 49 : translation by " C. B."

his house, watching him at prayer.[1] There is an ancient
tradition that the two were joint authors of the " Te Deum,"
which was long believed to have been improvised by them
as Augustine came out of the baptismal waters. He has left
on record in his *Confessions* the impression made upon his
heart by the singing of the hymns and canticles in Ambrose's
church. He was so moved by it that he wept. " I did
abundantly weep at the singing of Thy hymns, formerly
panting for Thee, and at last breathing in Thee, so far as the
air can play in this house of grass." [2] Again and again he
refers to the help he received from song. Amid the manifold
temptations that beset him, he found strength and inspiration
in the hymn-singing, and his belief that through its gracious
medium " the weaker minds are stimulated to a devotional
frame " was based on his own experience. " I perceive that
our minds are more devoutly and earnestly elevated into a
flame of piety by the holy words themselves when they are
sung, than when they are not ; and that all affections of our
spirit, by their own diversity, have their appropriate measures
in the voice and singing, wherewith by I know not what
relationship they are stimulated." And yet, even so, he feared
the subtle beguilement of sweet sounds, and wished at times
they could be banished both from his ears and from the church,
saying, " When it happens to me to be more moved by the
singing than by what is sung, I confess myself to have sinned
criminally, and then I would rather not have heard the
singing." Many others all down the ages have felt the same
insidious danger, and some have gone so far as to banish all
singing from public worship. But as for Augustine, he wins
our love, whether lamenting the temptations of the senses, or
yielding to the devout emotions which music can incite, because
his life was a canticle of praise.

[1] McCabe's *St. Augustine and His Age.*
[2] *Confessions*, Book IX, chap. vii. The latter part of this quotation is
ambiguous. Probably Augustine means " so far as a body such as mine,
which is as frail as the grass, can receive Thee." See Isa. xl. 6–7 and
2 Cor. v. 1.

Perhaps the most interesting Christian singer contemporary with Ambrose and Augustine was the noble Spaniard, Prudentius. We know very little about him. The facts of his life are set out with modesty and reserve in the preface and epilogue which he appended to his poems. There we learn that in young manhood he became a lawyer, " and with deceitful pleadings sinned," and that after leading a gay life he settled down as a magistrate, and at length received high military or civil appointments under the Roman Government. As the years lengthened he reviewed his past life, as so many have done before and since, with the regretful sigh *Cui bono?* and, turning his back upon the world, he retired into the quietude of nature, and at long last found his true vocation in inditing hymns of loving devotion to the Saviour, saying :—

> So here I humbly dedicate to Thee
> The rolling trochee and iambus swift ;
> Thou wilt approve my simple minstrelsy,
> Thine ear will listen to Thy servant's gift !

As a poet he is far more fascinating than Ambrose. Glover describes him as " the first really great Christian poet," and says the more one studies his contemporaries the more one admires him.[1]

His hymns, collected together under the title of *Cathemerinon, or Hymns for the Day*, are obviously not meant for public worship, but, as in the case of Keble and Whittier, selections have been adapted for such use. They are full of charm, revealing a lovable man, fond of his home and his garden, and keen to commend the Gospel to the educated men of his time. Their style is warmer, their theme more personal, than Ambrose's, and critics have traced in them the influence of Virgil and Theocritus. The Ninth Hymn, " For all Hours," is particularly pleasing.[2] It introduces the Greek trochaic metre into Christian hymnody. Let the reader compare the

---

[1] Glover's *Life and Letters in the Fourth Century*.
[2] The translation of this and the following selection is by Dr. R. M. Pope ; see his *Hymns of Prudentius*.

structure of the lines with Poe's " Raven " and Lowell's
" The Present Crisis."

Let me chant in sacred numbers, as I strike each sounding
    string,
  Chant in sweet, melodious anthems, glorious deeds of Christ
    our King.;
He, my Muse, shall be thy story ; with His praise my lyre shall
  ring.

        *   *   *   *   *

Of the Father's heart begotten, ere the world from chaos rose,
  He is Alpha ; from that Fountain all that is and hath been
    flows ;
He is Omega, of all things yet to come the mystic Close.

By His word was all created ; He commands, and Io ! 'tis done ;
  Earth and sky and boundless ocean, universe of three in one,
All that sees the moon's soft radiance, all that breathes beneath
  the sun.

        *   *   *   *   *

Sing, ye heights of heaven, His praises ; angels and archangels
    sing !
  Wheresoe'er ye be, ye faithful, let your joyous anthems ring,
Every tongue His name confessing, countless voices answering.

This is He whom seer and sibyl sang in ages long gone by ;
  This is He of old revealèd in the page of prophecy ;
Lo ! He comes, the promised Saviour ; let the world His praises
  cry !

        *   *   *   *   *

Now let old and young uniting chant to Thee harmonious lays,
  Maid and matron hymn Thy glory, infant lips their anthem
    raise,
Boys and girls together singing with pure heart their song of
  praise.

Let the storm and summer sunshine, gliding stream and sounding
    shore,
  Sea and forest, frost and zephyr, day and night their Lord
    adore ;
Let creation join to laud Thee through the ages evermore.

His " Hymn before Meat " may be described as the Vege-
tarians' Hymn. It recalls Virgil in its pastoral sweetness. He
prays that God's grace may be poured over his bread, and

Christ's sweet fragrance bless his bowl, and protests that no fowler's craft, no gin or mesh or net, shall lure fish or fowl to his table, nor shall the blood of slaughtered beasts pollute his meal.

> Leave to the barbarian brood
>   Banquet of the slaughtered beast ;
> Ours the homely garden food,
> Greenstuff manifold and good
>   And the lentil's harmless feast :
>
> Foaming milkpails bubble o'er
>   With the udders' snowy stream,
> Which in thickening churns we pour
> Or in wicker baskets store,
>   As the cheese is pressed from cream.
>
> Honey's nectar for our use
>   From the new-made comb is shed,
> Which the skilful bee imbues
> With thyme's scent and airy dews,
>   Plying lonely toils unwed.
>
> Orchard-groves now mellowed o'er
>   Bounteously their fruitage shed :
> See ! like rain on forest floor
> Shaken trees their riches pour,
>   High-heaped apples, ripe and red.

It is as refreshing as unexpected to find such simple and homely strains as these, amid the formal and disputatious hymnody of the early Latin Church.

Some lines in his " Hymn for the Epiphany " remind us that Prudentius lived in an age when martyrdom for Christ was something more than a mere memory.[1] Prudentius was widely read throughout Europe during the Middle Ages. Erasmus was among his admirers, and both Colet and Vives encouraged their pupils to study his poetry.[2]

The work begun by Ambrose of developing the music of the Church was continued in the sixth century by Pope Gregory, who called to his aid some of the most skilful musicians of his

[1] See p. 260.
[2] *The English Grammar Schools to 1660*, by Foster Watson.

time. He favoured an austerely plain type of music for liturgical use, scarcely more than a form of recitative, " a half-way
house between speech and song," though perhaps tolerating
rather freer airs for the hymns.[1] His collection of old and
new chants, known as Gregorian tones, was destined to influence the whole future of congregational song-worship. He
sent his music students to Gaul, to Germany and to England [2] ;
and so widespread was his influence that by general consent
he won the title of *Magister Cæremoniarum.*

The hymns written by Gregory's contemporary Fortunatus
introduce us to a new departure in the development of religious
poetry. He may perhaps be described as the first of the
Christian Troubadours. The lady of his muse was the
beautiful Queen Radegund, who had left a cruel husband and
founded a Convent at Poictiers, and for whom he formed, as
was the way with the troubadours, an extravagant, though
platonic, admiration. He was a great traveller, and because
of his refinement and the versatility of his interests, was a
welcome guest both in the homes of the nobility and the
seclusion of the monasteries. Perhaps, too, his songs ensured
him a welcome, for he sang gaily as he tramped the hills of
France. " I gave voices," he says, " to the forests, and the
forests replied to my song."

In the course of his travels he came to Poictiers, and found
a congenial friend in the Queen, who shared his literary
interests, and who persuaded him to accept the chaplaincy of
her convent and later the bishopric of the diocese. Now
Queen Radegund had received from the Emperor Justin II
a piece of the reputed true Cross, and it can readily be imagined
that the sacred relic called forth the superstitious veneration
of the clergy and people of Poictiers. The actual cross on
which our Lord suffered was believed to have been found by
Helena, the mother of Constantine, and fragments of it were
eagerly sought after and quickly distributed throughout the

[1] Smith and Cheetham's *Dictionary of Christian Antiquities.*
[2] See p. 117.

Christian world. When therefore the Queen heard that she
was to receive a piece of it, and that the holy fragment had
temporarily been left in the keeping of the Bishop of Tours,
she naturally desired that it should be received at her convent
with fitting ceremony. The great event is thus recorded by
Dr. Julian [1] :—

> Escorted by a numerous body of the clergy and of the
> faithful holding lighted torches, the Bishop started in
> the midst of liturgical chants, which ceased not to resound
> in honour of the hallowed wood of the Redemption.
> A league from Poictiers the pious cortège found the
> delegates of Radegund, with Fortunatus at their head,
> rejoicing in the honour which had fallen to them ; some
> carrying censers with perfumed incense, others torches
> of white wax. The meeting took place at Migné, at the
> place where, twelve centuries and a half later, the cross
> appeared in the air.

Here indeed was a theme worthy of a poet's pen, and
Fortunatus, quitting his nature songs and society verses,
composed for the occasion the " Vexilla Regis Prodeunt."
The Vexilla is, in Julian's estimation, " one of the grandest
hymns of the Latin Church, in which, in glowing accents, its
author invites us to contemplate the mystery of love accomplished on the Cross." It antedates by more than eleven
centuries Watts's tremendous lines on the same theme :—

> When I survey the wondrous Cross
> Where the young Prince of Glory died.

Dr. Neale's translation is generally adopted in modern
Hymnals.[2] Here is another taken from a Primer of 1685 :—

> Abroad the regal banners fly,
> Now shines the Cross's mystery ;
> Upon it Life did death endure,
> And yet by death did life procure.

[1] Dr. Julian is quoting from a French account. See *Dictionary of
Hymnology*, p. 1220.
[2] *Hymns Ancient and Modern* : " The Royal Banners forward go."

Pierced by a spear, to cleanse our hearts,
His side a sacred stream imparts ;
Which issues in a double flood,
A stream of water and of blood.

That which the prophet-king of old
Hath in mysterious verse foretold
Is now accomplished, whilst we see
That God is reigning from the tree.

Blest tree, most sacred and divine,
Which dost in royal purple shine,
Supporting an Incarnate God,
And rendered holy by thy load.

Blest tree, whose happy branches bore
The wealth that did the world restore,
The balance which the price did weigh
That spoiled the spoiler of his prey.

Blest Trinity, life's source and spring,
May every soul Thy praises sing !
Let those obtain a crown in heaven
To whom the cross hath conquest given.

Trench says that more than any other, this was the Crusaders'
hymn.

Another hymn of the Cross, written for the same occasion,
was the " Pange Lingua "[1]—" Sing, my tongue, the glorious
battle "—which in its second verse enshrines the old tradition
that the cross on which Jesus died sprang from a bough of the
forbidden tree [2] :—

Pitying did the great Redeemer Adam's fall and ruin see,
Sentenced then to death by testing fruit of the forbidden tree,
And He marked that wood the weapon of redeeming love to be.

We have now reached a point in our story where it is not
difficult to detect the beginnings of the intrusion of artistry
and of legendary lore into Christian hymnody. The early

[1] This must not be confused with another hymn, beginning with the
same words, by Thomas Aquinas.
[2] The legendary history of the " Holy Rood Tree " is fully told by
A. S. Napier : Early English Text Society's publication.

simplicity of the Ambrosian hymns begins to yield to artistic embellishments and enervating fantasies. Especially did the worship of the cross lead the Church into deep trials ; and soon a conflict equalling in intensity that for which Arius was responsible threatened to rend Christendom in twain.

The Iconoclastic controversy was the natural sequel to the veneration of the cross, such as was voiced, even though in the mildest provocative form, in the Radegundian hymns. The cultus, once begun, spread surely and insidiously year by year. At first, doubtless, nothing more than an act of simple ritual, deference to an idea rather than to an actual material representation, was intended. But the worship of the image grew, and Constantine's action in setting up a jewelled cross in his palace must have encouraged it.[1] The constant use of the sign of the cross, and the custom of displaying it everywhere, to which Chrysostom refers, " in houses, in market places, in deserts, on roads, on mountains, in groves, on hills, on ships and islands in the sea, on beds and dresses, on arms, on couches," while perhaps innocuous as isolated incidents, cannot but have played into the hands of the idol-worshippers. Miraculous powers were claimed not only for the actual supposed fragments of the sacred wood, but for pictures of it. The adorationists organized processions in which these pictures and other images were displayed to the superstitious multitude, and stories of miraculous happenings were spread abroad. On one occasion it was said that a crucifix had been heard to speak ; a picture of a saint was believed to distil balsam ; a father took an icon as sponsor for his child ; and the people actually ground images to powder and drank the dust in water, believing them to possess magical qualities.[2]

Again the forces of the Church were divided into rival

---

[1] The subject is dealt with in Smith and Cheetham's *Dictionary of Christian Antiquities* and in Smith and Wace's *Dictionary of Christian Biography*. A great deal of special literature is also devoted to it.

[2] See the article on " Iconoclasm " in Hastings's *Dictionary of Religion and Ethics.*

groups, " each more bent on proving the other wrong than to discover the mean of truth." The controversy that ensued was prolonged and fierce. In vain did authority forbid any kind of reverence to be paid to the images, and in vain did their destruction proceed. On one occasion a crowd of women were infuriated beyond endurance at the spectacle of a soldier defacing an image of the Saviour with an axe, and rushing upon him, they seized his weapon and clubbed him to death.[1] Rioting and massacres continued through the weary years, and infinite harm was done to the cause of pure religion, which both sides professed to serve.[2]

Looking dispassionately back across the centuries at these strange happenings, it is clear that the whole issue of the relation of art to worship was incipiently involved in the dispute. That issue is still a living one. Clement of Alexandria, on the one side, hinting at the value of pictorial art as an aid to worship, and his pupil Origen, on the other, seeming to fear it, are the representatives of two opposing tendencies upon which the Church has always held differing views. That the early Christians made use of simple decorative art both in their homes and in the catacombs is well known. The practice inevitably grew, and pictures of saints and martyrs, of Mary, and of the Saviour as the Good Shepherd and even as Orpheus, were in wide vogue ; while missals, mosaics and mural paintings were produced in profusion all over the Christian world.[3] In the Middle Ages wonderful artistic developments took place. Europe was studded with magnificent cathedrals, whose devout builders sought to make every detail symbolize some aspect of religious truth. Coloured windows beautified the churches and were regarded as the popular picture galleries of the people. Then came the great religious painters, who, in unbroken succession, from Giotto and Van Eyck to Millet and Holman Hunt, have expressed the religious idea through

[1] See the article on " Iconoclasts " in the *Encyclopædia Britannica*.
[2] See an article, " Curiosities of Christian History," by Croak James ; also Alice Gardner's chapter on " Ritual " in *Within Our Limits*.
[3] See the article on " Icons " in the *Encyclopædia Britannica*.

the captivating medium of colour. The art of music, developing later, took its place in the sanctuary along with its sister arts of painting, sculpture and architecture. The humble hymn itself is a form of art, depending for its power upon a certain quality of rhythmic beauty—the wedding of sacred words to sacred music.

It is not surprising that a puritanical suspicion of these " aids of worship " should have been aroused. A beautifully proportioned spire, a richly vaulted roof, an embroidered altar-cloth, bells and candles, tiaras and banners, are they, after all, among the things of ultimate value ? It was Milton's judgment that such material objects tend to take the mind away from the pure contemplation of God. They are but the trappings of worship, " empty pageantry " ; and their danger is that they may obscure the very truths they are meant to reveal. For what, after all, is required of us, but to do justly, and to love mercy, and to walk humbly with our God? " What have we to do any more with idols ? "

This then was the issue of the Iconoclastic controversy, which in the intervening centuries has called forth a vast volume of literature, in which the sacramental value of art has been debated from every conceivable angle.

The early protagonists with whom we are concerned, once again, as in the Arian quarrels, made use of hymnody as a weapon of attack and defence.

Two groups of poets, living in the seclusion of two famous monasteries, were particularly involved in the dispute when at its height. The first was the St. Sabas group ; and the second, and somewhat later, the Studium group, at Constantinople. Both used the Greek tongue.

The Laura of St. Sabas in those days was a weird and forbidding place. It was perched like an eagle's nest on the edge of a mighty rock overlooking the brook Kedron, and accessible only by ropes. The gorge at that point was known as the Valley of Fire ; it was of savage wildness and desolation, infested by wild animals and scarcely less wild mendicant

E

Arabs. Thither in the fifth century had Sabas come ; at first, it is said, living in a solitary cave from which he had ejected a lion ; one of a long line of hermits who thus sought to escape the pollution of the world.

The circumstances which brought the hymn-writers to this spot are of much interest. Early in the eighth century a certain citizen of the fair city of Damascus was walking in the slave market, when he saw a slave who had been doomed for death by his captors, and whose appearance attracted him. He bought him, and, finding him to be possessed of much learning, made him tutor to his son John. Years afterwards, this slave, whose name was Cosmas, asked leave to retire to St. Sabas, and there subsequently his pupil joined him, bringing with him his foster-brother, whose name also was Cosmas. Some years later John brought his nephew Stephen, then a little lad of ten, to live there too, and there he stayed for nearly sixty years.[1]

Here was indeed a nest of singing birds. John especially was eager to defend the veneration of icons, and he dedicated his great powers to that end. He protested defiantly against the excesses of the iconoclasts, wrote poems and treatises in defence of images, and urged all mothers to take their children by the hand and lead them to look on the sacred pictures and so lift their minds to God, which would, he said, be far better than letting them spend their time in carousals and buffoonery. The final vindication of the cause for which he contended is said to have been largely due to his gifted advocacy. Happily his hymns are not all controversial : some of them take us into a very heaven of peace and joy. His Resurrection hymn is still sung at Easter throughout the Greek Church. Some stanzas taken from it are well known in this country through Dr. Neale's translation :—

> 'Tis the Day of Resurrection ;
> Earth ! tell it out abroad.

[1] For the full story, see the *Life of St. John of Damascus*, by J. H. Lupton. Also Milman's *History of Latin Christianity*, vol. ii.

Another hymn, attributed to him by Neale, is known as
the " Stichera of the Last Kiss." It is sung towards the close
of the burial service, while the friends and relations in turn,
with the priest last of all, kiss the corpse. Here is a part of
it which throbs with deep feeling :—

> Behold and weep me, friends and brethren !
>   Voice, sense, and breath, and motion gone ;
> But yesterday I dwelt among you ;
>   Then death's most fearful hour came on.
> Embrace me with the last embracement ;
>   Kiss me with this, the latest kiss ;
> Never again shall I be with you ;
>   Never with you share woe or bliss.

> I go toward the dread tribunal
>   Where no man's person is preferred ;
> Where lord and slave, where chief and soldier,
>   Where rich and poor alike are heard :
> One is the manner of their judgment ;
>   Their plea and their condition one :
> And they shall reap in woe or glory
>   The earthly deeds that they have done.
> I pray you, brethren, I adjure you,
>   Pour forth to Christ the ceaseless prayer,
> He would not doom me to Gehenna,
>   But in His glory give me share !

The second member of the group, Cosmas, assisted his
foster-brother in the composition of hymns, and himself
wrote some of great power : " Cosmas, divine and glorious,
the spiritual harp, the divine lyre ; . . . thou hast rejoiced all
by the sweet and soft music of thy words." [1]

The little lad Stephen, coming to the monastery in childhood,
was, Neale tells us, the earliest of the hymnographers who lived
to see the final restoration of icons. The famous hymn " Art
thou weary ? " was suggested to Neale by some lines of
Stephen's which he found while exploring the treasures of
early Greek hymnody. It is one of the most powerful hymns
in the English language ; for its full power to be appreciated
it should be sung antiphonally.

[1] The quotation is from the Office for St. Cosmas in the Greek Church
books

The Studium group of hymnists flourished a little later than the Sabaites. Theodore and Anatolius were the most distinguished of the group. Theodore (born 759), for some time abbot of the Studium, came into conflict with Leo, the Armenian, over the Iconoclastic issue. For years he lay in noisome prison cells, and endured hardships unspeakable. Nothing, however, could daunt his spirit, and from his prison he sent out voluminous writings in defence of icons and ordered his supporters to march through the streets, bearing images and chanting hymns, in all these steps braving Leo's anger.

Neale thinks the verses that follow were probably written to celebrate a temporary victory won for his cause :—

> A song, a song of gladness !
>   A song of thanks and praise !
> The horn of our salvation
>   Hath God vouchsafed to raise !
> A monarch true and faithful,
>   And glorious in her might,
> To champion Christ's own quarrel,
>   And Orthodoxy's right !

*   *   *   *   *

> Now cries the blood for vengeance,
>   By persecutors poured,
> Of them that died defending
>   The likeness of the Lord :
> The likeness, as a mortal
>   That He vouchsafed to take,
> Long years ago, in Bethlem,
>   Incarnate for our sake.

> Awake, O Church, and triumph !
>   Exult, each realm and land !
> And open let the houses,
>   The ascetic houses, stand !
> And let the holy virgins
>   With joy and song take in
> Their relics and their icons,
>   Who died this day to win !

*   *   *   *   *

The God of vengeance rises :
  And Christ attacks the foe,
And makes His servants mighty
  The wicked to o'erthrow :
And now Thy condescension
  In boldness may we hymn,
And now in peace and safety
  Thy sacred Image limn.

O Lord of loving kindness,
  How wondrous are Thy ways !
What tongue of man suffices
  Thy gentleness to praise ?
Because of Thy dear Image
  Men dared Thy Saints to kill,
Yet didst Thou not consume them,
  But bear'st their insults still.[1]

The controversial note is only too obvious in these verses. They show that the writer, like many others, found it hard to maintain a spirit of loving sanity amid the heat of religious controversy.

To Anatolius (eighth century), thought to be a pupil of Theodore at the Studium, are attributed more than a hundred hymns, including " The day is past and over," " Fierce was the wild billow " and " A great and mighty Wonder." The first of these is a liturgical expansion of the simple Candlelight hymn quoted in an earlier chapter.[2] Julian gives an interesting account of its use in the great After-Supper Service of the Greek Church. The simplicity of an earlier time has given place to elaborate ritual, and the hymn is chanted in responsive fashion by a double choir as, at the lighting of the lamps, the singers march in procession round the nave of the great cathedral. The following hymn, by Robert Bridges, appears to some extent to be based upon it :—

Dark'ning night the land doth cover ;
  Day is over :
We give thanks, O Thou most high :

[1] Alice Gardner questions the authenticity of this hymn.
[2] See p. 41.

While with wonted hymn we adore Thee,
And implore Thee
For the light that doth not die.

Like a day our short life hasteth ;
Soon it wasteth ;
Cometh surely its sad eve :
O do Thou that eve enlighten,
Save and brighten ;
Nor old age of joy bereave.

Come no pain nor pity near it ;
Bless and cheer it,
That in peace we our peace win :
As Thou wilt, do Thou us gather,
Gracious Father,
Only without shame and sin.

Now we pray for rest, that sleeping
In Thy keeping,
We may joy in the sun's ray :
So through death's last darkness take us,
So awake us
To heav'n's everlasting day.

A third poet of the Studium, of a somewhat later date, was
Theoctistus (*c.* 890). The man who could write like this
must have loved his Saviour : there is no controversial note
here :—

Jesu, Name all names above,
Jesu, best and dearest ;
Jesu, Fount of perfect love,
Holiest, tenderest, nearest ;
Jesu, Source of grace completest,
Jesu purest, Jesu sweetest ;
Jesu, Well of power divine,
Make me, keep me, seal me Thine ![1]

One other writer of the same period must be mentioned.
Joseph " the Hymnographer," though not attached to the
Studium, was the founder of another monastery at Constan-
tinople, and, like Theodore, was banished for his defence of

[1] The translation is by Neale.

icons. His challenge to loyalty to the truth as a man sees it
has a sturdy ring about it :—

> Up and follow, Christian men !
>   Press through toil and sorrow !
> Spurn the night of fear, and then—
>   O the glorious morrow !
> Who will venture on the strife ?
>   Who will first begin it ?
> Who will seize the Land of Life ?
>   Warriors, up and win it !

Dr. Neale's two fine hymns, " Safe home, safe home in
port " and " O happy band of pilgrims," are based upon the
work of this writer.

And here let us pause to glance backward across the years
we have traversed and trace the direction in which Christian
hymnody was tending. First of all we see how intimate is
the relation of the Church's song to its history. Our hymnals
constitute, indeed, a rhymed commentary on the historical
story. Even when the Church was battling for very life, and
devout men were wellnigh overwhelmed in the conflict, song
never ceased. Doubtless many Christians, in the midst of
persecution, were tempted, like Israel of old, to hang their
harps upon the willows, and to cry " How can we sing the
Lord's songs in a strange land ? " Yet even as the children
of Israel found a theme for their poets in their very captivity,
telling each other in song that they could sing no longer, so,
as we have seen, no persecution or warfare, however tense,
and no controversy, however bitter, could silence the lips of
those who loved their Lord. For sorrow, as well as joy, seeks
emotional release, and finds it here. And it is a happy circumstance that the songs soar above the noise of the conflict, and
carry us with them into the empyrean, where the sunshine of
God's love shines on all alike and discord yields to concord.

But certain disquieting tendencies began to emerge. There
was, particularly, an ominous tendency to silence the voice of
the congregation, to rob them of their birthright of common
praise. This was done, in the first place, in the interests of

decency and order, and as a safeguard against heresy. In the Apostolic age the hymns were sung by the whole congregation, and original contributions were encouraged. Even in the time of Jerome this freedom seems to have continued, at any rate in some measure, for, in a letter to Marcellus, he says :—

> In Christian villages little else is to be heard but Psalms ; for which way soever you turn, either you have the ploughman at his plough singing Hallelujahs, the weary brewer refreshing himself with a psalm, or the vine-dresser chanting forth somewhat of David's.

But Jerome noticed the growing tendency to elaboration and specialization in worship-song, and we find him urging that the Christians should not imitate the comedians, "who smoothed their throats with sweet drinks in order to render their melodies more impressive, and that the heart alone can properly make melody to God."[1]

By the year 380 a decree of the Council of Laodicea shows how wide a departure had been made from primitive practice. The decree laid down the rule that " besides the canonical singers, who climb into the gallery and sing from the book, shall none sing in church."[2] A similar decree followed at Chalcedon in 451 : and in the following century the establishment, by Gregory, of his Choir-school at Rome probably finally silenced congregational singing.

The next tendency of importance is a departure from the severely objective content of the early hymns and the introduction of subjective sentiment and of non-scriptural themes. The " Vegetarian " hymn of Prudentius is a striking example of the latter tendency.[3] Gradually the door was opened to legendary lore, and an excess of veneration for the Virgin, who begins to supplant God as the central object of worship.

---

[1] Croak James's *Curiosities of Christian History*.
[2] Dr. Burn's *Life of Niceta of Remesiana*.
[3] It must not be forgotten, however, that this hymn was probably not written to be sung in church.

A further development is seen in the greater attention bestowed upon the artistry of hymn-writing. Many of the Greek hymns are acrostical and alphabetical in form, and rhyme begins slowly to assert itself.

In succeeding chapters we shall see how these tendencies grew, until they altered the whole character of the Christian hymn, and determined the limits of its use, for hundreds of years.

CHAPTER IV

CLAIRVAUX AND ASSISI

NEWMAN once expressed his keen regret that the monastic life, which held so dominant a place in organized religion for wellnigh a thousand years, had no Virgil to picture the even tenor of its way. The monks, he says, " turned their backs upon the wrangling forum, the political assembly and the pantechnicon of trades. . . . All they wanted was the sweet, soothing presence of earth, sky and sea, the hospitable cave, the bright running streams, the easy gifts which mother earth yields." It sounds idyllic, and in some degree it doubtless was so. How happy the lot of those who could separate themselves from the contaminating world around them, and dwell in an oasis of peace ! For that outer world, as the darkness of " the dark ages " settled down upon it, was not a desirable place to live in. Europe slowly fell into chaos ; its organized life was shattered to fragments by the oncoming hordes of barbarism ; fire and sword, sensuality and ignorance, engulfed a derelict Empire ; the Church itself sank again and again into an abyss of degradation ; and all things seemed hastening to their final doom. No wonder earnest-hearted men, harassed, disappointed, unable to see a gleam of light in the darkness, fled to solitude, as stricken deer to the waterbrooks, and sought within the sweet seclusion of the monastic walls the peace denied them in the world. Soldiers who fought in the trenches during the great European war speak of the song of the lark mingling with the awful diapason of battle. So from the quietude of the cloister many sweet songs arose above the discord, and from purified lips told a weary world, like the angelic choirs of old, of One who came to bring peace and good will to men.

This is not the place to review the rise and decline of

European monasticism. It is our delightful task rather, in these pages, to listen to the songs of aspiration and love, of hope and praise, which were poured out from the hearts of men and women who, by the beauty of their lives, transfused and sweetened the monastic system.

The story largely gathers round certain outstanding poets or groups of poets, and to them we must look as pointing, so to speak, the main line of march. Their work reached its culminating point in the twelfth and thirteenth centuries, with the two groups of writers who gathered round Bernard of Clairvaux and Francis of Assisi. After that time a decline set in, and the grand note was missing until Luther came to re-sound it.

At their best the hymns of the monastery ministered to all that was true and holy in men's lives. They are solemn and majestic in tone, and their music, sounding across the centuries, still brings joy and strength to Christ's people.

Perhaps the most notable departure, so far as form is concerned, from the hymnody of the early Church, is seen in the introduction of rhyme, which has so greatly enriched and beautified the worship-song of Christendom. Rhyme was not an entirely new element. It appears in Hilary and the Ambrosian hymn-writers, and may even occasionally be found in Virgil and Ovid and Horace.[1] Milton, in a notable passage, objected, as we have seen Johnson did, to its intrusion into the domain of sacred poetry. He described it as " the invention of a barbarous age, to set off wretched matter and lame metre." It is worthy of note, in passing, that although Milton—no doubt in obedience to a true instinct—discarded it in his great epic, he made use of it in many of his other poems. In his paraphrase of Psalm cxxxvi, he used not rhyme only, but the equally effective artistry of the refrain :—

> Let us, with a gladsome mind,
> Praise the Lord, for He is kind :
> For His mercies aye endure,
> Ever faithful, ever sure.

[1] For examples, see Trench's Introduction to his *Sacred Latin Poetry*.

Trench has stated with convincing power the case for rhyme as an aid to hymnody. It is by no means a mere embellishment, though doubtless it may become so. " It is rather," says Trench, " like music, like dramatic representation, the natural result of a deep craving of the human mind." Nor must its practical usefulness as an aid to memory be forgotten. In an age when few could read, it is not to be wondered at that leaders of religious thought availed themselves of so powerful a subsidiary aid to the propagation of their evangel.

Before turning to the writings associated with the two great names suggested by the heading of this chapter, let us briefly glance at a few of the more notable Latin hymns of earlier date, chiefly of the ninth century. Of typical Ambrosian hymns (by which is meant those written after the style of Ambrose), none is more notable, or displays more perfectly their austere simplicity and loftiness of thought, than the " Jam lucis orto sidere." Its authorship and its date are alike unknown, but whoever wrote it, the fact that, after at least a thousand years, such a hymn, coming to us from another community and tongue, is still in constant use, bears witness to the true communion of saints, independent of time, or creed, or nationality. It is a simple prayer to live each day well. Of many translations, the following by Neale is perhaps the best :—

Now that the daylight fills the sky
We lift our hearts to God on high,
That He, in all we do or say,
Would keep us free from harm to-day :

Would guard our hearts and tongues from strife ;
From anger's din would hide our life ;
From all ill sights would turn our eyes ;
Would close our ears from vanities :

Would keep our inmost conscience pure ;
Our souls from folly would secure ;
Would bid us check the pride of sense
With due and holy abstinence.

So we, when this new day is gone,
And night in turn is drawing on,
With conscience by the world unstain'd
Shall praise His Name for victory gain'd.

Two famous hymns on the Holy Spirit are believed to date
from the ninth century. The " Veni Creator Spiritus " is of
exceptional historical interest. It finds a place, in two renderings (one by Bishop Cosin, " Come, Holy Ghost, our souls
inspire," and the other, of sixteen verses, by an unknown
author, " Come, Holy Ghost, eternal God "), in the English
Prayer Book, and is the only metrical hymn officially recognized
by the Anglican Church. It is sung at the coronation of
kings, the consecration of bishops and the ordering of priests.
It is associated with the great name of Dryden through his
translation " Creator Spirit, by whose aid." Selborne gives
a delightful account of its origin.[1] It is related that the monk,
Notker, was moved by the sound of a mill-wheel to compose
a " sequence " on the Holy Spirit, which, when finished, he
sent as a present to the Emperor Charles, who in return
sent him back, by the same messenger, the hymn " Veni
Creator."[2]

The other Pentecostal hymn, the " Veni Sancte Spiritus,"
or " The Golden Sequence," " Holy Spirit, Lord of Light,"
has been characterized by Trench as the loveliest of all the
hymns in the whole cycle of Latin sacred poetry.

Notker (ninth century), to whom reference has just been
made, claims our interest. He was a monk at the Benedictine
Abbey of St. Gall, a noted centre of German literature, art
and music, and especially famous for its choir-school.[3] Two
of his friends joined him there, and as they were so often seen
together, passing long hours in the Scriptorium, cultivating
their mutual love of poetry and music, the monks called
them " the three inseparables." Notker was a favourite of

[1] See his article on " Hymns " in the *Encyclopædia Britannica*, pp. 185–6.
[2] The Emperor referred to was not Charlemagne, but his grandson.
[3] For the history of this important centre of culture, see *The Abbey of St. Gall*, by J. M. Clark.

the Emperor Charles the Fat. On one occasion the Emperor
sent a request to him for advice on the conduct of his spiritual
life. The monk was in the garden, watering and weeding
plants, when the royal messenger arrived. " Tell the
Emperor," he said, " to do as I am doing now." " Yes,"
said the Emperor, when receiving the advice, " that is the
sum of all."

Notker is of importance to our story, as he is practically the
inventor of sequences.[1]   In the Church of St. Gall, at certain
intervals in the services, it was customary for the choir to
lengthen out the closing syllable of the Alleluia, sometimes
to the extent of fifty or a hundred notes. Apparently, also, in
spite of the choir-school, the singing was far from perfect, for
we read that sometimes it sounded like " a great roar, as
though carts were tumbling down steps headlong." Notker
set about improving this state of affairs. Fortunately for
him, a visitor came to St. Gall from the French monastery of
Jumièges, where the difficulty with the singing of the Alleluia
had been overcome by the simple device of fitting words to
each note.[2]   This Notker proceeded to do for his own monastery. His sequences at first met with opposition, but the
Emperor was on his side, and soon a series, adapted to nearly
all the festivals of the Church's year, were produced. Here is
the " Joyful Sequence of the blessed St. Notker for the Epiphany
of Christ," the " Cantemus Cuncti," in Neale's translation [3] :

The strain upraise of joy and praise,
                Alleluia.

To the glory of their King
Shall the ransom'd people sing
                Alleluia.

[1] A sequence was originally a prolonged succession of notes sung on
the last syllable of the Alleluia. Later it came to mean " a composition
in rhythmical prose or accentual metre, said or sung, in the Western Church,
after the Alleluia and before the Gospel " (Murray's *Dictionary*).
[2] An Irish monk, Mœngal, is also reported to have given Notker a pattern
sequence.
[3] Julian rejects a theory that Godescalcus was its author.

And the Choirs that dwell on high
Shall re-echo through the sky
   Alleluia.

They through the fields of Paradise that roam,
The blessed ones, repeat through that bright home
   Alleluia.

The planets glitt'ring on their heav'nly way,
The shining constellations, join and say
   Alleluia.

Ye clouds that onward sweep !
Ye winds on pinions light !
Ye thunders, echoing loud and deep !
Ye lightnings, wildly bright !
In sweet consent unite your
   Alleluia.

Ye floods and ocean billows !
Ye storms and winter snow !
Ye days of cloudless beauty !
Hoar-frost and summer glow !
Ye groves that wave in spring,
And glorious forests, sing
   Alleluia.

First let the birds, with painted plumage gay,
Exalt their great Creator's praise and say
   Alleluia.

Then let the beasts of earth, with varying strain,
Join in Creation's hymn, and cry again
   Alleluia.

Here let the mountains thunder forth, sonorous,
   Alleluia.
There let the valleys sing in gentler chorus
   Alleluia.

Thou jubilant abyss of ocean cry
   Alleluia.
Ye tracts of earth and continents reply
   Alleluia.

To God, who all Creation made,
The frequent hymn be duly paid :
   Alleluia.

This is the strain, th'eternal strain, the Lord of all things
  loves :   ·   Alleluia.
This is the song, the heav'nly song, that Christ Himself
  approves :   Alleluia.

Wherefore we sing, both heart and voice awaking,
                                    Alleluia.
And children's voices echo, answer making,
                                    Alleluia.

Now from all men be outpoured
Alleluia to the Lord ;
With Alleluia evermore
The Son and Spirit we adore.

Praise be done to the Three in One,
                        Alleluia !   Alleluia !

That glorious song of praise is based on Psalm cxlviii, and
should be compared with the " Benedicite." It is full of the
joy of the open air, of mountain spaces and forest solitudes,
as is the fair land from which it comes.

The Advent hymn, " O Come, O Come, Emmanuel," is
said to have similarly been evolved from the lengthening out
of the notes of the letter " O."

Sequences in great number continued to be written for many
generations after the time of Notker, and were brought to final
perfection, so far as poetic form is concerned, three hundred
years later, by Adam of St. Victor.

No two names in the whole history of Christianity in the
Middle Ages stand out with greater prominence than Bernard
of Clairvaux and Francis of Assisi.

Bernard (b. 1091) was, until recently, generally regarded as
the author of that exquisite mediæval hymn, the " Jesu dulcis
Memoria," best known to us through Caswall's translation,
" Jesu, the very thought of Thee." To him also it has been
customary to attribute a number of other hymns, including

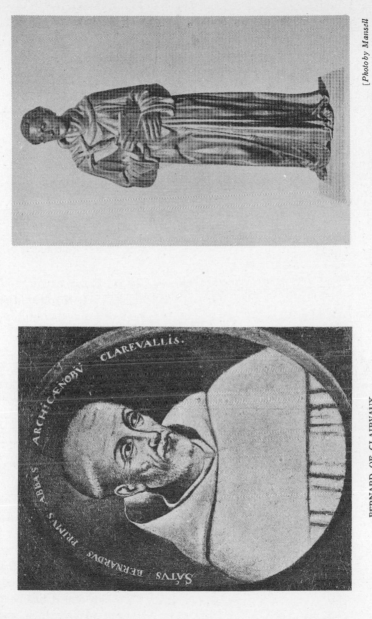

[*Photo by Mansell*

FRANCIS OF ASSISI
(Statue by Donatello)

BERNARD OF CLAIRVAUX
(*By permission of Librairie Lecoffre, Paris*)

With Abélard a new spirit of religious questioning dawned
on the Western world.   When he began to lecture in Paris
on religious themes, bringing the fundamental ideas of Christian
truth to the test of reason, throwing them into the arena of
public discussion, and attracting crowds of young enquiring
minds to hear him, Bernard was alarmed : " A horror of great
darkness fell upon him." Two principles were at stake : two
avenues of approach to the faith—the way of intuition and
the way of reason.   Apparently two paths, they surely at last
converge.

> Mind and soul, according well,
> May make one music.

At first, Bernard refused to meet Abélard.   Faith, with
him, says Vaughan, " receives the treasure of truth, as it were,
wrapped up (*involutum*).   Understanding may afterwards
cautiously unfold the envelope, and peep at the prize, but
may never examine the contents first, to determine whether
it shall be received or not." [1]   How then could he bring
himself to enter the public arena where the dearest objects
of his faith would be stripped naked to the public gaze ?
How endure his rival's " foolology," as he disdainfully described
Abélard's reasoning ?—Abélard, the frigid intellectual, who,
he declared, " is prepared to give reasons for everything, even
for those things beyond reason and contrary to it ! " [2]

Our concern, however, is not with Abélard's polemics, but
with his poetry.   There is a tradition that in his youth he
was one of a company of troubadours, such as made their
fatherland joyous with harp and song.[3]   Duffield records that
in early life he wrote " wild, unhallowed verses," and that
later he composed songs to his lover Héloïse, and set them
to such stirring tunes that soon all the world was singing
them.[4]   His hymns were written at the request of Héloïse

---

[1] Vaughan's *Hours with the Mystics.*
[2] For a full treatment of the matter, see Cotter Morison's *Life and Times
of St. Bernard* ; also S. J. Eales' *St. Bernard.*
[3] Rémusat's *Abélard,* vol. i, p. 54, n.
[4] Duffield's *Latin Hymns.*

for use in the Abbey of the Paraclete, of which she became the Abbess. He dedicated them " to my dear sister, dear while in the world, but more dear now in Christ." They include hymns on the Creation, Scripture history, the Trinity, the Virgin, and the life and work of Christ. The first hymn, which is a long sequence in praise of all created things, contains a section of special human interest, in which a contrast is drawn between the lot of a rich man in his well-furnished house and the homeless poor. The following is a fairly literal translation [1] :—

He who cannot furnish himself with a fire in winter is warmed
    by the sun ;
For his lamp at night, the poor man has the moon and the stars :
The rich man lies on couches of ivory ;
The poor man, lying on the springing turf,
Is delighted by the songs of the birds,
And he breathes the fragrance of the flowers.
The rich man constructs an expensive house,
—Which is bound some day to come to the ground—
Its vault painted with a make-believe sun and stars :
The poor man lies in his most beautiful room, under a real sky,
Which God has painted for him, with a real sun and stars.

Here is his " heaven " hymn, which is in wide use in this country, thanks once more to Neale :—

O what their joy and their glory must be,—
Those endless Sabbaths the blessed ones see !
Crown for the valiant : to weary ones rest :
God shall be all, and in all ever blest.

What are the Monarch, his court, and his throne ?
What are the peace and the joy that they own ?
Tell us, ye blest ones, that in it have share,
If what ye feel ye can fully declare.

Truly " Hierusalem " name we that shore,
" Vision of Peace " that brings joy evermore :
Wish and fulfilment can sever'd be ne'er,
Nor the thing pray'd for come short of the prayer.

[1] Abélard's *Opera*, ed. Cousin, vol. i., p. 300.

We, where no trouble distraction can bring,
Safely the anthems of Syon shall sing;
While for Thy grace, Lord, their voices of praise
Thy blessed people shall evermore raise.

There dawns no Sabbath; no Sabbath is o'er;
Those Sabbath-keepers have one, and no more;
One and unending is that triumph-song
Which to the Angels and us shall belong.

Now in the meanwhile, with hearts raised on high,
We for that country must yearn and must sigh:
Seeking Hierusalem, dear native land:
Through our long exile on Babylon's strand.

Low before Him with our praises we fall,
Of whom, and in whom, and through whom are all:
Of whom, the Father; and in whom, the Son;
Through whom, the Spirit, with these ever One.

Not far from Clairvaux was the great Abbey of Cluny, where Abélard, at the conclusion of his dialectical debate with Bernard, found a hospitable asylum on his journey from Paris to Rome, and where, through the kindly offices of Peter the Abbot, he and Bernard became somewhat reconciled. The magnificence of Cluny was in striking contrast to the simplicity of Clairvaux. It was the most influential and magnificent religious establishment in France. Hundreds of lesser monasteries owed allegiance to it; it boasted enormous wealth; its abbot lived in princely state; its furnishings and its table were luxurious. Outside its walls there was oppression, poverty, disease, degradation, war. Who can abide these contrasts? They exist still, though perhaps the colours, the lights and shades, are not so strongly painted. Stately cathedrals still overshadow filthy slums; the peace and dignity of the cathedral-close still jostle the squalor and sensuality of the overcrowded city. Bernard of Clairvaux came thundering against Cluny, and his anger found an echo in the breast of at least one of the monks there. Sick at heart, this poor monk retired to his cell, and there penned a poem satirizing the whole crazy business. He had no remedy to offer on this side the grave, but on the other he was sure the balance would be adjusted. He entitled his poem " On Contempt of the World," and by way of preface placed the warning words " Little children, it is the last time." Who he was is not quite certain. He also, like the great Abbot of Clairvaux, bore the name of Bernard. Some say he came from Morlaix, and that he was of Cornish descent. His satire attracted wide notice, and was frequently quoted in later times by religious reformers when exposing the corruptions of Church and State. We know it through Neale's masterly translation, and especially through the verses beginning " Jerusalem the Golden," where we have a wonderful picture of a heaven where all wrongs will be righted, and joy and peace will come to full fruition :—

> The home of fadeless splendour,
> Of flowers that fear no thorn,
> Where they shall dwell as children
> Who here as exiles mourn.

The structure of Bernard's verses, considering the age in which they were written, is highly intricate. The rhymes seem to tumble over one another ; here, for instance, is the couplet with which the poem abruptly opens :—

> Hora Novissima, tempora pessima sunt ; vigilemus !
> Ecce minaciter imminet Arbiter Ille supremus.

Let the words be read aloud, and it will be seen that the poet has interwoven six rhymes into the couplet. This measure is maintained through several hundred lines. The writer is sure he could not have achieved so hard a task unless " the Spirit of Wisdom and Understanding " had been with him, and had " flowed in upon so difficult a metre." [1]

In judging of the value of this hymn for congregational use to-day, the circumstance of its origin should be taken into account, and it should be remembered that it comes from a

[1] The reader is referred to *The Rhyme of Bernard de Morlaix*, by J. M. Neale.

time when many believed that Christ would soon return to the world, and thoughts of the coming apocalyptic judgment filled their imagination.

At the very time that Bernard of Clairvaux was acting as arbitrator between rival claimants to the papacy (in 1130), a youth named Adam of Brito was admitted as a monk into the great Abbey of St. Victor, in Paris, and there he passed the rest of his life. He was there when the Victorine theologians set before themselves the task of reconciling the rival schools of thought represented by Abélard and Bernard. Adam was a born poet. Trench and Neale agree in their estimate that he was the greatest Latin hymn-writer of the Middle Ages. But such a verdict all depends on the angle from which his work is viewed. If literary grace, the mastery of alliteration and of the intricacies of rhyme—in short, an almost uncanny power in the musical manipulation of words—is the test, Adam can out-Herbert George Herbert himself. The English reader who scans his lines can easily detect that fact, even if he cannot read a word of Latin. And no doubt more important qualities distinguish his hymns.[1] But there is an excess of artistry; and if judged by the test of the permanent value of his hymns for public worship, Adam of St. Victor must be said to have failed. A quotation from one of his sequences will be of interest. Its theme is the warfare which the Church militant must ceaselessly wage against her spiritual foes :—

> The world, the flesh, and Satan rage,
> Their diff'ring wars against us wage ;
> And when their phantom-hosts come on,
> The Sabbath of the heart is gone ;
> And storms confused about us low'r
> Of hope and fear, and joy and woe :
> And scarcely ev'n for one half-hour
> Is silence in God's house below.[2]

[1] Julian's *Dictionary of Hymnology*, p. 648.
[2] See *The Hymnal Noted*; the hymn commencing " The Church on earth with answering love."

Bernard of Clairvaux died in 1153. Less than thirty years later Francis of Assisi was born. In his youth the troubadours were roaming over Southern France and Northern Italy, taking joy and festivity with them on their wanderings. They were often men of culture, and their writings form a conspicuous part of the literary product of their age. Their principal theme was that which has inspired the folk-songs of all nations more ardently than any other : they wrote " all for the love of a ladye." Francis in his youth was attracted to them. His biographers picture him as a lover of romance, given to gaiety, fond of song and jest, everyone's favourite. His whole life may be likened to a canticle of joy and praise. He and his Brothers lived together in utter simplicity and peace. They were fond of calling themselves God's Jongleurs, and as they worked on the farm, or travelled from village to village, they sang along the footpath way, and we may be sure their songs brought joy to many careworn, labouring men and women, who, we are told, often went out in joyful procession, with green boughs, flags and music, to meet them.[1]

Towards the close of his short life (for he died at forty-five) Francis composed his Canticle of the Sun on this wise. Soon after receiving the Stigmata he set out from Monte Verna for Umbria. As he left Verna he bade farewell not only to the monks, but to the rocks and trees, the flowers and the birds (including " brother hawk," the daily visitant to his cell), and prayed God's blessing on the mountain. Exhausted, and threatened with blindness, he pressed on, singing all the way. He reached St. Damian, and there Sister Clare came to nurse him. One day, after a meal, Clare noticed him wrapt in ecstasy, and on coming to himself she heard him cry, " Praise be to God." In that hour of mystic contemplation and rapture he had composed the Canticle. It is a glorious song of praise for all created things. The " fire " verse is of peculiar interest, for it recalls the incident of the cauterization of his eyes with hot irons—an operation from which at

[1] Matthew Arnold's *Essays in Criticisms*, First Series.

first he naturally shrank, but to which he submitted with beautiful humility, making the sign of the Cross over the irons and saying :—

Brother fire, you are beautiful above all creatures : be favourable to me in this hour : you know how much I have always loved you : be then courteous to-day !

A few weeks later, when told that the Bishop and the Governor of Assisi were quarrelling and that the town was in an uproar, he added another verse :—

Praised be my Lord for all those who pardon one another for love's sake ;

and when they heard it the hearts of the disputants were touched, and they became friends.

When death drew near, he asked the Brothers who were standing round his bed to sing the Canticle, and, after they had done so, he added one further verse of praise for Sister Death. At vesper-time he breathed his last, and men say that as his spirit went to God an innumerable company of birds alighted on the roof of his cell and sang as if to greet him in heaven.[1]

Such notable critics as Renan and Matthew Arnold have recognized the greatness of Francis's Canticle. Renan spoke of it as the most perfect utterance of modern religious sentiment (perhaps a too superlative estimate, for the hymn is limited in its scope), and Arnold described it as the utterance of all that is most exquisite in the spirit of its century. Here is Arnold's translation [2] :—

O most high, almighty, good Lord God, to Thee belong praise, glory, honour and all blessing !

[1] The story of the Canticle is fully and charmingly told by Sabatier in his *Life of St. Francis*.
[2] A metrical translation has recently been made by Dr. Draper, set to the fine old German air *Lasst uns Erfreuen*. See *Hymns of the Kingdom*.

Praised be my Lord God with all His creatures, and specially
our brother the sun, who brings us the day and who brings
us the light; fair is he and shines with a very great splendour: O Lord, he signifies to us Thee!

Praised be my Lord for our sister the moon, and for the stars,
the which He has set clear and lovely in heaven!

Praised be my Lord for our brother the wind, and for air and
cloud, calm and all weathers, by the which Thou upholdest
life in all creatures!

Praised be my Lord for our sister water, who is very serviceable
unto us, and humble and precious and clean!

Praised be our Lord for brother fire, through whom Thou givest
us light in the darkness; and he is bright and pleasant and
very mighty and strong!

Praised be our Lord for our mother the earth, the which doth
sustain us and keep us, and bringeth forth divers fruits and
flowers and many colours, and grass!

Praised be my Lord for all those who pardon one another for
love's sake, and who endure weakness and tribulation;
blessed are they who peacably shall endure, for Thou, O
most Highest, shalt give them a crown!

Praised be my Lord for our sister, the death of the body, from
which no man escapeth. Woe to him who dieth in mortal
sin! Blessed are they who are found walking in Thy most
holy will, for the second death shall have no power to do
them harm.

Praise ye and bless the Lord, and give thanks unto Him and
serve Him with great humility!

Among Francis's band of disciples was Brother Pacifico, a
talented poet, who had won renown, and had even been
crowned with the laurel by the Emperor himself. Legend
tells that one day this man entered a church where Francis
was preaching and saw two flaming swords, which formed
the sign of the Cross, appear on the preacher's cloak. He
thereupon joined the master and helped him to write popular
religious verses, going with him into the villages and market

places, where the people wept with delight as they listened to the impassioned songs of the two young enthusiasts. When by and by Francis sent his disciples into foreign fields, he chose Brother Pacifico for France, judging that his poetic gifts would ensure him a hearing in a country where the troubadours and their songs were always welcome. Nor was he mistaken in his choice. The French heard " God's minstrels " so gladly that a similar mission was determined upon to England.

To St. Francis's circle we owe the two great hymns, the " Stabat Mater " and the " Dies Iræ." " These two," says Milman, " the one by its tenderness, the other by its rude grandeur, stand unrivalled." Tenderness and grandeur ; the soft influences of womanhood and chivalry ; the enervation of a monastic life spoilt by luxury ; the clash of war and dread of impending doom ; all these contending influences had a part to play in the life of Europe in the twelfth and thirteenth centuries, and all are reflected in its hymnody.

Thomas of Celano, the reputed author of the " Dies Iræ," was at Assisi during the lifetime of St. Francis, and afterwards wrote the master's biography.[1] His hymn, more than any other in the whole realm of Christian hymnody, deals in masterly fashion with the terrible themes of death and the judgment. Its author, like Dante, seems to have himself been in the purgatorial fires. He lived in an age when ecclesiastics sat as judges, and their tender mercies often were cruel. The methods to which they resorted included the ordeal and the trial by battle, the rack, the stake, the dungeon, and even burial alive. When Thomas was a lad his own city had been burned to the ground in a great feud between the Papal and the Imperial forces, and many of its inhabitants were transported. It is not improbable that these events burnt themselves into his mind. Terror, the gloom of the law courts,

[1] The authorship of the " Dies Iræ " is discussed in Julian's *Dictionary*, pp. 296 and 1629. It is concluded that it was almost certainly written in Italy in the thirteenth century, and that Thomas of Celano was acquainted with an earlier poem on the same subject.

the awful judgment seat, the prisoners' cry for mercy, are all transferred in his imagination from the Italian stage to the kingdom of the spirit and to the throne of God.[1] Few hymns have excited such widespread interest. A large literature gathers round it. One writer has noted more than two hundred and thirty translators who have turned it into English. It profoundly impressed such great writers as Crashaw, Johnson, Scott and Macaulay. Goethe introduced it with much power into the Minster scene in *Faust*, and Mozart has rendered it in his *Requiem*. It is entirely unsuitable for congregational use, yet few editors of hymnals care to omit it. W. J. Irons' translation "Day of wrath! O day of mourning!" is usually chosen for this purpose. Unfortunately no translation can reproduce the awful triple beats, as of a tolling bell, which make the original Latin lines so impressive :—

> Tuba mirum spargens sonum,
> Per sepulchra regionum,
> Coget omnes ante thronum.

Crashaw's adaptation is little known; here are some of his powerful stanzas :—

> O that fire ! before whose face
> Heaven and Earth shall find no place.
> O those eyes ! whose angry light
> Must be the day of that dread night.
>
> O that trump ! whose blast shall run
> At even round the circling sun,
> And urge the murmuring graves to bring
> Pale mankind forth to meet his King.
>
> * * * * *
>
> O that Book ! whose leaves so bright
> Will set the world in severe light.
> O that Judge ! whose hand, whose eye
> None can indure, yet none can fly.

[1] This line of thought is suggested by W. W. Nevin in the Introduction to his translations of the hymn.

Ah, then, poor soul, what wilt thou say ?
And to what patron choose to pray ?
When stars themselves shall stagger, and
The most firm foot no more can stand ?

But Thou giv'st leave (dread Lord) that we
Take shelter from Thyself in Thee ;
And with the wings of Thine own dove
Fly to the scepter [1] of soft love.

Dear, remember in that Day,
Who was the cause Thou cam'st this way.
Thy sheep was stray'd ; and Thou wouldst be
Even lost Thyself in seeking me.

*   *   *   *   *

O hear a suppliant heart, all crush't
And crumbled into contrite dust.
My hope ! my fear ! my Judge ! my Friend !
Take charge of me and of my end.

The " Stabat Mater " must be dealt with in the next
chapter, as it is desirable to place it in relation to the Marian
cultus of which it is the finest flower.

[1] " Scepter " here symbolizes the seat of supremacy.

CHAPTER V

AN INTERLUDE

IT is difficult to say where the history of the Christian hymn begins or ends. There is no fixed boundary-line. The history of the Church cannot be separated from the general history of mankind. "We include in ' ecclesiastical history,' " says Stanley, " the life of the most insignificant bishop or the most wicked of Popes, not the life of the wisest of philosophers or the most Christian of kings. But such a limitation is as untenable in fact as it is untrue in history. . . . The range of the history of the Church is as wide as the range of the world which it was designed to penetrate." [1] And so with the hymns of the Church. Just as a great river is fed by many streams, and in its course nourishes and refreshes the multitudinous life along its banks, so the worship-song of Christendom is helped by, and in its turns helps, many subsidiary interests that are, in varying degrees, incidental to its growth. Thus, before we are aware, we find our interest enlisted in such delightful themes as the origin of the dance, the folk-lore and folk-songs of primitive peoples ; angelology, carols and the miracle plays ; legends of the Madonna ; lullabies, charms and dirges ; troubadours and wandering minstrels ; and (as we have already seen) the divine arts of music, painting and sculpture.

Trench, in presenting to the members of the English Church his translations of *Sacred Latin Poetry*, expressed his determination to exclude anything that might tend to check the current of their sympathies, or " entangle them unawares in admiration for ought which is inconsistent with their faith and fealty to their own spiritual mother." And he particularly . desired to omit anything that savoured of superstition, or

[1] Stanley's Introduction to his Lectures on *The Eastern Church*.

breathed " a spirit foreign to that tone of piety which the English Church desires to cherish in her children."

Such themes as religious charms and dances might, perhaps, be held to come under Trench's ban. But they are, after all, a part of the human story. Through such humble and childlike media men and women have expressed their religious interest, and we must not fear to study their origins and the part they have played in the human drama. Many different colours find a place in every artist's pictures.

The most famous of all charms that have found an entrance into the Christian Church is the Sign of the Cross. Athanasius, in his *Treatise on the Incarnation*, urged the young Christian when tempted to resort to this charm. " In the very presence of the deceit of demons and the imposture of oracles and the marvels of magic, let him use the Sign of the Cross which is laughed at among them, and he will see how by its means demons flee, oracles cease, all magic and witchcraft is brought to nought." St. Anthony also, in warning some monks who came to him for instruction to beware of the Greek oracles, said, " Have no dealings with them, but rather sign yourselves and your houses and pray, and you shall see them vanish. For they are cowards, and greatly fear the Sign of the Lord's Cross." [1] It is worthy of remark that the Jewish tendencies towards the use of incantations and magic led to a famous protest at Ephesus [2] ; but the tendency seems difficult to eradicate. The Sign of the Cross, along with such signs as the lorica,[3] the phylactery, and the more heathenish horse-shoe and red-hand, show themselves tenacious in their hold upon the superstitious mind of the people. In this country certain rhymes were long believed to have special powers. Some of Anglo-Saxon origin are of great interest. Halliwell gives one of thirty-six lines which was used against dangers of the

[1] " Vita S. Antoni," par 35, in the Athanasius volume of the *Nicene and Post-Nicene Fathers*.
[2] Acts xix. 19.   [3] See p. 112.

night, such as cramp and thieves.[1] Here is one against nightmare :—

> In nomine Patris, up and downe,
> Et Filii, et Spiritus Sancti, upon my crowne,
> Crux Christi upon my brest,
> Sweet Ladie, send me eternall rest.

A delightful old Cornish charm, still to be seen in cottage bedrooms, says :—

> From Ghoulies and Ghoosties,
> Lang-leggety Beasties,
> And things that go Bump in the night,
> Good Lord, deliver us !

And so we come to the famous " White Paternoster," [2] " a waif from the fabric of early Christian popular lore," which has long kept its hold on the popular imagination :—

> Matthew, Mark, Luke and John,
> Bless the bed that I lie on !
> Four corners to my bed,
> Four angels round my head,
> One to watch and one to pray,
> And two to bear my soul away.

In a German version there are fourteen guardian angels :—

> Two to my left hand,
> Two to my right,
> Who watch me ever
> By day and night ;
> Two at my head,
> Two at my feet,
> To guard my slumber
> Soft and sweet ;
> Two to wake me
> At break of day,
> When night and darkness
> Pass away ;
> Two to cover me
> Warm and nice,
> And two to lead me
> To Paradise.

---

[1] Halliwell's *Popular Rhymes and Nursery Tales.*
[2] Cesaresco's *The Study of Folk-Songs.*

The " White Paternoster " is not far removed from some of the " Vesper " verses which to-day are in regular use in our places of worship :—

> May angels guard us while we sleep,
> Till morning light appears !

Angels occupy a large place in the pages of our present day hymn books. They introduce us into a strange, transcendental world. They figure prominently in the Old Testament. Jehovah has them at His command : they wait continually upon Him, " hearkening unto the voice of His word." In the Book of Daniel (Oesterley suggests under the influence of Persian thought [1]) the writer pictures vast armies of them, " ten thousand times ten thousand and thousand thousands." There is, as one would expect, a tradition that the Psalmist learned from them the divine art.

> 'Twas they of their art taught David to sing,
> And faith evermore hath knelt at his spring :
> Through them the world doth with music abound,
> Of viols and reeds and horns of rich sound.

In the New Testament they were entrusted with the annunciation to Mary ; they brought the news of the birth of Jesus to the shepherds ; they comforted the Saviour after His temptation and after the agony in the garden ; they announced His resurrection to the wondering women ; and in a series of wonderful pictures in the Revelation they are seen serving and praising God. In the early Church they were venerated, and there was much speculation upon their nature. The English religious poets follow their Hebrew forerunners : Milton, especially, after the pattern of Daniel, marshals myriads of them on his mighty stage—the good spending the happy hours in joyful song before the throne

---

[1] Oesterley's *Immortality and the Unseen World.*

G

of God, or speeding o'er land and ocean at His bidding ; the evil, " in thick array of depth inmeasurable," moving, at Satan's high command,

> In perfect phalanx to the Dorian mood
> Of flutes.

Some notable hymns by recent writers are addressed to the guardian angels who are thought to be deputed to watch over us from infancy to old age, helping us in life's upward struggle. Such are Faber's " Dear Angel, ever at my side," and the Angels' Song in Newman's " Dream of Gerontius " :—

> My Father gave
> In charge to me
> This child of earth
> E'en from its birth,
> To serve and save ;
> Alleluia !
> And saved is he.

> This child of clay
> To me was given
> To real and train
> By sorrow and pain
> In the narrow way,
> Alleluia !
> From earth to heaven.

Neale, too, as we should expect, often makes a place for guardian angels in his hymns :—

> Around the throne of God a band
> Of glorious Angels always stand ;
> Bright things they see, sweet harps they hold,
> And on their heads are crowns of gold.

> *   *   *   *   *

> Lord, give Thy Angels every day
> Command to guide us on our way,
> And bid them every evening keep
> Their watch around us while we sleep.

Angels had their part assigned to them in the early liturgical dialogues which were the forerunners of the mediæval Mystery Plays. In this country, as early as the tenth century, within the walls of the monasteries, the Resurrection scene was enacted in dialogue fashion by the priests. One, dressed in a white robe, and carrying a palm, sat at the sepulchre ; three others, representing the women, approached as if seeking something, and were asked, " Whom seek ye ? " The three replied, in unison, " Jesus of Nazareth." And so the familiar conversation proceeded, until at last the cloth was held up in the face of the clergy, to demonstrate that Christ had risen indeed, when they sang the " Te Deum " and " all the bells chimed out together." A similar ceremony, dating from the same period, was enacted at St. Gall. Here we have the origin of the " Victimae Paschali " hymn, upon which some of our best-known present-day Easter hymns are based.[1] Other dialogues represented the walk to Emmaus, the incredulity of Thomas, and the Nativity. Sometimes grotesque humour and buffoonery were admitted into the sacred plays during their performance in the churches. At Beauvais and elsewhere, in the thirteenth century, the famous " Donkey Festival " was enacted. A beautiful girl, carrying a doll-image of the Holy Child, rode on a richly caparisoned ass to the church, where, accompanied by the bishop and clergy, she made her way to the altar, the people singing a hymn of welcome, to a jolly song-tune :—

> From the Eastern regions far,
> See the holy donkey comes,

and ending with the chorus *Hin-ham, Hin-ham, Hin-ham,* to represent the braying of the ass.[2]

When from these simple beginnings the Mystery Plays

---

[1] This hymn will be found in *The English Hymnal*, beginning " Christians, to the Paschal Victim." See also *The Religious Drama*, chap. ii, by Gordon Crosse.

[2] Isaac Disraeli's Essay *Ancient and Modern Saturnalia* gives details of profanities of a like nature.

proper emerged, the playwrights introduced hymns and carols into their plots. In Bayle's Play, *God's Promises*, for instance, each act ends with a verse of " The Great Os " Sequence (known to us in its metrical form, " O Come, O Come, Emmanuel "), which was sung by a choir to an instrumental accompaniment.

In the Coventry Nativity Play the shepherds sing the carol " As I out rode this enderes' night " ; and in a further scene the mothers, after Herod has threatened to kill the boy babies, sing a lullaby to the following lovely air :—

Lul - ly, lul - la, you lit - tle tiny child; By - by, lul - ly, lul - lay. You lit - tle tiny child; Lul - ly, lul - la, By - by, lul - ly, lul - lay.

We are witnessing, as we try to relate these events to our main story, the ineradicable tendency of the common people to create their own hymnody, crude and homely though it may be ; and their refusal to allow the ecclesiastics to silence them in the churches. The joy of life wells up eternal in the human heart, and must find its natural expression.

This popular movement was conspicuously aided by the troubadours, minnesingers, minstrels and gleemen—for they went by many names—who figured so joyously in the social life of the Middle Ages. In Provence, that land of sunshine and gaiety, the troubadours, in court and manor, in farm and fair, sang their songs of love and chivalry. After the Crusades their numbers rapidly increased, and the people eagerly learned their songs—songs which so vividly mirrored the life and interests of their time that their authors have been described as " painters from real life."

Many of the Provençal troubadours were aristocrats. Kings and nobles have been numbered among them ; and even some clergy, at the risk of excommunication, joined their ranks. Their songs are delightfully varied in character. Some attack the vices of the Court and the Church ; some are popular romances ; others—and this type tended to predominate—are passionate love-songs. The worship of womanhood became a cult with the troubadours. Each had his favourite heroine, who was not necessarily his own lover, but often the wife or daughter of some nobleman whose smile or patronage the singer desired to obtain. The step from secular to sacred love was natural. Songs to Diana and Venus developed by easy gradations into Hymns to the Virgin ; the Princess of the earthly Court became the Queen of Heaven. Ecclesiasticism viewed these happenings with mixed feelings. Did the *trouveres* sing in honour of Mary and the Saints ? Then let them be encouraged ! Did they satirize the failings of the priests ? Then let them be condemned ![1]

In Germany, the Minnesingers wrote in more serious vein. They were a numerous clan ; Miss Winkworth says that more than two hundred of them are still known by name. Walter von der Wogelweide (of the Birds' Nests) is the chief of them, and upon him his fellow-bards bestowed the name "the sweetest of all nightingales." He mistrusted the organized religion of his time, and wrote songs lampooning the Pope, which greatly delighted the populace. In a song "To the Archangels "[2] he roundly rates Gabriel, Michael and Raphael for not coming to the help of his Anti-papal partisanship :—

> I ought to greet you angels too,
> But that I'm far too wise to do :
> What to the heathen have ye wrought of ill ?
> Since all unseen ye are and voiceless still,

---

[1] Camden described these satirical verses as " bobbing rhymes." Some were written by priests.
[2] *The Poems of Walter von der Wogelweide*, Introduction by W. A. Phillips.

Tell us, to help the work, what have ye done ?
If silently I too could wreak
God's vengeance, think not I would speak :
I'd leave you gentlemen alone !

Sir Michael, Sir Gabriel,
Sir foe of devils Raphael,
Wisdom is yours, and strength, and art of healing :
And three angelic hosts behind you wheeling
Haste to obey your orders joyfully.
If you want praise, then show some sense !
The heathen mock your impotence :
Praised I you now, they'd mock at me !

In Volgelweide, as in many other of the Minnesingers, the
transition from the praise of earthly to heavenly love is clearly
seen. First he idealizes womanhood, and sings of the effect
of pure love on a man's character :—

Whoso the love of a good woman heeds
Will be ashamed of evil deeds.

His democratic sympathies make him impatient of the social
snobbery which distinguishes between " women " and " ladies."

Ladies there are unwomanly ;
    Of women none could say the same
A woman's face is fair to see,
    And fair to speak a woman's name.
However it with ladies fare,
Women the while all ladies are ;
    A mockery is doubtful praise,
    As " Ladyship " may be :
But " Womanhood " is woman's crown always.[1]

Here is his " Morning Prayer," translated by Miss Winkworth :—

In safety may I rise to-day ;
Lord God, defend Thou all my way,
Where'er I go or ride throughout the land.
O Christ, now suffer me to prove
The mighty power of Thy dear love,

[1] Translated by W. A. Phillips.

And for Thy mother's sake guard me on every hand :
  As holy angels from on high
Once guarded Thee when Thou didst lie,
  Thou ancient God, a babe of days,
Before the ox and ass so meek and still ;
  When Joseph ever good and true
  To Thee and them gave tendance due,
  With faithful care that still hath praise ;
So care Thou, Lord, for me, in me fulfil
  Thine own commands, and keep me in Thy ways.

In England, the Gleemen, or Minstrels, as they were called, were light-hearted, merry fellows, carrying about the country-side not merely glees, but glee itself.[1] No festival seemed complete without them, and everywhere they met with a popular welcome. Bishop Percy, in his famed *Reliques*, has made a collection of their songs. He says they sometimes assisted at Divine service in the churches, presumably leading the chanting with voice or instrument, wearing the clerical tonsure as they did so. Thus familiarizing themselves with the worship of the Church, they introduced Latin lines or words into their popular songs, and interlarded sacred and secular in their love-ditties.

The monks, many of whom wrote verses in the retirement of the monasteries, interested themselves in the minstrels' songs, and doubtless sometimes helped to write or improve them. Percy says there are innumerable records that the singers were welcomed into the monasteries. The earliest-known English part-song, " Sumer is icumen in," was com-posed by a monk of Reading Abbey. Each group of writers no doubt tended to encroach on the other's ground, as such surviving folk-songs as " I'll sing you One, ho ! " and " The Twelve Days of Christmas," with their strange jumble of sacred and secular, seem to illustrate.

Towards the end of the sixteenth century the minstrels in this country fell into sad disrepute. Becket, who, as Chan-cellor, had been liberal to them, when he became Archbishop

[1] C. A. Harris, in *The Story of British Music*.

turned them unpaid away from Court, and well-conducted monasteries would no longer entertain them.   Queen Elizabeth finally gave them their *coup de grâce* by classing them with " rogues, vagabonds and sturdy beggars," and adjudging them to be punished as such.   Their connection, in this country, with hymnody may appear to be slight, but there can be no doubt that they had a share in helping forward the movement for the provision of people's vernacular hymns which came to a head at the Reformation.

The worship of the Virgin Mary was greatly stimulated by the song-literature of the troubadours.   It is difficult to say from what source the cultus first sprang.   The feminine element in mythology and in religion seems to respond to an elemental human craving.   Eve, Astarte, Isis, Demeter, Diana, Cybele, Venus or Aphrodite, and many others, are types of that dominant idea of a mother goddess, a woman who extends her sympathy and care to the sons of men.   The dim, unformed feelings of veneration for these shadowy figures were gathered up, so Catholic writers aver, " into the pure, dignified, tender image of the Madonna." [1]

However it originated, there can be no doubt that the Crusades of the eleventh and twelfth centuries, followed by the love-literature of the troubadours and the appearance of Dante's great poem and Giotto's marvellous pictures, led to a widespread increase in the worship of the Virgin.   She becomes the Queen of Heaven and the Mother of God. Innumerable churches and chapels are built in her honour ; guilds are formed ; pictures of amazing beauty are painted ; flowers and even tiny insects are named after her [2] ; poets sing her praises ; legends and stories are told of her ; and in all the popular response is passionately enthusiastic.

No form of Marian adoration met with more ready favour than the Carols which were written around the cradle.[3]

[1] Anna B. Jameson's *Legends of the Madonna.*
[2] E.g., Marigold, Rosemary, Lady-bird, etc.
[3] This paragraph and some that follow are largely reprinted from an article of mine in *The Friends' Quarterly Examiner*, October 1921.

Carols differ in many respects from hymns. They are less formal, and in their joyful abandon are more expressive of popular feeling. Though sometimes trivial and even non-sensical, their scenic and picturesque qualities, no less than their strong human appeal, have always endeared them to the common people. A Carol—the Italian *Carola*—like the English *Round-a-lay*, as the word clearly implies, is essentially a song-dance.

From time immemorial dancing has entered into religious ceremonial. All primitive people have their sacred dances, which are indispensably associated with the great crises of life, such as birth, puberty, marriage, death, victory and harvest. Our English sword-dance, in all probability, was originally a nature dance to promote fertility.[1] The Greeks introduced the dance into nearly all their religious festivals ; the rites of Dionysius anticipated the more elaborate dances of their later drama. The Jews danced at their social, religious, and military festivals. Jesus saw the children dancing in the market-place, and He it was who told us that the return of the prodigal son was celebrated with music and dance. Dancing, we know, was permitted in the ritual of the early Christian Church, for there are rules dating from as early as the sixth century regulating the custom. The leaders of the mediæval Church looked on it with suspicion, as savouring of heathenism and the tavern, but they were unable wholly to suppress it.[2]

It is still the custom in Spain for the choristers, on certain festivals, to dance round the lectern of Seville Cathedral, striking their castanets to the movement of their bodies ; whilst in our own country, at York, until the seventeenth century, an apprentices' dance took place in the nave of the Minster. It is therefore not surprising to find that numbers of mediæval Carol melodies are built up on charming old

[1] The Report of the Adult Education Committee appointed by the Board of Education : chapter on the Drama.
[2] Oesterley's *The Sacred Dance* should be consulted for a full treatment of this subject. It is a learned and fascinating book.

dance measures, including the gavotte, the bourrée, and the gigue. Here is one such [1] :—

It is pre-eminently to Francis of Assisi that we owe the softening and humanizing influences which produced the beautiful Carolry of the Middle Ages. With him and his circle of friends, unmarried men though they were, the domestic aspect of the birth-story became conspicuous, making a moving appeal to the popular imagination.

Francis saw how well the narrative of St. Luke could be dramatized so as to teach in pictorial fashion the doctrine of the Incarnation. For years he pondered how best this might be done, and at length obtained the Pope's permission to introduce a stage version of the sacred story into the churches with which he was associated. He was to spend that Christmas in the village of Grecia, near Assisi. There, in the little church, he prepared a stable, having borrowed from a friendly farmer an ox and an ass and a bundle of hay. When the day arrived, the villagers flocked in crowds to see the re-enactment of the wondrous story, and stood by the manger reverently listening as Francis and his brethren sang simple Carols to the Christ Child. The legend says that Francis stayed in the church all night, his heart full of unspeakable joy, and as he watched he thought he saw the tiny Child stretch out His little arms towards him, as if to bless him.

Francis's example spread rapidly, and to countless others Jesus became in a new sense a " little brother," hallowing all things simple and innocent. In many churches curious customs accompanied the visit of the Carollers. Thus in

[1] The three ships are the camels that carried the wise men across the desert to Bethlehem. The air, in *three* time, is taken from Sandy's Carols.

Germany, in the fourteenth century, the priests, impersonating Joseph and Mary, invited each other to take turns at rocking the cradle. Sometimes the " Præsepium," as the manger was called, was set up in a farmhouse, and the rocking was done by children, who doubtless danced round the crib with innocent merriment, singing as they danced.

Lullabies, Shepherds' Songs, Songs of the Wise Men, Legends of the most fantastic character, formed the staple of the Carols which sprang up on all hands. Much of it seems to us to-day to be highly fanciful and unrestrained, but, as we have seen, there were elements in it which endeared it to the common people.[1] It was of a different order—more popular and spontaneous—than the polished literary products which followed from the pens of learned and gifted poets such as (in this country) Milton and Ben Jonson, Vaughan and Wither. Two or three specimens of artistically constructed Marian poems of the fifteenth and sixteenth centuries cannot, however, fail to be of interest. Here is the ever-welcome " I sing of a Maiden." Saintsbury remarks on its infinite sweetness and solemnity, and the extraordinary appropriateness of the sound to the sense :—

> I sing of a maiden
> That is makèless,[2]
> King of all kingès
> To her son she ches.[3]
> He came all so stillè
> There His moder was,
> As dew in Aprillè
> That falleth on the grass.
> He came all so stillè
> To His moderès bower,
> As dew in Aprillè
> That falleth on the flower.
> He came all so stillè
> There His moder lay,
> As dew in Aprillè
> That falleth on the spray.

[1] For an interesting treatment of the subject, see E. J. Brailsford's *The Spiritual Sense in Sacred Legend.*
[2] Without a mate.　　　　　　　　　　[3] Chose.

> Moder and maiden
> Was never none but she ;
> Well may such a lady
> Goddes moder be.

The following, suggested by an Old German song of the sixteenth century, plays round the word " Rosemary " :—

> I know a Rose, full fair to see,
> Within a Lady's bower :
> It is the joy and pride of me,
> This Rose-Marie,
> And like none other flower.

> May, June, July, may boast to be
> The time for lovely roses,
> When maids and men, thro' Christentie,
> From bush and tree,
> Cull buds to make them posies.

> But mine doth follow other rule ;
> For well I can remember,
> My Rose-Marie, at time of Yule,
> When winds blow cool,
> Bare fruit in mid-December.[1]

Robert Southwell's charming carol was first published in 1596 :—

> Behould a sely [2] tender Babe,
> In freesing winter nighte,
> In homely manger trembling lies ;
> Alas, a piteous sighte.

> The inns are full ; no man will yielde
> This little Pilgrim bedd ;
> But forced He is with sely beastes
> In crib to shroud His headd.

> Despise not Him for lying there,
> First what He is enquire ;
> An orient perle is often found
> In depths of dirty mire.

---

[1] By the Rev. George Ratcliffe Woodward, M.A., Mus.Doc., in *Carmina Mariana*, Second Series, edited by Orby Shipley.
[2] Simple ; innocent ; holy.

Waye not His crib, His wodden dishe,
Nor beastes that by Him feede ;
Waye not His mother's poore attire,
Nor Joseph's simple weede.

This stable is a Prince's courte ;
The crib His chaire of State ;
The beastes are parcell of His pomp,
The wodden dishe, His plate.

Of the Marian hymns which have come down from olden
times and are still sung, the two most conspicuous are the
" Ave Maris Stella " (Hail, thou Star of Ocean), of unknown
antiquity, and the " Stabat Mater," to which reference was
made at the close of our last chapter. There are two " Stabat
Mater " hymns, one concerning the Mother of our Lord at
the cradle, and the other at the Cross. For long the latter,
the " Stabat Mater Dolorosa," was attributed to Jacopone da
Todi, a mystic who lived a little later than Francis, and who
was the greatest poet of the Order. The stories told of him
bear a strong resemblance to those about the ever lovable
Brother Juniper. Both were willing to become fools for
Christ's sake. There is a legend that when applying for
admission to the convent at Todi, Jacopone stripped himself
to the waist, put on an ass's skin and went on all-fours in self-
abasement. He roamed Umbria as " God's Troubadour,"
singing songs of exhortation and love to the people, songs
which were popular through the succeeding two centuries.
Evelyn Underhill places him high among the great contem-
plative Franciscan mystics ; " persons whose enthusiasm
and love set other loving spirits on fire." [1] One of
his " Laude " is written to show the people " How it
is the highest Wisdom to be reputed mad for the Love
of Christ " :—

Wisdom 'tis and courtesy,
Crazed for Jesus Christ to be.

[1] Evelyn Underhill's *Life of Jacopone* ; also her *Mystics of the
Church*.

No such learning can be found
In Paris, or the world around ;
In this folly to abound
Is the best philosophy.

*   *   *   *   *

He who enters on this dance
Enters Love's unwalled expanse.[1]

His poem " The Soul's Complaint " rises into an almost
uncontrollable ardour of love. English devotional poetry
shows nothing comparable to it, unless it be Crashaw's " The
Flaming Heart." The poet's heart is utterly consumed by
the love of Christ ; burnt up like a furnace ; slain by bliss ;
tormented by sweetness ; dumb and maddened by an excess
of joy. When he hears the Christ bidding him to control
his frenzy, he answers that he cannot do so ; thoughts of the
agony and bloody sweat, the wounds and the cross, drive him
all distraught. There is no limit to Christ's love : why, then,
should he curb his own ? :—

Thyself from Love Thy Heart didst not defend,
   From Heaven to Earth it brought Thee from Thy
      throne ;
Beloved, to what sheer depths didst Thou descend,
   To dwell with man, unhonoured and unknown :
In life and death to enrich us without end,
   Homeless and poor, with nothing of Thine own,
   Thou here didst come alone ;
      For Thou wert called
      By Love unwalled
That all Thy heart did move.

And as about the world Thy feet did go,
   'Twas Love that led Thee always, everywhere :
Thy only joy, for us Thy Love to show,
   And for Thyself no whit at all to care.

*   *   *   *   *

Love, Love, O Love, the world's wild voices cry,
   Love, Love, O Love, the clamorous echoes spread,
Love, Love, O Love, so deep Thy treasures lie,
   We hunger more, the more we taste Thy bread :

[1] This and the succeeding verses are taken from Mrs. Theodore Beck's
translations.

Love, Love, O Love, Thou circling Mystery,
  Who enters Thee at Love's deep heart is fed ;
Thou'rt Loom and Cloth and Thread :
      O sweet to be
      Clad all in Thee,
And ceaseless chant of Love.

Love, Love, O Love, Thy touch so quickens me,
  Love, Love, O Love, I am no longer I :
Love, Love, O Love, Thyself so utterly
  Thou giv'st me, Jesu, that I can but die.
O Love, O Love, I am possessed of Thee,
  Love, Love, O Love, O take me in a sigh !
Love, glad and spent I lie.
      O Love, my Bliss !
      O Lover's Kiss !
O quench my soul in Love !

The intensity of the poem, as Miss Underhill suggests, is
almost unendurable. The passionate human love of the
troubadour is heated a thousandfold in the burning fiery
furnace of divine love.

In the " Stabat Mater " (which is now thought to be from
another's pen) the feeling is more subdued. Nevertheless, it
melts the heart, as it describes, in language of simple pathos,
the sad figure of Mary standing at the cross ; the mother
mourning for her boy, as the sword pierces her heart :—

          Is there one who would not weep,
          Whelmed in miseries so deep,
            Christ's dear Mother to behold ?
          Can the human heart refrain
          From partaking of her pain,
            Of that Mother's pain untold ?

CHAPTER VI

THE BEGINNINGS OF SACRED SONG IN
THE BRITISH ISLES

CHRISTIANITY first reached Britain in the second century, but the earliest surviving specimen of sacred poetry of importance in the Anglo-Saxon tongue dates from the latter half of the seventh century. Before that time any hymns that may have been sung by the little communities of Christians in England were almost certainly in Latin, though doubtless tinctured with vernacular elements; and in that tongue the service books remained for many centuries. But, as we have already seen, the Latin language gradually crumbled, and under the pressure of human needs a vernacular literature slowly supplanted it.

The purpose of this chapter is to trace, in broad outline, the early developments of our native hymnody. So far as Church music is concerned, Burney (who has a quite sufficient fondness for satire) says that for the credit of our country it is best to allow the subject to rest undisturbed and not to sweep the cobweb veil and reveal the nakedness of the land. In the realm of devotional poetry there certainly is not much to boast of. Quite the most interesting surviving product of the first six centuries in these islands comes to us from Ireland. " St. Patrick's Breastplate " is an astonishingly powerful hymn. Perhaps it may be spoken of as a charm, for it is one of a large number of Irish poems which were recited to drive away all manner of evil things. A " Lorica," as such a hymn was called, was a kind of spiritual coat or breastplate, which not only charmed away disease and danger, but secured a place in heaven for him who " wore it ever night and day." A Lorica usually was written in three parts; first came an invocation to the Trinity and to the angels; then an enumeration of the various parts of the body to be safeguarded ; and lastly a list of the dangers from which immunity was sought. Patrick's Lorica or Breastplate contains allusions to pagan customs, which seem to show that it is related, though at far remove, to a pre-Christian charm or rune. It was indeed by no means uncommon for the priests to sanction Christian versions of heathen incantations, the purpose doubtless being the same as that which led to the building of Christian churches on the site of heathen temples. The primitive mind was won over slowly, and by tottering steps, to a purer faith.[1]

Patrick (fourth century) is said to have composed his hymn as he was going up to a great debate with King Loegaire at Tara. An ambush, the legend says, was set to kill the saint, but sudden darkness came down and hid him and his companions from their enemies, who thought they were fawns. Hence for long the hymn was known as " The Deers' Cry." Stripped of its legendary associations, it is a beautiful hymn of trust in God's abiding care.[2] It is written in the ancient Irish dialect. Mrs. Alexander, in translating it, has had the requirements of congregational singing well in mind.

> I bind unto myself to-day
>   The strong name of the Trinity,
> By invocation of the same,
>   The Three in One, and One in Three.
>
> I bind this day to me for ever,
>   By power of faith, Christ's Incarnation ;
> His baptism in Jordan river ;
> His death on Cross for my salvation ;
> His bursting from the spiced tomb ;
>   His riding up the heavenly way ;
> His coming at the day of doom ;
>   I bind unto myself to-day.

---

[1] See the article on " Irish Hymns " in Hastings's *Dictionary of Religion* ; also J. Earle's *Anglo-Saxon Literature*.
[2] Dr. Whitley Stokes's *Tripartite Life of St. Patrick* should be consulted.

I bind unto myself the power
  Of the great love of Cherubim;
The sweet " Well done " in judgment hour;
  The service of the Seraphim,
Confessors' faith, Apostles' word,
  The Patriarchs' prayers, the Prophets' scrolls,
All good deeds done unto the Lord,
  And purity of virgin souls.

I bind unto myself to-day
  The virtues of the star-lit heaven,
The glorious sun's life-giving ray,
  The whiteness of the moon at even,
The flashing of the lightning free,
  The whirling wind's tempestuous shocks,
The stable earth, the deep salt sea,
  Around the old eternal rocks.

I bind unto myself to-day
  The power of God to hold and lead,
His eye to watch, His might to stay,
  His ear to hearken to my need:
The wisdom of my God to teach,
  His hand to guide, His shield to ward;
The word of God to give me speech,
  His heavenly host to be my guard.

Against the demon snares of sin,
  The vice that gives temptation force,
The natural lusts that war within,
  The hostile men that mar my course;
Or few or many, far or nigh,
  In every place, and in all hours,
Against their fierce hostility,
  I bind to me these holy powers.

Against all Satan's spells and wiles,
  Against false words of heresy,
Against the knowledge that defiles,
  Against the heart's idolatry,
Against the wizard's evil craft,
  Against the death-wound and the burning,
The choking wave, the poisoned shaft,
  Protect me, Christ, till Thy returning.

Christ be with me, Christ within me,
  Christ behind me, Christ before me,
Christ beside me, Christ to win me,
  Christ to comfort and restore me,

Christ beneath me, Christ above me,
  Christ in quiet, Christ in danger,
Christ in hearts of all that love me,
  Christ in mouth of friend and stranger.

I bind unto myself the name,
  The strong name of the Trinity ;
By invocation of the same,
  The Three in One, and One in Three :
Of whom all nature hath creation ;
  Eternal Father, Spirit, Word ;
Praise to the Lord of my salvation,
  Salvation is of Christ the Lord.

Next to Patrick, in the story of Ireland's conversion to
Christianity, comes Columba (sixth century).   But Columba,
though born of an Irish royal line and founder of more than
one famed monastery in Ireland, actually achieved his great
conquests as a Christian missionary from his Scottish island-
home at Iona.   Some of his biographers picture him as a mild
and gentle saint, and others as a born fighter and avenger of
the oppressed.   Whichever estimate may be the more accurate,
there can be no question of the importance of the services
which, with the help of Oswald and Aidan, he rendered to the
faith among the impressionable people of the north.   He
ranks among Ireland's famous bards.   He was not only a
poet himself, but he maintained the most friendly relations
with the wandering minstrels whom he must often have met
on his travels ; and when they visited any monastery where
he lived, he would never allow them to leave until they had
sung their songs to the accompaniment of the harp.

Montalembert has preserved two or three poems, first
written in the Irish dialect, which have long been attributed
to Columba, but which, while doubtless interpreting his sentiments, are probably (in the form that has survived) of a later
age.   Two of them sing, in simple measures, the charms of
Derry and of Arran,[1] his favourite Irish monasteries.   Their
plaintive strains suggest an exile's lyre.   The one in praise of

[1] Now spelt *Aran*.

Arran may be freely rendered in modern form somewhat as
follows :—

> O Arran, O Arran, my Sun !
> My heart is with thee in the west !
>
> To sleep in death beneath thy soil,
> To lay my body there to rest,
> Will be as sweet as if I slept
> With Paul and Peter ever blest.
>
> Where Arran's bells sound o'er the sea,
> O there for ever would I be !
> For when their music fills the air
> My life is all felicity.
>
> O Arran, O Arran, my Sun !
> My heart is in the west with thee.

The other, to his beloved Derry, may, in part, be freely
rendered thus :—

> In Derry's groves of oak I see
> An angel white on every tree ;
> There is my home, my hermit's cell ;
> There God, whose home is heav'n, doth dwell.
>
> Durrow and Derry, sweet to see !
> And fair and pure is Raphoë !
> Drumhome I love, with fruitful grove,
> And Sords and Kells I fondly love :
>
> But sweeter, fairer than them all
> Is the salt sea and the wild gull's call :
> And when I row across the sea,
> Where Derry's streams wind through the lea,
> Delightsome peace takes hold on me.[1]

Columba's hymns, including a rhymed creed, are in Latin.
One, in Irish, that has long been ascribed to him, and that he
is said to have chanted as he fled from Ireland after defeat
in battle, is too good to be smothered in the uncertainties of

---

[1] I have based these free adaptations on Montalembert's French versions
in his *Les Moines d'Occident*, Book XI, chap. i.

authenticity, and we may be grateful to Moorsom for having given us an adaptation.[1]   It is prefaced with the words " Alone upon the mountains " :—

> Alone with none but Thee, my God,
>   I journey on the way ;
> What need I fear when Thou art near ?
>   O King of night and day !
> More safe am I within Thy hand
> Than if a host did by me stand.

* * * * *

> My life I yield to Thy decree,
>   And now to Thy control,
> In peaceful calm, for from Thine arm
>   No power can wrest my soul.
> Could earthly omens e'er appal
> A heart that heeds the heavenly call ?

> The child of God need fear no ill,
>   His chosen dread no foe ;
> We leave our fate with Thee, and wait
>   Thy bidding where we go.
> 'Tis not from chance our courage springs,
> Thou art " Our Trust," O King of Kings !

In England our story begins with the landing, in 597, of Pope Gregory's missionaries, under the charge of his trusted friend Augustine.   Gregory was a rich, learned and public-spirited citizen of Rome, who relinquished office and wealth for the seclusion of the monastery, and ultimately became Pope.   Probably during the monastic period of his life the incident occurred which has won him undying affection among English people the world over.   He had planned to buy some English youths " to be given to God in a monastery."   Probably it was a part of his cherished ambition to Christianize our country.   And at last the opportunity presented itself to him. One day, as he was walking in the market-place in Rome, he saw a group of fair-haired, blue-eyed, light-complexioned English lads on sale as slaves.   He asked the name of their

---

[1] *Renderings of Church Hymns*, by R. M. Moorsom.

race, and was told " *Angli* " ; so beautiful were they that he answered they should be called *Angeli*. Their home was *Deira* ; they should be saved *de ira Dei* ; their King was *Alle* ; in his country they should sing Alleluia.[1] He was unable to pursue his plans at the moment, but years afterwards, when he was Pope, he chose a company of forty monks to undertake the great adventure. They arrived on the coast of Kent early in the year 597, and at once sought an interview with King Ethelbert. After a delay of some days they set out for the meeting which was to be fraught with such tremendous import for the future of the English nation, chanting the Litanies they had been wont to use in Rome as they journeyed. After the interview the King told them that they might settle at Canterbury. On entering the city they sang a prayer which it was said Gregory himself had composed during a time of plague, and their Hallelujahs, in alternate choirs, were raised to heaven, led by the sweet-voiced Honorius, the youngest of their party.

Among the few books that Augustine brought with him— books which Stanley has described as " the mother books of England "—was a Psalter ; and we may perhaps conclude that in St. Martin's church in the ancient city, where they met to worship, were heard the first strains of sacred Latin song in an English church, to the solemn setting of their loved Gregorian tones :—

We beseech Thee, O Lord, by Thy pity, to spare in Thy wrath this city and Thy holy house. Hallelujah !

As soon as the missionaries were settled at Canterbury, further groups, which included trained musicians, were despatched to York and Rochester, to whom Gregory gave instructions regarding the services, saying : " I should like you carefully to select whatever you have found, either in the Church of Rome, or in that of Gaul, or in any other which

---

[1] The incidents connected with Augustine's mission are related in the *Cambridge Mediæval History*, vol. ii.

may better please Almighty God ; and to introduce into the Church of the English what you have been able to gather together." [1]

It is improbable that any vernacular hymns had been written at so early a date as the Augustinian mission. The services were doubtless in Latin.

Less than a century after the landing of Augustine the first clear note of Anglo-Saxon sacred song was struck by Cædmon, the poet-herdsman of Whitby, who thus won for himself the great and enviable name of " The Father of English Sacred Poetry." High on the cliffs of Yorkshire, looking out across the grey northern seas, the saintly Hilda had founded a religious settlement. Attached to her monastery, a herdsman tending the cattle, was Cædmon. One night, in his old age, while on duty in the stables, Cædmon fell asleep, when an angel appeared to him in a vision and said to him, " Sing me something." Cædmon answered, " I cannot sing. That is why I left the feast and came here." " But thou must," the angel said. " Then what shall I sing ? " was the reply. " Sing the origin of created things." Cædmon then obeyed the heavenly vision, and was taken into the monastery ; and there, Bede tells us, " Whatever he had learned from scholars concerning the Scriptures, he forthwith decked out in poetic language with the greatest sweetness and fervour," so that when the brethren heard it they said that truly God had indued him with heavenly grace.

Happily Cædmon's first hymn is preserved to this day in Bede's *Ecclesiastical History*, written about half a century after the poet's death. Some lines from it can be seen inscribed on a beautiful modern runic cross on the edge of the cliff at Whitby, close under the shadow of the mighty ruined abbey, which stands in pleasant pastures where the cattle, as in the poet's day, still browse. Standing there, the same far-reaching panorama of sea and river, green vale and purple moor, upon which Cædman must often have looked, captivates our senses,

[1] *Epistles*, Book XI, 64.

While with an eye made quiet by the power
Of harmony, and the deep power of joy,
We see into the life of things.

Here is Cædmon's hymn :—

Now must we praise
The Guardian of Heaven's
Realm,
The Creator's might
And His mind's Thought.
The Glorious works of the
Father,
How of every wonder
He the Lord Eternal
Laid the Foundation.

He shaped erst
For the sons of men
Heaven as their roof.
Holy Creator.
The Middle World He
Mankind's Guardian
Eternal Lord
Afterwards prepared
The Earth for men.
Lord Almighty.

After Cædmon, others essayed to write religious verse. He was the best, but, says Bede, many imitated him, and Northumbria from the seventh to the eleventh century was seldom without its poets, whose songs helped to familiarize the Bible to the Anglo-Saxon people.[1]

The most important scholar in England in the seventh century was the Venerable Bede, who spent the greater part of his placid life in the newly established monastery at Wearmouth, never journeying further afield than York. Doubtless Bede spent many happy hours in the library, among the books and church-music which the abbot had collected. He joined in the psalmody of the daily services in the church, and occupied himself from time to time in the writing of Latin hymns, in various metres and rhythms, singing them to the accompaniment of his Saxon harp.

His last great work was a translation into Anglo-Saxon of the Gospel of St. John. While he was engaged upon it he was seized with a fatal illness, but he pressed on with his task, singing day and night, with joy and thanksgiving, psalms and anthems and his own hymns. Once " he spoke, in the Saxon language, of the awful departure of the soul from the body " :—

[1] Spence Watson's *Life of Cædmon.*

[*Photo by Frith, Reigate*

CÆDMON'S CROSS

```
Before the need-fare ¹ ........No man becometh
Of thought more prudent.....Than is needful to him
To consider.................Before his departure
What, to his spirit,.........Of good or evil
After his death-day..........Will be adjudged.
```

When his last moments came, and the final sentence of his book had been dictated to the boy who attended him, he set himself to meet death with tranquillity, " for," Cuthbert records, " so long as the spirit was in the body he continued to sing ' Glory be to the Father ' and other spiritual songs, and ceased not, with outstretched hands, to render thanks to the true and living God."

It is impossible to say how much native religious verse was written in the dim centuries between Cædmon's time and the Norman Conquest. There are interesting stories of ecclesiastics and even kings disguising themselves as minstrels—of Bishop Aldhelm, on the bridge at Sherborne, singing songs of secular and sacred import, if haply he might persuade the people to listen to the evangel ; and of King Alfred harping in the camp of the Danish invaders and even at the royal table itself, the while he espied the disposition of their army —but although we may assume from these incidents that our Anglo-Saxon ancestors voiced their emotional life in sacred song, very little has survived. Much of it doubtless perished in the Danish invasions.

Notable among the material that has survived is the " Dream of the Holy Rood "—one of a group of poems attributed to Cynewulf, a rather mythical figure, who, according to Saintsbury, " out of dead runes, buried beneath charades and acrostics, has been resolutely manufactured and equipped with life." ² There is no mistaking the dramatic power of the " Dream." The poet pictures himself as falling asleep and in a vision seeing a tree, glistening with light and radiant with jewels, which, as he gazes, changes to a Cross that drips

---

¹ Need-fare = a compulsory journey : death.
² Professor Saintsbury's *History of English Prosody*.

with blood, and that speaks to him of One who once was
stretched upon it to rescue man from death and sin. And
this is what the Holy Rood says [1] :—

> Long years have passed since foemen hewed
>   And felled me where I stood ;
> They bore me to the hill of scorn,
>   Far from my native wood.
> 'Twas there I saw the Lord of Hosts
>   Ascend in princely might,
> I felt His limbs upon me stretched ;
>   Earth trembled at the sight ;
> Resolved to rescue lost mankind
>   The steadfast Hero came,
> And strong in His Almighty power
>   Embraced the tree of shame.
> He touched me with His hand of love,
>   I thrilled in every arm,
> Yet durst not scathe the murderous band,
>   Nor shelter Him from harm.
>
> With Him I bore that outrage sore,
>   I felt the driven nail,
> I saw the blood that from His wounds
>   Upwelled as life did fail ;
> Oh, wan and fearful was the shade,
>   For day had turned to night ;
> And ministering Spirits rose,
>   And Nature quaked in fright.
> The King, the Ruler of the world,
>   The Christ was on the Cross,
> The Lord of life was lying dead ;
>   Creation wept her loss.

Succeeding stanzas proceed to relate how, in after generations,
men came to revere the Cross they once despised, covering it
with gold and gems and bringing it world-wide honour. As the
poem draws to a close, its fantastic elements are forgotten, and
it becomes instinct with unalloyed devotional feeling :—

> I who was once a cross of pain,
>   And loathsome to all eyes,
> Now tower above, an honoured sign,
>   Majestic to the skies :

[1] R. M. Moorsom's adaptation gives the spirit of the poem in a form
that will be appreciated by " the ordinary reader."

> And healing virtue ever flows
> For all who hither turn,
> And seek in penitence and faith
> The way of life to learn.

To attempt anything in the nature of a review of the religious poetry of the English tongue throughout the later middle ages would necessitate a separate volume. Continuous attempts were made, right up to the time of the Reformation, to introduce vernacular elements into the Church services. A Service book of the eleventh century is to be seen in the British Museum in which the hymns are in Latin, but with an interlinear English translation.[1] A Breviary of the same period, used at Worcester, contains Psalms and hymns in both languages, some of them being set to music. Late in the thirteenth century a metrical Psalter was issued, apparently in the Yorkshire dialect ; and in the fourteenth century more than one vernacular Psalter appeared, one from the pen of Richard Rolle, who also wrote " canticles of divine Love." [2]

Here is a Marian hymn of about 1210, " A Good Orison of our Lady," in which (like earlier specimens already referred to [3]) the love-language of the troubadours is transferred to the mother of our Lord [4] :

> O holy Mary, mother sweet of Christ,
> Light of my life, dear Lady mine,
> In praise of thee I bow on bended knee,
> And all my heart's blood offer thee.
> Thou art my light of soul and joy of heart,
> My only hope and stay thou art ;
> 'Tis meet I honour thee with all my might,
> With songs of praise by day and night,
> For thou hast helped me in all manner wise,
> And brought me into Paradise ;
> For this, my Lady sweet, my thanks I give,
> And will thee thank as long as I may live.

[1] Wordsworth and Littlehales's *Old Service Books of the Church of England.*
[2] Saintbury's *History of English Prosody.*
[3] See p. 101.
[4] I am indebted to Mr. J. H. Pafford for this version of the opening lines of the Orison. The original reading is in G. E. MacLean's *Old and Middle English Reader.*

The following " Song on the Passion " bears evident French influences. It is from a collection of the thirteenth century [1] :

> Summer is come, and winter gone,
>   Groweth the day both fair and long,
> And now the birdes every one
>   Gladden themselves with merry song.
>   Yet with care my heart is bound
>   All amidst the joy that's found
>   In the land,
>   All for a Child
>   That is so mild
>   In hand.
>
> Tender is He, in sooth, and good,
>   And great in heart, and wise in thought,
> And far o'er brake, and bank, and wood,
>   Long while in love He sought me out.
>   And, behold, He hath found me
>   For the apple of a tree
>   Y-bound.
>   He brake the thong
>   That was so strong
>   With His wound.
>
> Jesu is that Childes name,
>   And King He is in every land ;
> Yet of that King did they make game,
>   And smote Him with a ruthless hand :
>   They hung Him on the cruel tree,
>   They gave Him woundes two and three.
>   Yea, all
>   Mocking looked up
>   And gave the cup
>   Of gall.

As the Reformation drew nearer, a growing number of paraphrases of the Psalms, of the Commandments, and of the Creeds, appeared, as well as devout hymns to the Virgin and to the Saviour.

Here, finally, is a delightful miniature taken from a Service-book used in Salisbury Cathedral. It is in the nature of a

---

[1] C. J. Abbey's *Religious Thought in Old English Verse,* chap. ii.

Lorica, with its prayer for preservation from specific dangers and temptations of the senses, and it breathes a spirit of obvious sincerity :—

> God be in my head, and in my understanding ;
> God be in mine eyes, and in my looking ;
> God be in my mouth, and in my speaking ;
> God be in my heart, and in my thinking ;
> God be at mine end, and at my departing.

Religious poetry of this character obviously has very little connection with our modern English hymn. However naïve and reverential it may be, it is lacking in the essential hymnic qualities. The fact of the matter is that the fate which had overtaken the congregational hymn throughout Western Christendom was fully shared in this country. The worship-song passed into the hands of the priests, or degenerated into trivialities, as organized religion lost its inner power. When at length a native hymnody came to birth, its genesis was not to be found, so far as investigations have yet shown, in pre-Reformation England. It was at Wittenberg and Geneva, after the cataclysmal disruption of the Reformation, that the fountain of praise was unsealed that was destined to make glad the hearts of the people of God in this, as in other, lands.

CHAPTER VII

LUTHER AND CALVIN

THE Reformation cleansed the Church, and in doing so established the right of the people to participate in the singing.

The sixteenth century, therefore, may be regarded as the turning-point in the history of Christian hymnody. Not the least service rendered by Luther and Calvin to the cause of personal religion was the re-establishment of vernacular congregational singing. The fact that the singing, for centuries before the great crisis, had been almost exclusively reserved for priests and trained songmen, and that the hymns were written in an unfamiliar tongue, was a symptom of the almost mortal disease that had overtaken organized religion. With Luther, hymnody came once for all out of its monastic prison, and lifted its glad, free carol in every town and hamlet of the Fatherland. Not that Luther was the first in the field. We have already seen how, across the Alps, the Umbrian peasantry exchanged songs with the Franciscan Friars, and how the love-literature of the troubadours gradually took on a religious tone. But, broadly speaking, hymnody had become the special preserve of the clergy, and the people had been bowed out. The content of the hymn had also become more and more formal and liturgical, lacking the simple, human appeal of an earlier age.

There was, undoubtedly, a plausible case to be made for the use of Latin in the liturgical and Scriptural offices of the Church. A recent apologist for such a rule expresses the fear that to translate the teachings of the Church from their ancient tongue into a variety of modern ones is to dilute and sometimes completely to change their meaning. If the translation is effected in six languages, the shade of meaning may be different in each. " Think," he says, " what danger there might be of changing that Truth which cannot be changed, if the doctrines and devotions of the world's Church were left to be expressed by the changing words of countless tongues." [1] If a Roman Catholic priest of the present day feels like that, how much more must the leaders of Christian thought during " the dark ages " have apprehended the danger, if danger there was ! For when the Roman Empire died, its language, in the popular sense, may be said to have died with it, and religious leaders were confronted with a linguistic dilemma of which many of them felt the great complexity. Thus, as early as the fourth century, Bishop Ulphilas, when undertaking his translation of the Scriptures into Gothic, could find no words for expressing Christian ideas. [2]

For long generations the new languages which sprang into being remained fluid, and subject to constant irruptions and changes in the meaning of only half-stabilized words. Under these circumstances the leaders of the Church felt that safety lay in the ancient Latin tongue ; they were unwilling to entrust the jewel of truth to any upstart linguistic stripling.

This attitude may have been all very well in the fourth century, but to perpetuate it to the end of time was another matter. Yet Rome persisted. Calvin actually records the case of an archbishop who threatened with incarceration, and even severer penalties, any person who should repeat the Lord's Prayer aloud in any but the Latin tongue. [3] When Wyclif translated the Bible into English, Convocation at Oxford intervened to forbid any unauthorized person to translate any portion of it " under pain of excommunication and the stigma of heresy " ; nor was anyone allowed to possess a copy without licence from a bishop. " It is a perilous thing," the Oxford prohibition says, " as the blessed Jerome testifies, to translate the text of Holy Scriptures from one idiom into another, inas-

[1] *Why in Latin?*, a Tract by Father Bampfield : Catholic Truth Society.
[2] L. Pearsall Smith's *The English Language* shows how the thirteenth century introduced into the English tongue many new words representing the inner aspects of Christian faith and experience. It is an ever-growing vocabulary.
[3] Calvin's Tract on *The Necessity of Reforming the Church.*

much as in the translations themselves it is no easy matter to keep the same meaning in all cases, like as the blessed Jerome, albeit inspired, confesses that he often went astray in this respect." [1]

More than a hundred years after Wyclif, Tyndale left the country and hid himself near Worms, in order to translate the New Testament. Its appearance was duly followed by the episcopal prohibition of the Bishop of London, who declared that the " crafty " translator had " prophanated the majesty of the Scripture, which heretofore hath remained undefiled, and craftily abused the most holy word of God and the true sense of the same," and who described the translation as " pestiferous and most pernicious poison." [2]

So far as the Church services were concerned, it was urged that the liturgy was an offering not by the people, but for them ; and that the Church being the spiritual home of people of all nations and tongues, a universal language alone was fitting to her world-wide mission. Concessions were made to the extent that the sermon, the catechism and the confession might be in the vernacular. In the case of confession, obviously the priesthood made a virtue of necessity : it would be difficult to confess one's sins in an unknown tongue ! Occasionally, too, hymn-singing in the vernacular seems to have been allowed. But the general position was as has been stated. The priests kept the singing almost entirely in their own hands, and in the traditional language of the Roman Church.

Calvin and Luther cut that knot. Calvin, in his downright way, declared that if a man sang in an unknown tongue, he might as well be a linnet or a popinjay. " There seems something monstrous," he said, " in this determination to hold converse with God in sounds which fall without meaning from the tongue." " Even if God," he added, " did not declare His displeasure at such a mockery, Nature herself, without a monitor, rejects it."

Luther's attitude was somewhat less uncompromising. He

---

[1] A. W. Pollard's *Records of the English Bible.*   [2] *Ibid.*

appreciated the ancient Latin hymns, and the sedate music to which they were set, and encouraged their continued use, believing in their educational value.[1] And, as we shall see, he supplemented them with a series of notable ones written in the mother tongue, which were broadcast to aid the cause of reform.

The congregational hymn, as we know it to-day, is a direct product of the Reformation ; though, as Dr. Benson has been at pains to point out, Luther is not its sole originator.[2] That honour must certainly be shared by Hus and Calvin, and by a number of humbler people who sympathized with their reforming zeal, and who clearly saw that a vernacular hymnody, side by side with a vernacular Bible, was needful, not only for fostering private devotion, but as an aid to the missionary work of the Church.[3]

The ground had to some extent been prepared for Luther by the writings of the mystics Eckhart, Suso and Tauler, and their followers. To these men religion was not institutional, priestly, ritualistic, but a personal experience of God's presence in the heart. That was the only pathway to the reform of the abuses which threatened to overwhelm organized religion. That and that alone could invest it with power and bless it with peace. Tauler and Suso clothed this essential message in tender poetic form. Here is a vernacular poem by Tauler, full of joy and trust in God's unfailing care :—

> As the bridegroom to his chosen,
> As the king unto his realm,
> As the keep unto the castle,
> As the pilot to the helm,
> So, Lord, art Thou to me.

> As the fountain in the garden,
> As the candle in the dark,
> As the treasure in the coffer,
> As the manna in the ark,
> So, Lord, art Thou to me.

[1] A. C. McGiffert's *Life of Martin Luther.*
[2] L. F. Benson's *The English Hymn,* chap. i.
[3] Moffatt's Introduction to his translation of the New Testament.

As the music at the banquet,
    As the stamp unto the seal,
As the medicine to the fainting,
    As the wine-cup at the meal,
    So, Lord, art Thou to me.

As the ruby in the setting,
    As the honey in the comb,
As the light within the lantern,
    As the father in the home,
    So, Lord, art Thou to me.

As the sunshine to the heavens,
    As the image to the glass,
As the fruit unto the fig-tree,
    As the dew unto the grass,
    So, Lord, art Thou to me.[1]

John Hus and other leaders of the " Bohemian Brethren "
also wrote hymns in the vernacular and set them to popular
airs, and scattered them far and wide through the land, until
at length the authorities took alarm and issued orders prohibit-
ing their use.   They might as well have told the tides to stand
still on the shore.

With the appearance of Luther the cause of reform leapt
forward on a grand and effective scale.   To him, as Schaff
summarizes the situation, " belongs the extraordinary merit
of having given to the German people in their own tongue the
Bible, the Catechism, and the Hymn Book, so that God might
speak *directly* to them in His word, and that they might
directly answer Him in their songs." [2]

The Brethren, watching Luther's work from Bohemia, sent
one of their number, Michael Weiss, to Wittenberg, with a
copy of their Confession of Faith, and the hymns which they
had taught the people, with the sweet and homely tunes to
which they had been wont to sing them.[3]   Their hymn book

[1] The translation is by Frances Bevan.   The authenticity of this and
other poems attributed to Tauler is in question.

[2] Julian's *Dictionary of Hymnology*, p. 414.

[3] One of these melodies was introduced by Balfe into *The Bohemian
Girl*.   It will be found as a hymn-tune in *The Fellowship Hymn Book*,
No. 231.

(translated by Weiss into German) pleased the great Reformer. " It is," he said, " the work of a good poet."

The occasion which led Luther to the writing of hymns is significant. In 1523 two youths were burnt to death, in the Grande Place at Brussels, for professing the reformed faith. They had died bravely, singing the " Te Deum." When the fire was lighted one was heard to say, " Now I seem to be on a bed of roses." Their faithfulness filled Luther with joy, nor can he have failed to realize that some day he might have to face as stern a call. His heart was stirred, and he penned his first hymn in honour of the two young martyrs—a worthy prelude to the noble chorus he soon was to raise to heaven. The hymn, entitled " A New Song of the two Martyrs for Christ, burnt at Brussels by the Sophists of Louvain," quickly spread all over Germany and the Low Countries, and did much to prepare the people to receive the teaching of the great Reformer. This is how it opens :—

> By help of God I fain would tell
> A new and wondrous story,
> And sing a marvel that befel
> To His great praise and glory :
> At Brussels in the Netherlands
> He hath a banner lifted,
> To show His wonders by the hand
> Of two youths, highly gifted
> With rich and heavenly graces.

The closing lines also show Luther rejoicing rather than lamenting over the crisis thus precipitated upon God's people. He recognized it to be the darkest hour that preceded the light, the dawn of summer after the blight of winter :—

> Springtime is even at our door,
> The winter now hath vanished ;
> The tender flow'rets spring once more,
> And He, who winter banished,
> Will send a happy summer.

Faith was indeed, alike to Luther and to the young heroes whose death inspired his song, the assurance of things hoped for, the evidence of things not seen.

Luther's poetic gift, so dramatically aroused, soon found further employment in the cause of reform. In 1541 a service of intercession against the Turks was held at Wittenberg, for which Luther prepared special prayers and wrote a special hymn. To him, as to many others in those stern times, the Pope and the Turk were Anti-Christ—the one his spirit and the other his body. So he prayed :—

> Lord, help us in Thy word and work ;
> Restrain the murderous Pope and Turk,
> Who fain would tear from off Thy throne
> Christ Jesus, Thy beloved Son.

This hymn early found its way into the English Psalter—for the fear of the Turks was fully shared by Englishmen—and had a long run of popularity here.

But another consideration, of a different order, moved Luther to write his hymns, and it is a motive which has animated many other hymnists through the centuries. In his preface to his hymn book he says, " These songs have been set in four parts for no other reason than because I wished to provide our young people (who both will and ought to be instructed in music and other sciences) with something whereby they might rid themselves of amorous and carnal songs, and in their stead learn something wholesome."

It is delightful to think of Luther and his circle of friends as they gathered round his fireside, or strolled round the little orchard which had been secured for him by his wife's frugality, snatching a few happy hours from the turmoil of life to refresh themselves with sweet human fellowship. At one time it would be chess ; at another a browse among the books in the delightfully untidy library, or a merry sing-song over a glass of good German beer. The careful wife, " My Lord Katie " as he playfully called her, would be there, her little children by her side : Justus Jonas, his fellow-professor at the University, and his colleague Paul Eber, would often look in ; and sometimes his lifelong friend Spalatin—the friend who supported him at Worms and was destined to stand by him at the hour of death—would doubtless leave the court to join them. These, with a few other friends who shared their love of poetry and music, formed themselves into "a house choir," and sought far and near for suitable verse and music for the people's hymn book upon which Luther had set his mind. Walther, a musician and poet of capacity, and Speratus, a fellow-worker for Church reform, had been associated with him in the venture since his bachelor days. Never did Walther tire of singing the praises of music ; never did he weary of listening to its sweet strains, which found an answering echo in his own happy and joyous temperament.

Chief among them, both as poet and musician, was Luther himself. D'Aubigné pictures him playing on his lute and singing with a full deep voice. Walther testifies that in that delightful home circle Luther was as happy and cheerful as a boy, laughingly telling how he had learned his skill in fitting words to music from his beloved Virgil. Luther lamented his own lack of the poetic gift, but for the special purpose which he had in view he excelled them all. His hymns are characterized by a rugged strength, a native vigour and direct-ness, and an engaging simplicity and homeliness which at once won for them a place in the hearts of the common people. They are in striking contrast to the trivialities and prettinesses of the lighter versifiers who spun their fantastic ditties to the Virgin and the saints. They throb with life and earnestness ; and the chief of them—the immortal "Ein Feste Burg"—is as the sound of mighty thunders. Those of his friends, though not bearing such obvious marks of genius, are often charac-terized by the same grave and solid qualities. Here are some verses from Eber's prayer to Him who is "the only refuge in time of trouble" :—

> When in the hour of utmost need
> We know not where to look for aid,
> When days and nights of anxious thought
> Nor help nor counsel yet have brought :

Then this our comfort is alone,
That we may meet before Thy throne,
And cry, O faithful God, to Thee
For rescue from our misery :

To Thee may raise our hearts and eyes,
Repenting sore with bitter sighs,
And seek Thy pardon for our sin,
And respite from our griefs within :

For Thou hast promised graciously
To hear all those who cry to Thee,
Through Him whose Name alone is great,
Our Saviour and our Advocate.[1]

Jonas's paraphrase of Psalm cxxiv has similar echoes of the fears and persecutions to which this band of brave and saintly men were subjected all through life :—

If God were not upon our side
    When foes around us rage,
Were not Himself our Help and Guide
    When bitter war they wage,
Were He not Israel's mighty Shield,
To whom their utmost craft must yield,
    We surely must have perished.

Luther's first hymn book was published in 1524. It only contained eight hymns, four of which were his own and three by his friend Speratus. It was soon followed by others, with more from Luther's pen. The music to which these hymns were set is referred to elsewhere in these pages.[2] Suffice it to say here that both words and music marked an epoch. As a Church-musician Luther may be described as a second Gregory. He broke the tradition of a thousand years and established a new one ; but in doing so he was wise enough to retain much that was good of the old era and carry it forward into the new. His influence on the work of the great Christian musicians of Germany has been marked. Notably does Bach derive inspiration from him. Bach invests the congregational

[1] Translated by Miss Winkworth in *Lyra Germanica*.
[2] See p. 286.

chorale with an artistic beauty and power such as only genius
can command.

The new hymns, with the magnificent chorales to which
they were set, were eagerly learned by the German people.
We read of crowds singing them in the market-places, and of
musicians playing them on blow-horns from church steeples.
In Magdeburg, an old man sang them in public and was
imprisoned, but the burghers rose in a body and demanded
his release.   A beggar, singing one of them at Luther's door,
delighted him by relating that they were being carried as far
away as the Baltic—" a shout of deliverance was sounding "
there.[1]   They sang themselves directly into the hearts of the
people, to the dismay of the priests, who complained (and with
truth) that Luther was singing the people into Protestantism.
Next to the Bible, few influences did more for the Reformation,
as contemporary observers abundantly testify.[2]   If evidence
were wanting to show the immeasurable power of the modest
hymn as " a popular instrument of religious culture," it is
abundantly forthcoming in this simple record.

Calvin, like Luther, favoured congregational singing, and
wished to begin the innovation with the children in his church,
who were formed into choirs and encouraged to attend singing practice for some hours each week.   " It was," says the
caustic Burney, " the only amusement he seems ever to have
allowed his followers." [3]   But such a verdict is too sweeping.
Calvin by no means underrated the power of good music, and
quoted with approval Plato's verdict that there is scarcely
anything in the world that exercises such an influence upon
men, or so potently affects and fashions their morals.   But
he stood for dignity to the point of severity in Church music.
He did not approve of the French tendency to introduce light
airs, such as were wedded to bacchanalian and frivolous love-
songs, into the sanctuary.   For the same reason he objected
to organs and to four-part singing.   He feared such intrusions

[1] D'Aubigné's *History of the Reformation.*
[2] Dr. Frere's article on " Hymns " in the *Encyclopædia Britannica.*
[3] Burney's *History of Music.*

as a departure from the simplicity which he felt should characterize worship, and as tending to draw the mind away from the deep things of God to merely sensuous pleasures. His views on the subject are stated in his *Institutio*, published at about the time that Luther was issuing his later hymn books :—

> If the singing come not from the heart it is worth nothing, and can only awaken God's wrath. Singing in itself is good and useful ; our tongues must praise God, and, as we honour Him by a common faith, we must also unite in glorifying Him before men, that they may hear our confession of His name and be inspired with the desire of following our example. Singing in the Church has been practised from the earliest times ; the Apostle Paul recommended the use of spiritual songs. But neither the ear nor the spirit must be distracted. Augustine remarks that he preferred the style recommended by Athanasius, which was rather speaking than singing ; but the latter awakened feelings in the highest degree edifying to his soul. With proper moderation, therefore, the use of singing is holy and useful. Those melodies which are introduced merely to give pleasure are not agreeable to the majesty of the Church, and must be infinitely displeasing to God.[1]

To meet the need as he felt it, Calvin sought the help of the best available musicians. Thus it comes about that to his influence we owe the chaste and noble " psalm-tunes " of the order of the Old Hundredth, which, originally reaching us from Geneva, set the standard of congregational singing in this country for many generations.[2]
When we turn from the tunes to the hymns, we find Calvin's attitude strongly differentiated from Luther's. The two men were alike in their determination to purify Church praise. Referring to the Catholic Church, Calvin writes : " What shall

---

[1] *Institutio*, Lib. III, c. 20, secs. 31, 32.   [2] See p. 289.

LUTHER

By permission of Ernest Benn, Ltd.)

CALVIN'S AUDITOIRE, GENEVA
Showing the pulpit from which Calvin and Knox preached

I say of the blasphemies which ring in the public hymns, and which no pious man is able to hear without the utmost horror ? Adulation of, and prayers to, Mary and the saints, and of individuals whom they, on their own judgment, have admitted into the catalogue of saints ! " When Calvin came to the task of providing a worthy substitute for use in his own church, he took his stand with Zwingli and insisted that the Scriptures alone should constitute the content of the worship-song. " We shall find nothing better," he said, " than the words of God." He particularly favoured the Psalms, which he believed the Holy Spirit had dictated to David, and which he described as an anatomy of all parts of the soul. Marot, the French poet, and his friend Beza, a Burgundian man of letters, metricized the whole Book of Psalms for him. Bourgeois furnished many tunes, some of which, in spite of Calvin's warning, were adaptations from songs, and it is said that when Calvin " saw them walking chastely with David," for the only time in his life the stern Reformer laughed.[1]

The strict position thus taken by Calvin is more readily understood if it is remembered that the newly found Bible was believed by the Reformers to be the one sure safeguard against a reversion to Rome. The sacred writings, in their estimation, furnished the Church with " an all-sufficient well-spring of praise," and if once Christian people wandered beyond its pages, they would be in danger of returning to those beggarly elements from which they had so hardly escaped.

The verdict of time has been in Luther's favour ; but we may at least thank Calvin that, largely owing to his stand for nothing but Scriptural praise, the Bible has formed the real groundwork of English hymnody, to its incalculable advantage.

The work accomplished by Luther and Calvin was but the beginning of a great outburst of Christian song. This was far more noticeable in Germany than in France. It is true that the Geneva Psalter for a few brief years enjoyed a feverish

---

[1] This is recorded by Schweitzer in his *Life of Bach*. See also for this subject G. W. Stewart's *Music in the Church*.

welcome in Paris. Marot was a favourite court poet, " the prince of poets and the poet of princes." Psalms were dedicated to the King, and " Aux Dames de France." To the fair ladies of the French court and aristocracy he made an eloquent appeal for support in his efforts to purify the song-literature of their times, and begged them to sing not of human love, but of Love divine. He rejoiced to think that rich and poor might perhaps soon be heard singing the sweet strains of his " holy song-book " instead of the licentious ditties to which they were addicted :—

> Thrice happy they, who shall behold,
> And listen in that age of gold !
> As by the plough the labourer strays,
> And carman mid the public ways,
> And tradesman in his shop shall swell
> Their voice in Psalm or Canticle ;
> Shall sing to solace toil ; again,
> From woods shall come a sweeter strain,
> Shepherd and shepherdess shall vie
> In many a tender Psalmody ;
> And the Creator's name prolong
> As rock and stream return their song !
> Begin, then, ladies fair ! begin
> The age renew'd that knows no sin !
> And with light heart, that wants no wing,
> Sing ! from this holy song-book, sing !

Royalty and nobility responded by choosing particular psalms as their favourites. The Queen chose " Rebuke me not," and the King " Stand up, O Lord, to revenge my quarrel " to a dance tune of Poitou ; and singing psalms in verse became a fashionable diversion.[1]

The subsequent history of hymnody in France is in striking contrast with that of England and Germany, as a glance at the articles on the subject in Julian will quickly show. France, the land of the " Te Deum," of Hilary, of Bernard and the Victorines, has since the Reformation produced few hymn-writers of distinction. Two of her leading poets, Racine and

---

[1] See an amusing article on " Psalm-Singing " in Disraeli's *Curiosities of Literature.*

Corneille, wrote a few ; Mme Guyon and Fénelon stand high among mystical poets ; and Malan is the Charles Wesley of the French Reformed Churches. But it is to Germany that we must look to see the rich harvest of the seed sown at Wittenberg and Geneva.

The Thirty Years War, which fulfilled Luther's worst fears of a violent aftermath of the Reformation and shook society to its very foundations, produced some of Germany's noblest hymns. The troubles of the times quickened many earnest-hearted men's love for their religion and drove them to seek in God a peace denied them in the world. Rinkhart's " Now thank we all our God," Lowenstern's " Lord of our life and God of our salvation," and Heermann's " O Thou the true and only Light," are among these war-time songs. But the chief writer of this school, and in many respects the greatest of German hymnists, is Paul Gerhardt (b. 1607). He is, says Miss Winkworth, " the typical poet of the Lutheran Church, as George Herbert is of the English." His are largely hymns of individual experience, and Frere forms the true estimate of them in placing them in the middle ground between the rugged homeliness of Luther and the introspective emotion-alism of the later pietists. Here is a lovely evening hymn, characteristic, in its spirit of childlike simplicity and peace, of much of Gerhardt's work .—

> Now woods and wolds are sleeping,
> And darkness fast is creeping
>   O'er byre, hearth and hall :
> But thou, my soul, ere slumber,
> For blessings passing number
>   Exalt the Giver of them all.
>
> Though all around be darkling,
> Yet golden stars are sparkling
>   From out yon azure spheres :
> So may I shine in lustre,
> As one of that fair cluster,
>   When call'd to quit this vale of tears.

O tarry thou beside me ;
Jesu, my joyaunce, hide me
  Beneath Thy sheltering wing :
And would the fiend infest me,
Forbid him to molest me,
  But bid Thine Angels round me sing.

Ye also, O my dearest,
My friends and kindred nearest,
  God rest you safe from harm !
His Angel-hosts attend ye,
Their golden shields defend ye
  From nightly danger and alarm.[1]

We shall meet with the hymn-writers of Germany again
when we come to consider the work of the Wesleys.

---

[1] This translation of " Nun ruhen alle Wälder " is by the Rev. G. R. Woodward, M.A., Mus.Doc. ; see *Songs of Syon.*

CHAPTER VIII

THE METRICAL PSALMS

THE Reformation left a deep and abiding mark not only upon the song-worship of the English Churches, but upon religious literature in general. The sixteenth century saw three important new translations of the Bible Tyndale's version, the Great Bible, and the Genevan or Breeches version. It also saw the production of the first English Prayer Book, and the complete Anglicization of the Liturgy. Unfortunately, when the liturgical books were turned into English a clean sweep (with one single and notable exception)[1] was made of the ancient Latin hymns. This meant a quite needless impoverishment of our worship-song for at least two hundred years, for it was not until the time of the Wesleys that they began to come back into use again. Doubtless they were abandoned because of their Popish associations. Moreover, hymns in a tongue that all could understand were felt by the leaders of Reform to be needful for the fostering of the newly awakened devotional life of their converts. So we find that Coverdale and Whittingham, in their years of exile, not only had a share in the translation of the Genevan Bible, but also tried their hand, along with many of their fellow-exiles, at the translating or writing of hymns and paraphrases in the English tongue.

At first it looked as though Luther rather than Calvin would prove to be the father of English congregational singing. Coverdale's *Ghoostly Psalmes and Spirituall Songes*, published between 1530 and 1540, was largely Lutheran in its contents. Some of its " psalmes and songes " were set to German chorales, including the famous " Ein Feste Burg," and on its title page appeared the quaint dedicatory lines :—

[1] See pp. 77 and 146.

Be not ashamed, I warrande thee
    Though thou be rude in songe and ryme,
Thou shalt to youth some occasion be
    In godly sports to passe theyr tyme.[1]

The conception of Psalm-singing as a " godly sport " sounds
somewhat startling to us to-day, but Coverdale was merely
adopting Luther's view of the value of song as a popular
instrument of religious culture.

Dating from about the same period, but far more interesting than Coverdale's *Songes*, was the famous *Compendious
Book* of *Gude and Godlie Ballates* of the Wedderburn
brothers.   John Wedderburn, the most important of the trio,
had fled from Dundee to Wittenberg in 1539, and had there
enjoyed the friendship of Luther and Melancthon.   There
can be no doubt that he had watched the manner in which
the evangel of the Reformers was being sung in Germany
and carried far afield, to the accompaniment of popular ballad
measures.   Such a practice was by no means confined to
Protestant writers.   Abbey records that a collection of Roman
Catholic hymns, set to profane melodies, was printed in
Venice in 1512 ; and a version of the Psalms in Flemish, of
1540, actually had the first line of a ballad at the head of each
Psalm.[2]   So Wedderburn determined to follow suit, and he
soon set about his task in thorough-going fashion.   On his
return to his native land he brought with him a collection
of songs and ballads which, with his brothers' help, he had
compiled upon the Lutheran model, and which he commended
to the notice of the young people of Scotland and particularly
" such as are not exercised in the Scriptures."   Latin hymnody,
he said, was of no use to such folk, as it could not be understood : " but," he added, " when they hear it sung into their
vulgar tongue, or sing it themselves, with sweet melody, then
shall they love their God with heart and mind, and cause
them to put away baudry and unclean songs."   A large pro-

---

[1] *Memorial of Miles Coverdale*, published by S. Bagster, 1838.
[2] C. J. Abbey's *Religious Thought in Old English Verse*, p. 181.

portion of the contents of Wedderburn's collection are from German sources ; there are some carols, including the ever-delightful " In Dulci Jubilo," and Luther's " Vom Himmel Hoch," and also some satirical verses attacking, with rough humour, the vices and weaknesses of the Roman priesthood. The closing section of the book is the most interesting, consisting as it does of a number of religious parodies of popular songs and ballads. A favourite hunting-song of Henry VIII's, " The hunt is up "—a song still to be found in some English collections—was metamorphosed like this :—

Henry VIII's Version.

> The hunt is up, the hunt is up,
>   And it is well-nigh day,
> And Harry our King is gone hunting
>   To bring his deer to bay.

Wedderburn's Version.

> With huntis up, with huntis up,
>   It is now perfite day,
> Jesus our King is gone hunting ;
>   Who likes to speed they may.

A later verse, with some tang in it, adds :—

> The hunter is Christ, that hunts in haste ;
>   The hounds are Peter and Paul ;
> The Pope is the fox ; Rome is the rocks
>   That rubs us on the gall.

A love-song, " John, come kiss me now," is made to read :—

> John, come kiss me now ;
> John, come kiss me now ;
>   John, come kiss me by-and-by,
>   And make no more ado.
> The Lord thy God I am
>   That John does thee call ;
> John represents man
>   By grace celestial.

And here is another, that sings itself, in which again the earthly love is sublimated into the Divine [1] :—

> All my love, leave me not,
> Leave me not, leave me not,
> All my love, leave me not,
> Leave me not alone,
> With a burden on my back ;
> I cannot bear it, I am so weak ;
> Love ! this burden from me take,
> Or else I am gone !

> I cry to Thee, I cry to Thee,
> To leave me not, to leave me not ;
> I cry and I call to Thee
> To leave me not alone ;
> All they that laden be,
> Thou bid'st them come to Thee ;
> Then shall they savéd be,
> Through Thy mercy alone

> Faith, hope and charity !
> Leave me not, leave me not ;
> Faith, hope and charity,
> Leave me not alone ;
> I pray Thee, Lord, grant me
> These godly gifties three ;
> Then shall I savéd be,
> Doubt have I none !

Equally striking and naïve are two further songs, " Who is at my window ? " and " Say well and do well." It is a queer " hymn book " and one is not altogether surprised that officialdom, seeing it eagerly welcomed, as wandering minstrels carried it across the glens and mountains of Scotland, tried to suppress it. If such a book were to appear to-day there almost certainly would be an outcry against it. Respectability would insist on dignity in worship, and would talk of the cheapening of religion. But dignity may throttle spontaneity and zeal. Wedderburn was content to be God's Jongleur if haply he might save some. No one can fairly pass judgment

---

[1] In this and the earlier specimens I have modernized the original spelling.

on his songs who has not seen those they were meant to supersede. As we compare the two, we pass from obscenity to purity, from profanity to faith ; and though their language may sometimes be rugged and vulgar, yet, as one commentator says, " there is often present a yearning pathos as of soul speaking to soul, which transmutes and purifies their coarser elements, and transfuses the whole with a spiritual rapture " ;[1] and in any case they constitute the answer of a cruelly persecuted man to the oppression which organized religion meted out to him and the corruption into which it had sunk.

It is perhaps unjustifiable to claim, as some have done, that the *Compendious Book* is the earliest English hymnal ; but it certainly pointed the way along Lutheran rather than Calvinistic lines which English hymnody was ultimately destined to take.

How then did it happen that in England and Scotland not only did the Calvinistic psalmody become for many generations the sole vehicle of public praise, but an actual obstacle to the singing of hymns in our churches ?[2] The answer is to be found in the circumstance that the Marian exiles gravitated to Geneva rather than to Wittenberg, and fell under the spell of Calvin's powerful personality ; so that, when they returned home, they brought with them his rules for the conduct of public worship. John Knox, the most conspicuous and masterly man among them, made it his practice to defer to Calvin's judgment in all such matters. He spent much time while in exile in preparing a Psalter for use among the English-speaking Protestants, and when at length he and his fellow-exiles came home, they did so with songs of praise taken from the pure fountain of the Scriptures upon their lips. Among their little company was Knox's brother-in-law, William Whittingham, who, as we have seen,[3] was one of the translators of the Genevan Bible ; and William Kethe, immortalized

---

[1] *Cambridge History of English Literature*, vol. iii.
[2] For an interesting treatment of this matter, the reader is again referred to the admirable opening chapter of L. F. Benson's *The English Hymn*.
[3] See p. 141.

as the author of the justly renowned paraphrase of the
100th Psalm, " All people that on earth do dwell," which was
written expressly for the " Old Hundredth " tune to which
it is now universally sung.

The Psalter prepared for use in Geneva contained no less
than thirty-seven paraphrases by Thomas Sternhold. Sternhold, in the days before the persecution, had been an official
at the courts of Henry VIII and Edward VI. A story that
has survived tells how King Edward heard him singing Psalms
to an organ accompaniment, and expressed a wish to hear
more ; and when, later, he published some of them, they
were dedicated to His Majesty with the modest words, " Albeit
I cannot give Your Majesty great loaves or bring into the
Lord's barn full handfulls, . . . I am bold to present a few
crumbs which I have picked from under my Lord's board."

Soon after Knox returned to Scotland, the General Assembly
faced the question of Psalm-singing, and sanction was given
for the publication of " the whole Psalmes of David in English
meter." ¹ The date of the first complete Psalter, issued by
the publisher Day, is 1562. The appendices to this Psalter
have great historical interest, for they contain, besides the
Psalms, metrical versions of the Canticles, the Commandments,
the Athanasian Creed, the " Te Deum " and the Lord's Prayer ;
a few original English hymns, and an English version of the
old Latin hymn " Veni Creator Spiritus "—" Come, Holy
Ghost, eternal God." The " Veni Creator " was a legacy
from the pre-Reformation Service-books. It was the only
metrical hymn to survive the upheavals through which
Christianity was passing. It has had a continuous life of
a thousand years in our English Churches, and is a uniquely
precious link across the barriers of time and of creed.²

The reception given in England to the new psalmody was
from the first unmistakably cordial. Julian describes the
stages by which it won its way to the hearts of the people :—

¹ The wording of the title page, and other interesting information,
will be found in *The Metrical Psalms and Paraphrases*, by Thomas Young.
² See pp. 77 and 141.

At first (he says) the putting forth of the Psalter and the *Hymns* was a tentative measure only. This tentative measure evidently satisfied the Queen's Censors that the whole book was in accordance with the Reformed Teaching and Ritual, that it was calculated to do good to the people, and that it was acceptable to them and to the clergy at large. These authorities therefore deemed it right to raise the book from the position of a private manual into a public and authorized book for use in public worship. This they did by Licencing it to be printed and published with the full knowledge that it was to " bee soong of the people together, in Churches, before and after Morning and Evening prayer, as also before and after the Sermon." Its acceptance was universal and continuous.[1]

The scenes in London that marked the first singing of the Genevan psalms were fully as enthusiastic as those enacted in the streets of Paris or of Augsburg. Thousands gathered at St. Paul's Cross and sang them together after sermon ; the practice spread from town to town, and Sternhold's effusions were " roared aloud," according to Burney, like orgies, in almost every street, as well as church, throughout the kingdom. The Papists looked on with disapproval, and Jewel, who was an eye-witness, says that even the children retorted by laughing at the priests as they passed in the streets, and the bishops were called hangmen to their faces. Queen Elizabeth is said to have dubbed the psalms " Geneva Jigs," but she encouraged the Psalm-singers and even tried her own hand at paraphrasing, and gave her approval to the famous Injunction :—

For the comforting of such as delight in music, it may be permitted that in the beginning or end of Common Prayer either at Morning or Evening, there may be sung an hymn or such like song to the praise of Almighty God

[1] Julian's *Dictionary of Hymnology*, p. 1540.

in the best melody and music that may be devised, having respect that the sentence (sense) of the hymn may be understood and perceived.

This Injunction became at once the recognized authorization of the anthem by the choir and of the Genevan psalm by the people.[1]

Sternhold wrote most of his paraphrases in the old English ballad metre—the measure of " Chevy Chase " and of " The Bailiff's Daughter of Islington." In so doing, according to Dr. Johnson, he flattered himself that the courtiers would sing them instead of their loose and wanton sonnets. But he had in mind other people besides courtiers. He wanted the common people to sing them, and he was therefore content to sacrifice literary polish for straightforward lucidity and faithfulness to the language of the Scriptures. His own 18th Paraphrase, " O God, my strength and fortitude," and the 23rd, " My Shepherd is the living Lord," are forceful and reverent in feeling ; and many that followed from the pen of other paraphrasers during the succeeding century or so have likewise endeared themselves to God's people and still retain a place among the classics of devotion.

A form of devotional literature that occupied the field in the religious life of this island for more than two hundred years, and that counted among its contributors many writers of mediocre capacity, could hardly be expected to maintain a uniformly high standard of excellence. Moreover, the limitation of its theme within the restricted boundaries of a manual that had originally been compiled for use in the Jewish Temple was a handicap. Imagine a congregation of Christians singing such sentiments as these :—

> Lord, Thou hast given me the necks
> Of all my enemies,
> That so I might destroy all those
> That up against me rise.

[1] Benson's *The English Hymn.*

> They call'd for help, but none gave ear,
>   Nor came to their relief;
> Yea, to the Lord they call'd for aid,
>   Yet heard He not their grief.
>
> And still, like dust before the wind,
>   I drive them under feet,
> And sweep them out like filthy dirt
>   That lieth in the street.

Or again, even more vigorously pugilistic :— .

> O God, break Thou their teeth at once,
>   Within their mouth throughout;
> The tusks that in their great chaw bones
>   Like lions' whelps hang out.

Such fierce and sanguinary sentiments ought to find no place in a Christian Church. The writers of such Psalms might have had some excuse for violent language; but not so the followers of Him who taught us to forgive our enemies and to pray for them that despitefully use us. Yet, alas! every reader of Prothero's *Psalms in Human Life* knows to what unholy uses the Psalter has been diverted, and how its every page has been stained with the blood of violent and revengeful men.

Nor can much Christian edification have followed the singing of such queer lines as these—to choose one's quotations somewhat at random :—

> Why should the proud and wicked man
>   Blaspheme God's holy name,
> While in his heart he crieth " Tush " ? :
>   God cares not for the same.

or :—

> By reason of my groaning voice
>   My bones cleave to my skin,
> As pelican in wilderness
>   Such case now am I in;
> And as an owl in desert is,
>   Lo! I am such a one;
> I watch, and as a sparrow on
>   The housetop am alone.

Fortunately there is another side of the picture. All is not doggerel. The example set by the versifiers in exile and by Sternhold and his coadjutor Hopkins was in course of time followed by a succession of poets and would-be poets. In the reign of William III, Tate and Brady published their *New Version* of the Psalms. Tate was Poet-laureate and a friend of Dryden, and Brady was a Royal Chaplain and sometime incumbent of Stratford-on-Avon. Their book contained a plentiful supply of chaff, but perhaps a few more grains of golden corn than Sternhold's. " As pants the hart " and " Through all the changing scenes of life " are still highly prized, and Tate's Christmas Carol " While shepherds watched their flocks by night " (which appeared in a Supplement to the *New Version*) is a masterly adaptation of the Nativity story. Quite a number of the eminent poets of the period covered by the Old and New Versions also tried their hand at paraphrasing the Psalms, and when we meet with such names as Gascoigne and Sidney, Sandys and Wither, Herbert and Milton, we expect choice work, and now and again we meet with it. But on the whole it has to be confessed that the sixteenth and seventeenth centuries, richly as they influenced the religious and literary life of the nation, are poverty-stricken so far as its psalmody and hymnody are concerned.

But these paraphrases shall speak for themselves. First of all, let us see Sternhold at his best. Here is his version of Psalm xxiii :—

> My Shepherd is the living Lord,
>   Nothing therefore I need,
> In pastures faire with waters calm
>   He set me for to feed.
>
> He did convert and glad my soule
>   And brought my mind in frame,
> To walk in paths of righteousnesse
> ˙ For His most holy name.
>
> Yea, though I walke in vale of death,
>   Yet will I fear none ill ;
> Thy rod, Thy staffe doth comfort me,
>   And Thou art with me still :

And in the presence of my foes
   My table Thou shalt spread ;
Thou shalt, O Lord, fill full my cup
   And eke anoint my head.

Through all my life Thy favour is
   So frankly shew'd to me,
That in Thy house for evermore
   My dwelling place shall be.

It is interesting to contrast Sternhold's lines with the following version of the same psalm, by Francis Davison, whose father was privy councillor to Queen Elizabeth, and who claims that his paraphrases are " of a different composure from those used in the Church." Does he refer, one wonders, to their literary merit, or merely to their freer metrical form ?

God, who the universe doth hold
                  In His fold,
Is my Shepherd, kind and heedful—
      Is my Shepherd, and doth keepe
                  Me His sheepe
Still supplied with all things needfull.

He feedes me in fieldes which beene
                  Fresh and greene,
Mottled with Spring's flowry painting ;
      Through which creepe with murmuring crookes
                  Christall brookes,
To refresh my spirit's fainting.

When my soule from heaven's way
                  Went astray,
With earthe's vanities seduced,
      For His name sake kindly He
                  Wandering me
To His holy fold reduced.

Yea, should I stray throughe deathe's vale,
                  Where his pale
Shades did on each side enfold me ;
      Dreadles, having Thee for guide,
                  Should I bide,
For Thy rod and staff upholde me.

Thou my board with messes large
    Dost surcharge ;
My bowles full of wine Thou powrest,
And before myne enemies'
    Envious eies
Balme upon my head thou showerest.

Neither dures Thy bounteous grace
    For a space ;
But it knowes nor bound nor measure.
So my daies to my life's end
    I shall spend
In Thy courtes with heavenly pleasure.

George Herbert's version of the Shepherd Psalm " The God of Love my Shepherd is " is too well known to need quoting. It is a perfect gem.

George Sandys' style is vigorous. This is how he closes his paraphrase of Psalm xxxix :—

Man nothing is but vanity,
    Though crowned on high ;
Walks like a shadow, and in vain
    Turmoils with pain :
He heaps up wealth with wretched care,
Yet knows not who shall prove his heir :

His beauty wasted like a cloth
    Gnawn by the moth ;
Himself a short-lived vanity,
    And born to die.
Lord, to my prayers incline Thine ear,
And Thy afflicted servant hear.

Phineas Fletcher's Psalm cxxx is of special interest because in its closing verse we see a very early tendency to " Christianize " the Psalter, a process which was to be the dominating principle of Isaac Watts's epoch-making work in the following century :—

From the deeps of grief and fear,
    O Lord, to Thee my soul repairs ;
From Thy heaven bow down Thine ear ;
    Let Thy mercy meet my prayers.

Oh, if Thou mark'st
What's done amiss,
What soul so pure,
Can see Thy bliss ?

But with Thee sweet mercy stands,
    Sealing pardons, working fear :
Wait, my soul, wait on His hands ;
    Wait mine eye, O wait mine ear ;
        If He His eye
        Or tongue affords,
        Watch all His looks,
        Catch all His words.

As a watchman waits for day,
    And looks for light, and looks again ;
When the night grows old and grey,
    To be relieved he calls amain :
        So look, so wait,
        So long mine eyes,
        To see my Lord,
        My Sun, arise.

Wait, ye saints, wait on our Lord ;
    For from His tongue sweet mercy flows :
Wait on His cross, wait on His word ;
    Upon that tree Redemption grows.
        He will redeem
        His Israel
        From sin and wrath,
        From death and hell.

The Psalms and Scriptural Paraphrases had a long run.
An interval of nearly a hundred and fifty years elapsed between the publication of Day's Psalter and Watts's first volume
of hymns, and even then another equally long period was to
pass before throughout our churches hymns rather than psalms
became the accepted medium of praise.   Their influence upon
religious thought and emotion has thus been prolonged and
far-reaching.   It is impressive to remember that the Psalms,
which nurtured the inner life of the people of Israel long
before the coming of Christ, which furnished the primitive
Church with its first praise book, which were " recited weekly
in every monastery and convent in Europe . . . and by every

priest and deacon as a part of his daily duty " all through the centuries of monasticism, and are still daily sung in our English cathedrals, were given a new lease of life, and in a gracious and popular form, by the leaders of the Reformation, thus endearing them to countless believers in many lands and forming the groundwork, the well-spring, of our modern hymnals.

> There David standes, with harpe in hand,
> As maister of the Queere.

The little group of six hymns which found a place in the appendices to Sternhold's *Old Version* are specially important to our story. Their introduction there is an admission that from the first the inadequacy of the Psalms as the sole vehicle of Christian praise was recognized by the Reformers. It is thought that they were at first intended for private rather than public use : but, however that may be, their appearance is a landmark in the evolution of the English hymn. It shows that the Lutheran party elbowed their way in alongside the Calvinists, as if determined to provide a nucleus around which ultimately a vernacular English hymnody might be created. Benson is at pains to show that these appendices did not in actual fact lead the way toward an ultimate hymnal. They are, he thinks, merely an episode, of no great importance, in our story.[1] But they do at least suggest one direction in which the growing desire for a distinctly Christian hymnody was to be met.

The time has at last come when we can turn to trace the beginnings of our modern English hymnody, which, as has been made abundantly clear, is the direct offspring of the Reformation.

[1] Benson's *The English Hymn*, chap. i.

CHAPTER IX

A NEST OF SINGING BIRDS

THE principal sources from which our modern English hymnody drew its young life have now been brought under review. The hymns of the ancient and mediæval church; the homely songs of the German fatherland; the metrical psalms and paraphrases : these three fertilizing springs were destined to flow into one channel; a stream in the desert, a stream of joyful song; and many who were athirst drank of its waters and were refreshed. And now at length, the stream, enriched by the copious fountains of our native hymnody, was to become a mighty river, whose waters should flow for our healing from one generation to another.

The development of this English hymnody, which has now to be traced, proceeded along two well-defined channels.[1] Firstly, the scope of the metrical psalmody was gradually widened so as to accommodate its content to Christian truth; and secondly, a native school of devotional poets arose, who slowly discovered the distinction between a meditative poem intended for private reading and edification and a lyrical hymn to be sung in church. Probably the discovery would have been made earlier, but for the fact that Calvin's rule was so completely dominant. Seeing that no use would be made of them, it was hardly to be expected that many hymns would be written. The six which appeared in Day's Psalter [2] were of no literary merit.

Twenty years or so later, a book was issued by William Hunnis bearing the strange title *Seven Sobs of a Sorrowful Soul for Sin*. To his collection Hunnis himself made some

[1] I am again indebted to Dr. Benson's valuable book *The English Hymn* for guidance at this stage of my story.
[2] See p. 146.

original contributions, which are marked by a certain sweet simplicity. Here is one of them :—

> O Jesu sweet, grant that Thy grace
> Always so worke in mee,
> I may desire the thing to doo
> Most pleasing unto Thee.
>
> O Jesu meeke, Thy will be mine,
> My will be Thine also ;
> And that my will may follow Thine
> In pleasure, paine and wo ;
>
> O Jesu, what is goode for mee,
> I say best known to Thee :
> Therefore according to Thy will
> Have mercie now on mee.

Anyone acquainted with Farr's volumes will know that the devotional poetry of the age of Queen Elizabeth was of considerable variety and extent, and sometimes of much charm.[1] A pioneer hymn-writer of the period is George Gascoigne, an Elizabethan courtier, whose religious poems were all written in what he calls his " middle age," when he looked back with regret on the follies of his youth. Perhaps that is what accounts for their tinge of sadness, sometimes verging on morbidity. Some stanzas from his " Good Morrowe " are to be found in a few modern hymnals. It will be seen that they are on the border-line between a meditation and a hymn. Hymn-writing is seen in its infancy. We learn to walk before we can run.

> You that have spent the silent night [2]
> In sleepe and quiet rest,
> And joy to see the cheerefull lyght
> That riseth in the East :
> Now cleare your voyce, now cheere your hart,
> Come helpe me now to sing :
> Ech willing wight come beare a part,
> To prayse the heavenly King.

[1] *Select Poetry, chiefly devotional, of the Reign of Queen Elizabeth* : Collected and edited for the Parker Society by Edward Farr.
[2] The modern version usually begins : " Ye that have spent the quiet night."

> The dreadfull night with darkesomnes
>   Had overspread the light,
> And sluggish sleepe with drowsines
>   Had overprest our might :
> A glasse wherein you may beholde
>   Ech storme that stops our breath,
> Our bed the grave, our clothes lyke molde,
>   And sleepe lyke dreadfull death.
>
> Yet as this deadly night did laste
>   But for a little space,
> And heavenly daye, now night is past,
>   Doth shewe his pleasant face :
> So must we hope to see God's face
>   At last in heaven on hie,
> When we have changed this mortall place
>   For Immortalitie.

The poet, in succeeding verses, shows himself of the family of the nature-mystics. He draws the usual analogies between the natural and the spiritual worlds. Christ is the Sun ; the sky is heaven ; the earth, the tomb ; the rainbow, God's throne ; the clouds, our earthly trials ; the dew, God's grace, and so forth. Here are some quaint lines :—

> The carion Crowe, that lothsome beast,
>   Which cries agaynst the rayne,
> Both for hir hewe and for the rest
>   The Devill resembleth playne ;
> And as with gunnes we kill the crowe,
>   For spoyling our releefe,
> The Deville so must we overthrowe
>   With gunshote of beleefe.
>
> The little birdes which sing so swete
>   Are like the angells' voyce,
> Which render God his prayses meete,
>   And teache us to rejoyce.

Gascoigne wrote just before Spenser. Spenser (b. 1552) can only with difficulty be dragged by zealous editors in search of treasure into the charmed circle of hymn-writers. That air of virgin innocence and ethereal splendour which marks his poetry is all too rarely to be met in our hymn books. He

tells us that as he himself, with many other poets, had written
lewd songs in the hot days of youth, he now in later years
altered " the tenor of his string " and sang of heavenly Love.
Where else in the whole range of English literature is there
—as Palgrave describes it—a more splendid outburst of pure
lyrical enthusiasm than his and Milton's odes ? This glorious
sonnet from *Amoretti and Epithalamion* is in *The English
Hymnal* [1] :—

> Most glorious Lord of life that, on this day,
> Didst make Thy triumph over death and sin ;
> And, having harrowed hell, didst bring away
> Captivity thence captive, us to win :
> This joyous day, dear Lord, with joy begin ;
> And grant that we, for whom Thou diddest die,
> Being with Thy dear blood clean washed from sin,
> May live for ever in felicity !
> And that Thy love we weighing worthily,
> May likewise love Thee for the same again ;
> And for Thy sake, that all like dear didst buy,
> With love may one another entertain !
> So let us love, dear Love, like as we ought :
> Love is the lesson which the Lord us taught.

There are stanzas in the " Hymn of Heavenly Love " that
might well be placed to a similar use, such as :—

> O blessed Well of Love ! O Flower of Grace !
> O glorious Morning Star ! O Lamp of Light !
> Most lively image of Thy Father's face,
> Eternal King of Glory, Lord of Might,
> Meek Lamb of God, before all worlds behight,
> How can we Thee requite for all this good ?
> Or what can prize that Thy most precious blood ?

The following Morning Hymn is of about Spenser's time :
it has a pleasing open-air redolence about it : its author is
unknown [2] :—

---

[1] The lines are in the section of Sunday hymns : they were written for
Easter.
[2] *Ancient Devotional Poetry from Manuscripts of the Sixteenth and
Seventeenth Centuries.*

The birds that here so merrily do sing,
And make these woods with their sweet carols ring,
Methinks do meete to praise with one accord
Th' allmighty power of their most gratious Lord,
Who made them, and with plenty feedes them all,
From the greate Eagle to the Nightingall.

Then rise, my soule ! My harpe and voice, awake !
Before the day to God confession make ;
Sing a new song, extoll His providence,
And magnify His great beneficence ;
Let both thy viol and thy lute resound,
What grace in thy distresses thou hast found.

Begin thou first, and thou shalt quickly see
The Cherubins and Seraphins agree,
And joyne their voices to the Sphere's sweet sound,
To make both heaven and earth God's praise resound :
O joy ! when Angells join with men to sing
The praises due to our immortal King.

Robert Southwell, a charming singer of this period, belonged
to the " Society of Jesus." Religious intolerance in the
sixteenth century was by no means confined to the Romanists.
Southwell suffered martyrdom, along with many other Jesuit
Fathers, at the hands of the Elizabethan government. Some
of his poems were written in prison : they show us a man
who lived with God.

Yet God's must I remain,
    By death, by wrong, by shame ;
I cannot blot out of my heart
    That grace wrought in His name.

I cannot set at nought
    Whom I have held so dear ;
I cannot make Him seem afar
    That is indeed so near.

The following shows signs of that love of fantastic ornamentation which overtook the Elizabethan and Jacobean
lyrists, and which culminated later in the luscious poetry of
the George Herbert school. Yet it is as reverent in tone as
it is charming in style :—

I praise Him most, I love Him best, all praise and love is His ;
While Him I love, in Him I live, and cannot live amiss.
Love's sweetest mark, laud's highest theme, man's most desirèd
    light,
To love Him life, to leave Him death, to live in Him delight.
He mine by gift, I His by debt, thus each to other due,
First Friend He was, best Friend He is, all times will try Him
    true ;
His knowledge rules, His strength defends, His love doth cherish
    all ;
His birth our joy, His life our light, His death our end of thrall.[1]

Among other notable poems of the period which just escape
being hymns are Campion's well-known " Never weather-
beaten sail more willing bent to shore " and " F. B. P.'s "
haunting " Jerusalem, my happy home." Delightful to read,
the wistful " otherworldliness " of such pieces makes them
unsuitable for congregational singing.

It is different with George Wither. He, almost first among
our devotional poets, sees what are the essential requirements
of a good hymn. He does not see so clearly as Ken or Watts,
but he comes nearer than any of his predecessors to the real
thing. His *Hymns and Songs of the Church*, published in
1623, when he was thirty-five years of age, gained the Royal
favour, and he actually obtained a patent for its publication along with every copy of the metrical Psalms. Against
this concession the Company of Stationers protested, mixing
a good deal of venom with their protest, charging Wither
with making money out of the praises of God, and declaring
that the hymns were Popish, superstitious, obscene, and
" unfit to keep company with David's Psalms," and that in
any case such writings should be left to the clergy. Wither's
reply shows him to be more than a match for his detractors.
Of especial importance is his plea that the scope of the hymns
used in church should include those that illustrate " the
particular mysteries of the Christian faith." He animadverts
upon the inadequacy of the metrical Psalter, and boldly claims
himself capable of offering up a sweeter perfume to God,

      [1] Robert Southwell's *Complete Poems*, ed. by Dr. Grosart.

" making use with modesty of the gifts which were bestowed upon me to that purpose." Wither's hymns were eagerly bought by young people, and he became quite a popular poet. Doubtless their use was greatly aided by the delightful airs to which they were set by Orlando Gibbons.

Eighteen years later Wither published a further collection of hymns entitled *Hallelujah, or Britain's Second Remembrancer*. He addressed this book to the High Courts of Parliament, saying that he had directed to their notice " the sweet perfume of pious praises compounded according to the art of the spiritual apothecary." With engaging candour he told his readers that the hymns were all his own : he had copied no man, for he thought that by searching his own heart he would the better find out the message which would be most helpful to those whom he desired to profit. He prefixed a note— often full of humour—to each hymn, defining the occasion for which it was specially written—such as " To be sung when washing " or " When slandered " or " When we cannot sleep." In other instances he mentioned the special class of persons it was meant to help, such as " For Members of Parliament," " For a Physician," " For Lovers," " For Artists," " For a Widow delivered from a troublesome yoke-fellow," and " For a Musician who is more out of order than his instrument." The note " For a Merchant or Chapman " read :—

> By the use of this Hymn, Merchants may be kept heedful of the snares and temptations which they become liable unto by their negotiations ; and what peace and profit will ensue if they be just and merciful in their dealings.

Pope spoke of Wither as " sleeping among the dull of ancient days, where no critics damn." But if the critics neglected him, so much the worse for the critics. To-day, happily, we enjoy rather than damn him. Posterity owes him a debt for having so effectively widened the scope of the hymn : he leaves Augustine's definition far behind [1] and uses the hymn, not merely to praise God, but, as he himself said, to make us mindful of our duties. But the reader will wish to hear him. Here is the first hymn of his " Hallelujah "— " A general invitation to praise God." It is based on Psalm cxlviii :—

Come, O come ! in pious lays
Sound we God Almighty's praise ;
Hither bring in one consent,
Heart, and voice, and instrument.
Music add of every kind ;
Sound the trump, the cornet wind ;
Strike the viol, touch the lute ;
Let no tongue nor string be mute ;
    Nor a creature dumb be found,
    That hath either voice or sound.

Come, ye sons of human race,
In this chorus take a place ;
And amid the mortal throng,
Be you masters of the song.
Angels, and supernal powers,
Be the noblest tenor yours ;
Let in praise of God the sound
Run a never-ending round ;
    That our song of praise may be
    Everlasting as is He.

From earth's vast and hollow womb,
Music's deepest bass may come ;
Seas and floods, from shore to shore,
Shall their counter-tenors roar ;
To this concert, when we sing,
Whistling winds your descants bring ;
That our song may over-climb
All the bounds of place and time,
    And ascend from sphere to sphere,
    To the great Almighty's ear.

So, from heaven, on earth He shall
Let His gracious blessings fall ;
And this huge wide orb we see,
Shall one choir, one temple be ;

[1] See p. 27.

Where, in such a praise-full tone
We will sing what He hath done,
That the cursèd fiends below
Shall thereat impatient grow.
    Then, O come! in pious lays
    Sound we God Almighty's praise.

The hymn to be sung " When we are upon the sea " is full
of music and literary power :—

On those great waters now I am,
    Of which I have been told,
That whosoever thither came
    Should wonders there behold.
In this unsteady place of fear
    Be present, Lord, with me ;
For in these depths of water here
    I depths of danger see.

A stirring courser now I sit,
    A headstrong steed I ride,
That champs and foams upon the bit
    Which curbs his lofty pride ;
The softest whistling of the winds
    Doth make him gallop fast ;
And as their breath increased he finds
    The more he maketh haste.

Take Thou, O Lord ! the reins in hand,
    Assume our Master's room ;
Vouchsafe Thou at our helm to stand,
    And pilot to become :
Trim Thou the sails, and let good speed
    Accompany our haste ;
Sound Thou the channels at our need,
    And anchor for us cast.

His Evening Hymn " Behold the sun " has some tender
lines, and his Musician's Hymn contains the following needful
reminder—a reminder which might well be taken as a guiding
motto for every chapter of our studies in hymnology :—

He sings and plays
    The songs which best Thou lovest,
Who does and says
    The things which Thou approvest.

The lyrical poets of the Jacobean and Carolean period count George Herbert as their chief glory. The immediate circle surrounding Herbert may almost be said to constitute a family party, linked together by ties of blood or friendship or literary tastes, and presided over by the genial and kindly fisherman, Izaak Walton. It is rather a wonderful group, including as it does, besides Herbert himself, Donne and Wotton, Crashaw and Bishop King, Ferrar and Ken. The age in which these men lived is itself remarkable in the annals of English literature. The years of Izaak Walton's lifetime, which spanned almost a century, saw the production of the Authorized Version of the Bible, of Bacon's Essays, of Shakespeare's great masterpieces *Hamlet* and *Macbeth*, and of Milton's *Lycidas* and *Paradise Lost*. It was the time when the common speech of the people reached its zenith of beauty, redolent of nature and the open air and rich in natural, poetical feeling. The devotional poetry of the age is marked by a splendour of workmanship which has never been equalled before or since. Truth to tell, it is almost too rich for human nature's daily food, " sweet even to a sense of faintness," bewitching in its jewelled beauty ; but this excess of ornamentation is nearly always atoned for by the devoutness and sincerity of the writers' lines. The " George Herbert group " was drawn together, as has been said, around that prince of anglers Izaak Walton, who, if we may judge by the portrait which gazes at us from Houseman's canvas, was a genial and lovable companion.[1]

Donne, the earliest of the group—its father—was a friend of the Herbert family. He helped Herbert's mother to plan her son's education, and at his death bequeathed the young poet one of his famous rings, with its blood-stone, on which was engraven a figure of the Crucified not on a cross, but on an anchor. Wotton, who shared Walton's love of angling, was bound to Donne by lifelong ties. They had been close friends in their University days " and so it lasted till age and

[1] See the Frontispiece of *The Compleat Angler*, Washbourne's ed.

death forced a separation." Bishop King, too, was a mutual friend, and the writer of an elegy to Donne's memory. Then there was Crashaw. Only a youth at the time of Donne's death, and apparently not very intimate with Herbert, he was a personal friend of Izaak Walton.[1] He certainly shared Herbert's interest in Ferrar's monastic experiment at Little Gidding. Like Herbert, he often went there to refresh his faith, and tried to emulate the experiment at Cambridge. Crashaw's " Steps of the Temple " forms a kind of sequel to Herbert's " Temple " ; and it may well be, too, that Ferrar's lost hymns were based on Herbert's model. It was to Ferrar, it will be remembered, that Herbert bequeathed his own precious volume, saying that in it he would find a picture of the many spiritual conflicts that had passed between its writer's soul and God, and enjoining him to read it " and then if he can think it may turn to the advantage of any dejected poor soul, let it be made public ; if not, let him burn it, for I and it are less than the least of God's mercies."

Ken, the youngest, and from the hymnologist's standpoint the most important, member of the group, was an inmate of Izaak Walton's home through the impressionable years of adolescence. His sister Anne married Walton,[2] and when their parents died, she became as a mother to him. In that cultured and happy household he must often have heard his foster-father gossip of his latest fishing expedition, of his old friends Donne and Drayton and Wotton, and of George Herbert, whose life was revered in that home as a pattern of piety. The boy had the run of the library, where doubtless he became acquainted with the devotional poems of this circle of friends ; and it may well be that Walton sometimes read to him some of the hymns he himself, according to tradition, had written.

Such was " the Herbert group." It was a circle that enjoyed a sheltered and privileged life of culture and refinement. It

---

[1] *Thomas Ken,* by Dean Plumptre.
[2] She is the Kenna of *The Compleat Angler* : " Hear my Kenna sing a song," Part I, chap. v.

is true that more than one of these saintly men endured hardship, and one of them faced bitter tragedy : but on the whole they lived in the peaceful seclusion of the quiet parsonage or the episcopal palace, and tasted whatever sweets are to be found in the purer parts of the court itself.

It should be added that both Henry Vaughan and Richard Baxter had ties with the group. Vaughan not only ascribed his conversion to the example of Herbert's holy life, but took " The Temple " as the model for his poems. Baxter, when a lad, lived for a few weeks in the house of Sir Henry Herbert —George's elder brother—at Whitehall, in accordance with his mother's desire to secure him a place at court. Sir Henry was Master of the Revels at that time, and, as his young guest saw fashionable society enjoying " a stage-play instead of a sermon on the Lord's day," and heard the preachers attacking the Puritans, the youth soon returned home sadder and wiser for his experiences.

Invaluable as was the contribution which this galaxy of writers made to religious song, Ken was the only one of them, with the exception of Baxter, who understood how to write a good hymn. A few examples will show the limitations, in this respect, of the others. They are of importance to our story, not only because they bring us into the spiritual company of some of the sweetest singers of the Anglican Church, but because they form a connecting link between the psalmody of the English Reformation and the hymnody of modern times.

Donne's hymn, " To God the Father," set to a most grave and solemn tune, was often sung by the choristers of St. Paul's Cathedral, in his own hearing, bringing him, as he himself records, inexpressible tranquillity of mind :—

> Wilt Thou forgive that sin where I begun,
>   Which was my sin, though it were done before ?
> Wilt Thou forgive that sin, through which I run
>   And do run still, though still I do deplore ?
>   When Thou hast done, Thou hast not done ;
>   For I have more.

Wilt Thou forgive that sin which I have won
Others to sin, and made my sins their door ?
Wilt Thou forgive that sin, which I did shun
A year or two, but wallow'd in a score ?
When Thou hast done, Thou hast not done
For I have more.

I have a sin of fear, that when I have spun
My last thread, I shall perish on the shore ;
But swear by Thyself, that at my death Thy Son
Shall shine, as He shines now and heretofore :
And having done that, Thou hast done ;
I fear no more.

Eight or nine of George Herbert's poems have been made
to do duty as hymns, by John Wesley and others, but his
lovely paraphrase of Psalm xxiii " The God of Love my
Shepherd is " is the only one that has satisfactorily stood the
test. Of the others, the " Antiphon " makes the best hymn.[1]
As its title implies, Herbert intended that it should be sung
responsively by a soloist and chorus :—

CHORUS : Let all the world in every corner sing
          My God and King.

SOLO :   The heavens are not too high,
        His praise may thither fly ;
        The earth is not too low,
        His praises there may grow,

CHORUS : Let all the world in every corner sing
          My God and King.

SOLO :   The Church with psalms must shout,
        No door can keep them out :
        But, above all, the heart
        Must bear the longest part.

CHORUS : Let all the world in every corner sing
         My God and King.

Crashaw hardly finds a niche in our modern hymn books,
but how can we pass by so charming a singer without pausing

---

[1] *The English Hymnal* contains four of Herbert's poems ; the two here
mentioned, and also " Praise " and " The Elixir."

for a moment to listen to his music? His translation of the
" Dies Iræ " has already been noticed.[1] His Epigrams might
have come from Herbert's pen, so dainty and so worshipful
are they. This is his cameo of the two men who went up to
the Temple to pray :—

> Two went to pray? O rather say
> One went to brag, the other to pray.
>
> One stands up close, and treads on high,
> Where the other dares not lend his eye.
>
> One nearer to God's altar trod ;
> The other to the altar's God.

That is exquisite. Crashaw's most brilliant poems are those
to St. Theresa. Doubtless they are abnormally passionate,
but nevertheless the closing lines of " The Flaming Heart,"
where emotion throbs and burns at a white heat, are of amazing
power, like grand organ-tones of feeling :—

> O thou undaunted daughter of desires !
> By all thy dow'r of Lights and Fires ;
> By all the eagle in thee, all the dove ;
> By all thy lives and deaths of love ;
> By thy large draughts of intellectuall day,
> And by thy thirsts of love more large then they ;
> By all thy brim-fill'd Bowles of fierce desire ;
> By thy last Morning's draught of liquid fire ;
> By the full kingdome of that finall kisse
> That seiz'd thy parting Soul, and seal'd thee His ;
> By all the heav'ns thou hast in Him
> (Fair sister of the Seraphim !) ;
> By all of Him we have in Thee ;
> Leave nothing of my Self in me.
> Let me so read thy life, that I
> Unto all life of mine may dy.

Vaughan, who in point of time comes between Herbert and
Crashaw, seems to ante-date Wordsworth's " Intimations "
in his two poems on the days of infant innocence, " The
Retreat " and " Childhood." Less known, but of value to

[1] See p. 92.

us in these times when militarism is menacing European
civilization, are the lines bearing the title " The Men of
War." Palgrave says they were written as a protest against
the tyranny and persecution suffered under Cromwell and
the Puritans. They close in this fashion :—

> Seeing soldiers long ago
> Did spit on Thee, and smote Thee too ;
> Crown'd Thee with thorns, and bow'd the knee,
> But in contempt, as still we see ;
> I'll marvel not at aught they do,
> Because they used my Saviour so ;
> Since of my Lord they had their will,
> Thy servant must not take it ill.
>
> Dear Jesus, give me patience here,
> And faith to see my crown as near,
> And almost reach'd, because 'tis sure
> If I hold fast, and slight the lure.
> Give me humility and peace,
> Contented thoughts, innoxious ease,
> A sweet, revengeless, quiet mind,
> And to my greatest haters, kind.
> Give me, my God ! a heart so mild
> And plain, as when I was a child.
> That when Thy throne is set, and all
> These conquerors before it fall,
> I may be found—preserved by Thee—
> Amongst that chosen company,
> Who by no blood—here—overcame,
> But by the blood of the Blessed Lamb.

Vaughan's lines entitled " Peace " are still widely sung :—

> My soul, there is a country
>   Far beyond the stars,
> Where stands a wingéd sentry
>   All skilful in the wars :
> There, above noise and danger,
>   Sweet Peace sits crown'd with smiles,
> And One born in a manger
>   Commands the beauteous files,
> He is thy gracious Friend,
>   And—O my soul awake !—
> Did in pure love descend
>   To die here for thy sake.

Compared with these highly-strung numbers, Wotton's " How happy is he born and taught " sounds matter-of-fact. It is a social song rather than a hymn, but, for all that, it fills a useful place, with its note of sturdy independence, in some present-day hymn books. Baxter's " Lord, it belongs not to my care "—a song of trust in the prospect of trials and of death—is in another category. In form, it points the way to the true structure of a hymn. It is plainer and more restrained in tone than the polished and emotional work we have been reviewing.

The seventeenth century was a somewhat barren period in the history of hymnology. Milton and Dryden made some contribution, and such lesser writers as Crossman and Fletcher and Austin sang a few sweet songs. Herrick's *Noble Numbers*, which appeared in 1647, contained some hymns which were sung before King Charles at Whitehall. The pagan Devonshire parson could write incomparable songs, and perhaps if his life had been less irregular we might have counted him among our great hymn-writers. It is all one to him whether he is writing " unbaptized rhymes " of Julia's beads or sweet Corinna's kisses, or nobler numbers on more sacred themes : he is the same charming artificer from cover to cover. His " Thanksgiving to God for his House " is not deemed sedate enough—the more's the pity—to pass the scrutiny of the compilers of present-day hymnals. Yet how engaging, how delightfully human, it is !—

> Lord, Thou hast given me a cell
>   Wherein to dwell ;
> A little house, whose humble roof
>   Is weather-proof ;
> Under the spars of which I lie
>   Both soft and dry ;
> Where Thou my chamber for to ward
>   Hast set a guard
> Of harmless thoughts, to watch and keep
>   Me, while I sleep.

Some verses from his " Litany," beginning " In the hour
of my distress," are still sung in our churches, though the
humour has been kept outside :—

> When the artless doctor sees
> No one hope, but of his fees,
> And his skill runs on the lees,
> Sweet Spirit, comfort me !
>
> When his potion and his pill
> Has, or none, or little skill,
> Meet for nothing but to kill,
> Sweet Spirit, comfort me !

Turning over his pages and meeting lines of perfect beauty
such as this—

> We see Him come, and know Him ours,
> Who, with His sunshine and His showers,
> Turns all the patient ground to flowers

—we wish Herrick could have given more liberally to the
treasury of the Church's praise.

Before the century came to an end it gave us the first series
of hymns that actually won their way into use in the Church
of England. That honour belongs, not to Wither (for his
hymns seem to have been restricted to private use), but to
John Mason, an Anglican clergyman, whose *Songs of Praise*
were published in 1683. Mason was a good pastor to his
little flock, living a life of quiet piety and endearing himself
to his parishioners. His lyrical gifts were of a high order,
and it is not surprising to learn that he influenced both Watts
and Wesley. In the preface to his *Songs* he quoted a saying,
" If I were a Nightingale I would sing like a Nightingale ;
but now that I am a Man, I will sing the Praises of God as
long as I live ; and I would have you to sing with me." In
his third Song appear the oft-quoted lines :—

To whom, Lord, should I sing but Thee,
The Maker of my tongue ?
Lo ! other lords would seize on me,
But I to Thee belong.

Here is his " Song of Praise for the Evening " :—

Now from the altar of my heart
Let incense-flames arise ;
Assist me, Lord, to offer up
Mine evening sacrifice.
Awake, my love ; awake, my joy,
Awake, my heart, and tongue ;
Sleep not ; when mercies loudly call
Break forth into a song.

Man's life's a Book of History,
The leaves thereof are Days,
The letters Mercies closely join'd,
The title is Thy Praise.
This day God was my Sun and Shield,
My Keeper and my Guide ;
His care was on my frailty shewn,
His mercies multiply'd.

Minutes and mercies multiply'd
Have made up all this day ;
Minutes came quick, but mercies were
More fleet and free than they.
New time, new favour and new joys
Do a new song require ;
Till I shall praise Thee as I would
Accept my heart's desire.

Lord of my time, whose hand hath set
New time upon my score,
Then shall I praise for all my time,
When time shall be no more.

Within a decade of the appearance of Mason's little book,
a pamphlet was printed, without the author's knowledge,
headed, *A Morning and Evening Hymn, Formerly made
by a Reverend Bishop.* The Bishop was Thomas Ken, and
the hymns—now " a part of England "—the one, " Awake,
my soul, and with the Sun," and the other, " Glory to Thee,

my God, this night." [1] Ken's hymns were almost certainly written for the boys of Winchester School. They were included in a *Manual of Prayers*, with the injunction, " Be sure to sing the Morning and Evening Hymns in your chamber devoutly." Before Ken's time, the boys' usual morning hymn had been the " Jam lucis orto sidere "—" Now that the daylight fills the sky "—an ancient Latin Office hymn, upon which Ken's lines are to some extent obviously modelled. Any reference here to Ken's Evening Hymn would be incomplete without some mention of the parallel lines in Sir Thomas Browne's *Religio Medici*, published in 1643. The similarity is striking :—

> The night is come, like to the day
> Depart not Thou, great God, away.
> Let not my sins, black as the night,
> Eclipse the lustre of Thy light.
> Keep still in my horizon ; for to me
> The sun makes not the day, but Thee.
> Thou, whose nature cannot sleep,
> On my temples sentry keep ;
> Guard me 'gainst those watchful foes
> Whose eyes are open while mine close.
> Let no dreams my head infest
> But such as Jacob's temples blest.
> While I do rest, my soul advance ;
> Make my sleep a holy trance ;
> That I may, my rest being wrought,
> Awake into some holy thought ;
> And with as active vigour run
> My course as doth the nimble sun.
> Sleep is a death ;—O make me try,
> By sleeping, what it is to die !
> And as gently lay my head
> On my grave as now my bed.

There is no need to assume that Ken was a plagiarist. A much more likely explanation is that both hymns, as well as a third similar one by Flatman,[2] are based on ancient ones in the Roman Breviary.[3]

[1] The original form is " All praise to Thee, my God, this night."
[2] See pp. 203–4. [3] See p. 76.

Ken also wrote a third hymn, for midnight, which was intended to be stored up in memory for sleepless nights. " But have a care," Ken says, " not to fix your mind too much, for fear of hindering your sleep." He himself, in late life, suffered from insomnia, and his biographer tells us that he solaced himself by writing hymns which he described as " Anodynes, or Alleviations of Pain." [1]

> I some remission of my woes
> Feel, while I hymns compose.
>
> *   *   *   *   *
>
> And when my pains begin to rage
> I them with hymns assuage.

Some verses from the " Midnight Hymn " will be of interest. The version is from the *Manual* :—

> Lord, now my sleep does me forsake,
> The sole possession of me take ;
> Let no vain fancy me illude,
> No one impure desire intrude.
>
> Blest angels, while we silent lie,
> Your Hallelujahs sing on high,
> You, ever wakeful near the Throne,
> Prostrate, adore the Three in One.
>
> I now, awake, do with you joyne,
> To praise our God in hymns divine :
> With you in heav'n I hope to dwell,
> And bid the night and world farewell.
>
> My soul, how canst thou weary grow
> Of ante-dating heav'n below,
> In sacred hymns and divine love
> Which will eternal be above ?
>
> Lord, lest the tempter me surprise,
> Watch over Thine own Sacrifice ;
> All loose, all idle thoughts cast out,
> And make my very dreams devout.

[1] Plumptre's *Thomas Ken.*

All three hymns close with Ken's doxology, which is perhaps the most familiar stanza in the English language :—

> Praise God from whom all blessings flow,
> Praise Him all creatures here below,
> Praise Him above, y'angelick host,[1]
> Praise Father, Son and Holy Ghost.

These immortal hymns brought with them, as we who look back over the intervening years can clearly see, a pledge and assurance that a native hymnody had at length come to birth.

[1] Altered in 1712 to " ye heavenly host."

CHAPTER X

A PAUSE IN THE MUSIC

On the walls of Bristol Cathedral there is to be seen a tablet to the memory of Catherine Winkworth, who, through her *Lyra Germanica*, introduced the treasures of German hymnody to English-speaking communities throughout the world, and in doing so " opened a new source of light, consolation and strength in many thousand homes." A similar tribute might appropriately be paid to Sternhold and the paraphrasers who succeeded him. There can be no question that through them a new factor, most inspiring in its general influence, had been introduced into the public worship of the Protestant world. But every good gift of God is liable to abuse, nor is the sanctuary itself exempt from such a danger. Oblations may be vain, and the solemn assembly a mockery. When men are not honestly trying to make their lives conform to their religious expression, God does not hear their praises. " Take thou away from Me," the awful monitory Voice protests, " the noise of thy songs, for I will not hear the melody of thy viols." [1]

Such a danger crept insidiously into the worship-song of the Reformed Churches, and within a century of the publication of Day's Psalter a remarkable note of warning against insincerity in worship was sounded throughout the length of the land by George Fox, the founder of the Quakers. Fox was rugged and unpolished in manners, but burning with the zeal of a prophet and of the stock of the martyrs. As he travelled from place to place he ceaselessly arraigned the Churches, lifting up his voice both inside and outside of their walls, for the formalism and unreality which too often marked their services, protesting that they " fed upon words and trampled upon the life," and that their organized religion

[1] Amos v. 23.

" stood in forms without power." Others before Fox had
felt the same misgivings, and various dissenting communities
sprang up, under the conviction that the prescribed forms and
official associations of a State Church were inimical to pure
religion. Conspicuous among them was the group that
gathered round the person of John Smyth " the Se-Baptist." [1]
It is uncertain whether Smyth was ever an Anglican clergyman.
In 1600 he had accepted a Church appointment as " Lecturer "
at Lincoln; and while there he came more and more to
distrust the official priesthood and set forms of worship,
although so far he had raised no objection to congregational
singing. He soon moved to Gainsborough—where the Manor
was owned by a family who had protected Knox and other
Marian refugees—and, renouncing ordination, he became
pastor of a little group of dissenters there. The group was
one of several that had sprung up in the neighbourhood, all
moved by the same anxious desire to seek a freer and more
spiritual basis of Christian fellowship. Near by, at Scrooby,
their leader was John Robinson; and the two men formed
so intimate a friendship that their acquaintances spoke of
Smyth as the guide and Robinson the shadow.

The story of the persecutions meted out to these men in
England, of their flight to Holland, and of the subsequent
emigration of a party of them on board the *Mayflower* to
America, there to found a new and mighty nation, is among
the epics of religious history.

The attitude which John Smyth adopted towards congregational singing, when once he had broken with the " formal "
religion of the Anglican Church, was somewhat akin to that
afterwards taken by Fox. The order of service in his church
at Amsterdam did not permit of the use of books. Both the
Bible and the Psalter were forbidden, on the ground that the
Spirit is quenched and formalism fostered by their use; and
they were classed with pictures and images as idolatrous.
Smyth's rule regulating the singing reads :—

[1] So called because he baptized himself.

> Wee hould that, seeing singing a psalme is a part of
> spiritual worship, therefore it is unlawfull to have the
> booke before the eye in time of singing a psalme.

The principle for which he contended was that worship
must be spontaneous, the immediate and personal upreaching
of the soul towards God. " Saying set forms of worship by
rote," he insisted, " is quenching the Spirit, and reading forms
of worship out of a book is quenching the Spirit." Metre,
rhyme and musical measures came under the same ban : they
" quenched the Spirit " ; and singing from a book was a
" carnal formality." [1] Not all the Churches in Amsterdam
followed this stringent rule. Some allowed Psalm-singing,
which was spoken of as " conjoint singing," both before and
after the sermon. Ainsworth, who was the leader of one
group, wrote against Smyth's " challenges and cavils," and
in 1612 published a Psalter with tunes for use in his own church.
This is the famous Psalter which John Robinson adopted at
Leyden, and which was taken out to New England by the
Pilgrim Fathers, thus becoming the mother-book of American
church praise.[2]

Throughout the seventeenth century the General Baptists
in England maintained an almost unbroken opposition to
congregational singing. In 1678 singing apparently was
permitted if engaged in " one by one," but the singers were to
keep as nearly as possible to the sacred words, and were to
sing with cheerful voice. " Thus," said one of their number,
" he that hath a psalm becomes a useful minister in the House
of God." A little later even this measure of liberty was withdrawn, for in 1689 the General Baptist Assembly expressed
the view that such " carnal formalities'" were unsafe, and
decreed that the singing of one worshipper was " the same as
the singing of the whole." [3] It was not until the appearance

---

[1] *Smyth (or Smith) the Se-Baptist and the Pilgrim Fathers*, by W. H.
Burgess ; also *The Works of John Smyth*, by Whitley.
[2] Benson's *The English Hymn*, p. 101.
[3] *The Inner Life of the Religious Societies of the Commonwealth*, by
R. Barclay.

of Keach's pamphlet *The Breach Repaired*, in 1691, that these objections began to lose their hold in Baptist circles, and even then the controversy between singing and non-singing congregations almost rent the denomination in twain.

In many of the Brownist and Independent churches very much the same course of events was followed. Richard Baxter relates that some congregations near him derided singing by many scornful names, and could not endure it, their pastors being " fain to unite them to the constant and total omission of singing psalms." At Beccles, at Yarmouth, at Southwark and at other places records show that singing only cautiously came into vogue. It may be that in some cases silence was enjoined for fear of persecution, but the dispute, it is quite evident, touched deep issues.[1]

While these Free Church communities were maintaining this protest against formalism in worship, George Fox came on the scene. He and the early Friends took up a position which, while not absolutely denying a place to congregational Psalm-singing in meetings for worship, in practice involved its almost entire exclusion. Contemporary accounts of the regular Friends' meetings do not contain many references to singing, and we may safely conclude that it did not often take place. Nevertheless, Fox's *Journal* gives several instances of singing under the emotional stress of persecution.

Many times, in the long, sad story of religious persecution, the Psalms have sustained the courage of the martyrs, nerving them, with a strength greater than their own, to suffer and to die. In the Psalms " there are pages," says Prothero, " which are illuminated by the victories of weak humanity over suffering and fear and temptation ; and others which glow with the brightness of heroic constancy and almost superhuman courage." [2] The same songs from which Paul and Silas drew refreshment in their prison at Philippi lent courage to Luther at Coburg and to Mme Guyon in the Bastille.

[1] Curwen's *Studies in Worship Music*, First Series, chapter on " The Psalmody of the Baptists."
[2] Prothero's *The Psalms in Human Life*, chap. i.

Ridley at the stake at Oxford and More on the scaffold at Tower Hill met death with a Psalm on their lips. The persecuted Huguenots hiding in their forests and mountains, and the Pilgrim Fathers bidding a last farewell to the Old World, sought strength and consolation from the same source, and did not seek in vain. So that George Fox found himself in a noble succession when in Carlisle prison the jailor struck him and he responded with a song. " While he struck me," Fox records, " I was made to sing in the Lord's power ; and that made him rage the more. Then he fetched a fiddler, and brought him in where I was, and set him to play, thinking to vex me thereby ; but while he played I was moved in the everlasting power of the Lord God to sing ; and my voice drowned the noise of the fiddle, and made the fiddler sigh and give over fiddling and pass away with shame." [1]   Four years later, when he and his companions were driven out of Perth,[2] Fox writes, " As they guarded us through the town we got on our horses. James Lancaster was moved to sing with a melodious sound in the power of God ; and I was moved to proclaim the day of the Lord." Again, when Fox was being led to trial at Lancaster he was " moved to sing praises to the Lord, in His triumphing power óver all." In 1655, the *Journal* records that Elizabeth Cowart and Margaret Newby sang in the stocks at Evesham, nor could all the Mayor's threats deter them.

Singing, both individual and " conjoint," had also an occasional place in the meetings of the Friends almost from the beginning. In 1655 Thomas and Elizabeth Holme, at a meeting at Underbarrow, " were much exercised by the power of the Lord in songs and hymns and made melody and rejoiced, and the life was raised thereby and refreshed in many in the meeting." Some, however, the record adds, " did scruple." [3]   In the following year Humphry Norton— the Friend who wrote to Cromwell offering to go to prison

---

[1] Fox's *Journal*, 1653.   [2] Then known as Johnstons.
[3] Norman Penney's edition of Fox's *Journal*, vol. ii, p. 326.

in Fox's stead—gives an account of a meeting at Swarthmore where there was singing ; but again, as at Underbarrow, a critical note was sounded ; there was a " leightness " in the proceedings which troubled Norton. Some years later Fox gives an account of a meeting he attended at Cork, where " the power of the Lord was so great, that Friends, in the power and spirit of the Lord, brake out into singing, many together, even with an audible voice, making melody in their hearts." [1]

What was the character of the singing in these meetings ? Croese, in his *History of Quakerism* (1696), gives some interesting information on this point.[2] He says that Friends waited earnestly for the impulse of the Spirit before breaking into song. Then they sang sometimes one by one, unless it happened that they sang altogether. Then follows this passage :—

> They sing and praise, not by a regular pronunciation
> of words, or musical melody, far less by the numbers of
> metre or verse (which sort of singing is never lawful
> with them, but when one of 'em has an extemporary
> faculty to compose) but in the collision, sound, and
> stretching of the voice, almost as the Spaniards, or Moors
> in Afric, if you have ever heard 'em, as I have heard
> 'em both, frequently singing in their own countries. And
> thus not only one or two, but all that are present, do sing
> with a sweet and pleasant voice.[3]

Barclay gives further details, and from him we learn that the Psalms were sometimes used. " That singing of Psalms," he says, " was used by the saints, that it is a part of God's worship when performed in His will and by His Spirit, and that yet it may be and is warrantably performed among the saints, it is a thing denied by no Quaker (so called), *and it is not unusual among them*,[4] whereof I have myself been a witness,

[1] *Journal*, 1669. [2] Book II, p. 55.
[3] Croese can be extravagant and his records must usually be accepted with reserve. [4] The italics are mine.

and have felt of the sweetness of quickening virtue of the Spirit therein."[1] A pronouncement of the Yearly Meeting of the Society in 1675 states that "there hath been and is serious sighing, sensible groaning and reverent singing, breathing forth an heavenly sound of joy with grace and with the spirit of understanding"; and it is added that these utterances should not be quenched or discouraged unless they become immoderate.

Now what are we to conclude from this evidence ? It is clear that the Psalms were sometimes sung; as for the rest, was it akin to the inspirational utterances of early Christian times, a Pentecostal gift of tongues ? We must remember that the early followers of George Fox were experiencing an extraordinary exhilaration of spirit; they felt themselves to be caught up in a great emotional experience and in the rapture of it they at times became abnormal. Their very name was first given to them reproachfully because they trembled with a great spiritual travail. Such happenings as those recorded by Croese; "groanings," and "sighings," and "quakings," and "speaking with tongues," are the common accompaniments of great religious revivals, and can be matched in the records of many denominations besides the Friends.[2] These men and women were not mad. It is quite clear, now, that they were much more ready to detect abuses than to form any constructive plans for the right use of song in the religious life, but it is equally clear that some protest against the prevailing abuses was urgently called for. The utterances of representative Friends of the period show that, as we have already noted, they had no desire entirely to prohibit singing in worship. Here and there a clean sweep was advocated, as, for instance, at Reading, where a trustee of the Meeting House threatened to close the place, saying that "singing or speaking singingly

[1] *Truth Cleared from Calumnies.*
[2] This subject is touched upon in W. C. Braithwaite's Swarthmore Lecture, "Spiritual Guidance in Quaker Experience." See also *The American Friend*, 1907, for an account of some such happenings in a Friends' Church in America, with comments by "R. M. J." See also John Wesley's *Journal*, April 21, 1739, etc.

in prayer, preaching or with a vocal voice (*sic*) was an abomination "; but Barclay and other statesmanlike members of the Society took no such uncompromising position. Fox himself allowed a place for metrical psalmody. He said, " Those who are moved to sing with understanding, making melody to the Lord in their hearts, we own : if it be in meeter, we own it." [1]   Barclay admitted it to be " a part of God's worship " [2] : Burrough wrote, " Singing which is with the Spirit and with understanding of the Redeemed of the Lord, we own and witness." [3]

But, while not precluding its use, the Friends steadfastly witnessed against the prevalent degradation of the song-worship of the churches.[4]   Owing, doubtless, in a large degree, to the law which enacted that everyone must attend church, they saw all sorts of irreligious people participating in the singing, and it seemed to them to be rank blasphemy ; and even when those who sang were living irreproachable lives, they could not understand how the sentiments of many of the Psalms could be suited to Christian times and Christian feelings, or how Christian people could sincerely take them upon their lips. When they came to voice their protests, they did so in the aggressively strong language of their times.   Fox protested that both preachers and people sang lies when they spoke in David's words, while David's condition was not theirs.   George Whitehead declared that no one ever read in the Scriptures that the early Christians sang the Psalms " in rime and meeter, as priests and people do now, which were put into meeter by Thomas Sternhold, John Hopkins and others; nor that even the Churches of Christ had drunken clerks to give them forth what Psalms they were to sing, nor to give them such a tune to sing by as the priests and their hearers now usually have,

---

[1] *Truth's Defence against the Refined Subtilty of the Serpent*, by George Fox and R. Hubberthorn.   Also compare Fox's *Itinerary Journal*, Tercentenary edition, p. 214.
[2] *Apology*, Props. XI, XXVI.
[3] *Truth Defended*.
[4] See, *inter alia*, an article on " Puritan Singing in the Seventeenth Century," by Georgina K. Lewis, *Friends' Quarterly Examiner*, 1919.

whose song shall become howlings." [1] Another Friend, commenting on the ease and readiness with which people sang the penitential Psalms, scornfully remarked, " You sing that there is nothing in your hearts but sin and wickedness, which I believe you." [2]

But there were other cogent reasons leading the early Friends to adopt a critical attitude. At the very commencement of his travels, when a young man of twenty-four years of age, Fox had felt himself dedicated to the task of drawing men away from formal worship, including " praying and singing which stood in forms without power." Worship needed to be liberated from the swathing-bands of formalism. It ought not to depend upon a rigid liturgy or prearrangement which might impose upon the worshippers the necessity to voice what they did not feel, or to keep silence when they felt they had a message to deliver. " No worship ought to be made dependent upon the presence of any one man or order of men ; no service, or stated vocal utterance in the congregation, ought to be allowed to interfere with the operations of the Lord's free Spirit." [3] This basal principle governed the whole of worship, and thus determined the Friends' attitude alike to preaching and praying and singing. Hence arose a great fear of prearrangement and a distrust of ritual ; and hence, too, " the basis of silence " which so strongly differentiated the meetings of the Society from those of other Christian communities. Quite obviously such a conception of the ordering of public worship meant the practical exclusion of congregational hymn-singing. The singing of a hymn by an individual is still occasionally heard in a Friends' Meeting. " Conjoint " singing is also not altogether unknown ; but as

[1] *A Serious Account of Thirty-five Reasons why the People of the Lord called Quakers cannot go to worship at those Places called Churches and Chapels*, George Whitehead, 1661.
[2] *Some Considerations proposed to all you that sing David's Sundry Experiences*, Edward Cook, 1670.
[3] The quotation, which is from the *Yearly Meeting Epistle* of 1866, expresses the traditional view of worship, to which the Society throughout its history has attached primary importance.

GEORGE FOX

(After the painting by Sir Peter Lely in Friends' Historical Library, Swarthmore College, U.S.A.)

there are usually no hymn books available, and no previously selected tune, and often a very imperfect command of the melody, it is obvious that, in general, singing is not engaged in ; nor is it at all widely desired, for there is a fear that its introduction would jeopardize the principle, held by Friends to be vital, of spontaneity in worship.

The dread of insincerity in the worship-song of the Churches, which caused the early Friends to make so strong a stand, has been shared throughout the centuries by many notable leaders of religious thought and life. Even before the Christian era Plato had remarked upon the insidious power of music, if unrestrained, to enfeeble the moral sense. At first, he says, sweet and soft airs may temper the spirit like steel, but if a man " carries on the softening and soothing process, in the next stage he begins to melt and waste, until he has wasted away his spirit, and cut out the sinews of his soul ; and he becomes a feeble warrior." [1] We have seen how Augustine feared that the sweetness of Church music might beguile his senses and make him forget the words he was uttering ; and how Bernard of Clairvaux purposely wrote in uncouth measures for fear that the artistry of words would distract the mind. Chrysostom complains of the " theatricalities " introduced into the singing, when, he says " all should be grave and solemn " ; and Jerome makes a similar protest. Wyclif is more caustic. He says : " When there are forty or fifty in a choir, three or four proud and wanton rascals will so trick the most devout service that no man shall hear the sentence and all the others will be dumb and look like fools." Calvin in Reformation times, and Bishops Wordsworth and Heber in nineteenth-century Anglicanism, voiced the same fears. Plato, Augustine, Chrysostom, Jerome, Bernard, Wyclif, Calvin— these, indeed, form a goodly company of great souls to whom Fox might have appealed in his stand for reality in worship-song.

Before passing on to any further comments upon the Quaker

[1] *The Republic*, Book I, p. 410.

attitude to hymnody, one or two considerations are worth recalling. We are indebted to the Friends for helping us to a fuller realization of the value of silence. Sitting in the quiet peace of a Friends' Meeting, the worshipper is not hurried on from prayer to hymn, from hymn to reading, from reading to sermon, from sermon to benediction. To say, however, that silence is greater than speech is as absurd as to say that one season of the year is greater than another. Each has its divine office. Silence is to the heart what a fallow year is to the land : it is a fruitful and creative force. Silence is " a great virtue ; it covers folly, keeps secrets, avoids disputes, and prevents sin." [1] The mind collects itself in silence to hear God's voice. Waiting in stillness for what He will say to us—

> A sacred reverence checks our songs,
> And praise sits silent on our tongues.

To the Friends, silence was an essential element in spiritual worship. Penington, in writing of the " benefit of silent meetings," stated the case thus : " God is to be worshipped in spirit, in His own power of life. . . . His Church is a gathering in the spirit. . . . If any man speak there he must speak . . . as a vessel out of which God speaks ; as a trumpet out of which He gives the sound. Therefore there is to be a waiting in silence, till the Spirit of the Lord move to speak, and also give words to speak." [2] The subsequent history of the Society shows how even so sweet a gift as silence may be invested with an exaggerated importance ; and it is a fact worth recalling that Fox " did not pass those high encomiums upon silence which have passed current in later times. He did not, in his own career, forget that ' faith comes by hearing.' " [3]

It is highly suggestive to find Fox and other prominent

[1] William Penn's *Fruits of a Father's Love.*
[2] The Swarthmore Lecture for 1919, " Silent Worship," by L. Violet Hodgkin, deals helpfully with this subject from the Quaker standpoint.
[3] John Stephenson Rowntree's Essay, *Quakerism, Past and Present.*

leaders of the movement seeking to give expression to their tense emotions through the artistry of rhythm. Here we see this strange paradox—on the one hand, Quakerism dispensing with the aid of art and music and rhetoric in its worship, and prone to look upon these things as harmful ; and on the other hand, its pioneers instinctively discovering in the music of carefully ordered words a natural outlet for their over-wrought feelings. Thus Fox, after many stirring experiences in Ireland, " was moved to declare to Friends there in the ministry as follows " :—

> Sound, sound abroad, ye faithful servants of the Lord, and witnesses in His name, ye prophets of the Highest, and angels of the Lord ! Sound ye all abroad in the world, to the awakening and raising of the dead, that they may be awakened, and raised up out of the grave, to hear the voice that is living. For the dead have long heard the dead, the blind have long wandered among the blind, and the deaf amongst the deaf. Therefore sound, sound, ye servants, prophets, and angels of the Lord, ye trumpets of the Lord, that ye may awaken the dead, and awaken them that be asleep in their graves of sin, death, and hell, and sepulchres and sea and earth, and who lie in the tombs. Sound, sound abroad, ye trumpets, and raise up the dead, that they may hear the voice of the Son of God ; the voice of the second Adam that never fell ; the voice of the Light, and the voice of the Life ; the voice of the Power, and the voice of Truth ; the voice of the Righteous, and the voice of the Just. Sound, sound the pleasant and melodious sound ; sound, sound, ye trumpets, the melodious sound abroad, that all the deaf ears may be opened to hear the pleasant sound of the trumpet to Judgment and Life, to Condemnation and Light.

James Nayler had recourse to the same medium when thanking God for his recovery from his grievous fall. The following beautiful passage consists of a series of parallelisms after the manner of Hebrew poetry [1] :—

> Then didst Thou lay the foundations of the earth,
> And lead me under the waters :
> And in the deep didst Thou show me wonders,
> And Thy forming of the world.
> By Thy hand Thou led'st me in safety
> Till Thou shewedst me the pillars of the earth :
> Then did the heavens shower down,
> And they were covered with darkness ;
> And the powers thereof were shaken,
> And Thy glory descended :
> Thou filledst the lower parts of the earth with gladness,
> And the springs of the valleys were opened,
> And Thy showers descended abundantly,
> So the earth was filled with virtue.
> Thou madest Thy plant to spring,
> And the thirsty soul became as a watered garden :
> Then didst Thou lift me out of the pit,
> And set me forth in the sight of mine enemies.

Thomas Story, Penn's friend, lover of trees, sensitive soul, at whose preaching many broke into tears, wrote passages of even greater beauty, some of which he felt sure were "given to him by dictation from the Mind of Truth," and which Wm. Chas. Braithwaite judges to be worth, with one or two of Ellwood's pieces, all the rest of the poetry of the early Friends.[2]

This natural law of rhythmic relief for the emotions doubtless accounts for the habit of " intoning " their sermons which at one time was so deeply rooted in some Friends' Meetings as to become (according to one of their historians [3]) " a hallmark of proper guidance," and which could be heard in some meetings well on into the present century.[4] One story tells how at

[1] I have arranged the quotation in the style familiar to us in the Psalms, the more effectively to show how closely Nayler copied the Hebrew forms. See Sewel's *History*, 1795 ed., vol. i, pp. 272–3 ; also Nayler's *Confessions, Prayers and Praise*.
[2] William C. Braithwaite's *Later Periods of Quakerism*, pp. 466–9 ; also *Christian Discipline*, 1925, Part II, pp. 44–5.
[3] J. W. Graham.
[4] It was heard at the Yearly Meeting of the Society in London in 1927, on the occasion of the opening of Friends House, when a woman Friend from Iowa "intoned" both in prayer and speech.

Westminster Meeting, after Stephen Grellet had spoken, a woman rose and " chaunted most delightfully," and another tells of a young American Friend, who, when he first began to speak in Meeting, was encouraged by an Elder, who said to him, " If thou art faithful, dear young man, thou wilt learn the tune in time." One incident in relation to " intoning " is of especial interest. On one occasion, when Priscilla Green, an English Quakeress, was on a visit to America, the poet Longfellow went to hear her. " She spoke," he records in his diary, " with a sweet voice and very clear enunciation ; very deliberately, and breaking now and then into rhythmic chant, in which the voice seemed floating up and down on wings." [1] Such a tendency in worship is probably to be noted in all branches of the Church. Augustine in the fourth century noticed that the liturgical chanting at Alexandria was " more like speaking than singing," doubtless a form of rhythmic recitative ; and, after an interval of sixteen hundred years, it is still common to hear much the same phenomenon in public prayers.[2]

As time went on, and as the more rigid elements in Puritanism entered into Quakerism, the objection to hymn-singing was extended to music in general. The Puritans have no doubt been unjustly condemned as a race of gloomy fanatics who fled from joy and beauty as from some poisonous miasma. But one glimpse into the cultured home of Colonel Hutchinson and his charming wife—to say nothing of the artistic interests of Cromwell and of Milton—should warn us against so sweeping a generalization. The fact is that the Puritans of the Restoration period faced life and its duties in a spirit of high seriousness, and did not feel the same need of the pleasures of life as men of lesser mould around them. And beyond this, their breach with the popular amusements of their time was almost forced

[1] *Life of Longfellow*, by his brother, vol. ii, p. 304. It may be said that Longfellow's Ballad poetry, like all Balladry, when read, largely depends for its impressiveness upon a certain rise and fall of the voice.
[2] The subject of " Tones in Preaching " provoked some correspondence in the *Friends' Historical Journal* from 1916 onwards.

upon them, not by the neurosis which follows persecution, but by the degradation of the drama and of song and the cruel accompaniments of sport. What could sober-minded men and women have to do with the dramatic indecencies of the age of Wycherley, or the vacuities of the popular songs which " tended only to the corruption of youth ? " " I was moved," says Fox, " to cry out against all sorts of music, and against the mountebanks playing tricks on their stages ; for they burdened the pure life, and stirred up people's minds to vanity." [1] His critics made it a complaint against him and his colleagues that they would not join in their merriment, but, says Fox, " we told them that when they went to their sports, and games, and plays, and the like, they had better serve God than spend their time so vainly."

Some chapters in the story of the attitude of the Friends to music excite our amused interest as to-day, with our more liberal outlook, we glance backward. Solomon Eccles—the Solomon Eagles of Ainsworth's *Old St. Paul's*—although he had been wont to earn more than £130 a year and " live very high " by teaching music, yet burnt his viols and his virginals, with his music-books, on Tower Hill, convinced that all who practised such Babylon arts were " for the Lake, except they repented." John Mulliner, a Quaker barber, whose hobby was music, wrote a *Testimony against Periwigs and Periwig-making, and Playing on Instruments of Music*, sacrificing both his business and his recreation as vanities which only brought a false peace to his soul. A very early official warning against music was made at " yearley meeting, the 26th day of 10th month, 1681, at friends Meeting house in Scarborough," when it was reported that certain men were in the habit of going about the town at night-time, playing at the door of Friends' houses, saying " Good-morrow," and playing on instruments of music. The report was received with regret, and the meeting concluded that if the singers only intended to give the hour, or to tell the quarter of the wind, or to see the doors

[1] *Journal*, 1649.

were fast, it might be allowed : " but to say ' Good-morrow '
and to play on musical instruments, this friends should forbid,"
and should bear their testimony " against all such wanton,
brutish practices, tending only to satisfy and please vayne
and wanton minds with their foolish music." [1]

The Yearly Meeting Epistles, commencing at about the
middle of the eighteenth century and continuing for a hundred
years, contain repeated warnings against " pernicious amusements " and the many temptations which beset the members
of the Society to fall away from the strictness and plainness
of living which distinguished the generation of its founders.
Towards the middle of the nineteenth century music seems
to have been specially marked out as a pernicious evil. The
Epistle of 1846 says :—

> Our attention has been turned to the increased expo-
> sure of our young friends to the temptations of music ;
> which we believe to be, both in its acquisition and its
> practice, unfavourable to the health of the soul. Serious
> is the waste of time of those who give themselves up to
> it ; and what account can they render of those precious
> hours which might otherwise have been devoted to the
> glory of God and the good of their neighbour ? It does
> not, however, merely involve an absorption of time : it
> not infrequently leads into unprofitable, and even per-
> nicious associations, and in some instances, to a general
> indulgence in the vain amusements of the world.

The Epistle of 1854 dwelt on the particular dangers of
" sacred " music, which was held to delude the mind by
" producing an excitement mistaken for devotion, and making
an entertainment of the most awful events recorded in Holy
Scriptures." A correspondent wrote at about the same period
to *The British Friend* to lament that he had actually seen a
piano in a Friend's house. Another critic pointed out that

[1] *Friends' Historical Journal*, vol. ii, 1905, p. 82.

people flocked to church not to worship, but to listen to the music, and Cowper's lines on musical festivals were quoted with approval :—

> Ten thousand sit
> Patiently present at a sacred song,
> Commemoration mad, content to hear
> —O wonderful effect of music's power—
> Messiah's eulogy for Handel's sake.

Moved by similar considerations, Joseph Sturge threatened to refuse payment of a rate which was levied in Birmingham for the erection of a new Town Hall, if that building were to be used for the performance of oratorios.[1]

It is easy for us to smile at these idiosyncrasies and to congratulate ourselves that we are more tolerant than our fathers ; but no one can wade through the Quaker pronouncements, of which some few examples have here been given, however dismal they may be, without realizing that he is in the presence of men and women of heroic mould and nobility of life. It was their conviction that life had been given to them for great and lofty purposes, and that every moment was precious and must be redeemed from triviality. This it was that made them not merely willing but eager to lay aside every weight, and to renounce every risk of dissipating their spiritual energies upon interests of secondary importance, and which might " strike at the Divine Life in their souls." They desired, further, to witness to a certain way of worship, which would, as they hoped, strike at the roots of insincerity. They had the faults of their qualities, but it was their sheer unselfish earnestness that led them to an ascetic and even morbid condemnation of many things that we now recognize to be good gifts of God and an aid to fullness of life. We do not know what their attitude, in the earliest decades of their history, would have been towards hymnody, for there were then no hymns in public use, and Fox could have had no knowledge

[1] *Memoirs of Joseph Sturge*, Hy. Richard, chap. iii.

in his old age that even then there was living a youth who was destined to sing " a nobler, sweeter song " than any theme of David's—a song which, in God's good providence, was to " kindle a flame of sacred love " in many hearts.[1] They were mistaken in assuming that a read prayer must necessarily be an unreal prayer. In their eagerness to keep clear of formalism in worship, they failed in charity towards others who held different views. Many will think, with a critic within their own circle, that they fell into the common error of " desisting from using a means of grace for fear that they might not use it aright." [2] Their condemnation was too sweeping of a custom which, in spite of its weakness, almost every other branch of Christ's Church from Apostolic times has found to be of value in the building up of the faith. And they have never sufficiently appreciated the power of the simple hymn as an aid to the evangelist and a medium of religious education and fellowship.

It must not be forgotten, on the other hand, that the Friends of the present day feel that it is for them, abandoning all censorious judgment of other branches of Christ's Church, to witness to the value of a certain mode of worship. Every musician knows the value of a pause ; and shall there not, in the universal music which humanity is for ever raising before the throne of God, be an office for silence as well as for sound ? It would be an impoverishment and not an enrichment of the religious life of our country if the Society of Friends weakened in its testimony to the value of " the still life " through which, though no word be spoken and no song be sung, " fellowship is attained in the spirit of God." [3]

A few words should perhaps be added, before resuming the thread of our main story, upon recent hymnological developments in Quaker circles. Whittier is said to have remarked that " two hundred years of silence had taken all the ' sing ' out of the Quakers." But an examination of the contents of

[1] The reference is to Isaac Watts.
[2] Sl. Fothergill's *Essay on the Decline in Membership*, 1859.
[3] George Fox, 1657.

N

one of the standard hymnals of the present day reveals the fact that of four hundred and fifty hymns, almost one-tenth have been contributed by Friends—a somewhat surprising proportion.[1] Barton [2] and Ellwood are among them, but the one great name which Friends have contributed to the hymnody of the English-speaking world is that of Whittier. The rapidity with which recent editors have discovered hymnic treasures in Whittier's poetry is one of the most enheartening incidents in our story. Between thirty and forty hymns from his pen are now in use. He is one of the sweetest singers in the choir. Garrett Horder thinks his greatest hymn is " Our Master," a poem of thirty-nine verses, of which nearly every one has found its way into public worship. The affection in which it is held is equalled by the exquisite lines " Dear Lord and Father of Mankind." Here is Horder's selection from " Our Master " :—

> Our Friend, our Brother, and our Lord,
>   What may Thy service be ?
> Nor name, nor form, nor ritual word,
>   But simply following Thee.
>
> Thou judgest us ; Thy purity
>   Doth all our lusts condemn ;
> The love that draws us nearer Thee
>   Is hot with wrath to them.
>
> Our thoughts lie open to Thy sight,
>   And naked to Thy glance :
> Our secret sins are in the light
>   Of Thy pure countenance.
>
> Yet weak and blinded though we be,
>   Thou dost our service own ;
> We bring our varying gifts to Thee,
>   And Thou rejectest none.
>
> To Thee our full humanity,
>   Its joys and pains belong ;
> The wrong of man to man on Thee
>   Inflicts a deeper wrong.

[1] The reference is to *The Fellowship Hymn Book*.
[2] Barton's best-known hymn is " Walk in the Light."

Deep strike Thy roots, O heavenly Vine,
  Within our earthly sod,
Most human and yet most divine,
  The flower of man and God !

Apart from Thee all gain is loss,
  All labour vainly done ;
The solemn shadow of Thy Cross
  Is better than the sun.

Alone, O love ineffable !
  Thy saving name is given ;
To turn aside from Thee is hell,
  To walk with Thee is heaven.

We faintly hear, we dimly see,
  In differing phrase we pray ;
But dim or clear, we own in Thee
  The Light, the Truth, the Way !

Not only are " the silent Friends " thus becoming hymn-writers, but in many of their corporate activities, such as their " Mission " Meetings, their Boarding Schools, their Foreign Mission work, the Adult School Movement, and " Woodbrooke " Settlement, they have not only found that hymn-singing is a help, but have taken part in compiling quite a number of hymn books suited to such special needs.

The long period of distrust of music showed signs of giving way in the latter decades of the nineteenth century. A " Symposium " on the subject, in the *Friends' Quarterly Examiner*, 1879, clearly revealed the changed attitude. " It cannot be denied," one writer said, " that, equally with human speech, the power of song, however much abused, is a gift of God, and as such should be consecrated to Him." At last, in 1925, there came a full admission that Friends had, in the past, been more ready to discern the evil than the good in art in general, and that " every great work of art is one way in which the Divine Mind is revealed through men," and that without music, without the satisfaction of the delightful instinct for melody and rhythm that is deeply rooted in human nature, man's personality suffers loss. " To many music is a means of expressing the deepest things in their experience, and of bringing them into touch with God." [1]

The hymn-singing of to-day would be more effective as a means of religious culture if the admonitory counsels and sober fears of the Friends were taken more completely to heart by the Churches. The danger of formalism and unreality in public worship is ever present with us.

Men of earnest heart and purpose will increasingly cease meeting together for worship unless, with an unquestioned integrity, every part of the " service " rings true.

[1] *Christian Discipline*, 1925, Part II, pp. 81–2 ; also p. 11.

CHAPTER XI

CRESCENDO

IN the Library of York Minster there is a volume entitled *Musick's Monument*, dated 1676, which gives a vivid and humorous account of the singing in parish churches in general and in York Minster in particular, at the very time when George Fox was lamenting its unreality. The author, Thomas Mace, was thoroughly satisfied with the few Psalm tunes then in use (in spite of the fact that there were scarcely more than a dozen to choose from), and declared " they are so excellently good that I will be bold to say art cannot mend them or make better." But the singing distressed him. It was entirely satisfactory in the Minster, " the most remarkable and excellent that has been known or remembered anywhere in these latter days "; but as for the ordinary parish churches, " 'Tis sad," he says, " to hear what whining, toting, yelling or screeching there is in many country congregations." Mace's remedy was to introduce organs to aid the human voice. He contended that the young people of a village could learn to play that instrument in a fortnight, " and thus, little by little, the parish will swarm with organists." [1] Needless to say, the proposal to call in the aid of organs, or indeed of any musical instrument, met with strong opposition. Lightwood tells a story of a countryman of that period, who, when he heard the organ in church, " fell a'dancing and jigging all up the aisle, having never heard anything like it before except the bagpipes in an alehouse." [2] Puritan sentiment objected to organs because of their Romish and Laudian associations, and lengthy and bitter controversies ensued in many places when it was proposed—as someone caustically described it—

[1] Curwen, in his *Studies in Worship Music*, vol. i, chap. i, has some interesting information on this subject.
[2] J. T. Lightwood's *Hymn Tunes and their Story*.

" to praise God by machinery." The difficulty was increased by the almost entire absence of books in the pews, the natural consequence of the illiteracy of the people. Hence arose the practice of " lining out," that is to say, the clerk read out the psalm line by line and the people then sang it from memory. This custom had been officially sanctioned in 1645 by an order of the Westminster Assembly, which read, " Where many in the congregation cannot read, it is convenient that the minister, or some other fit person appointed by him and the other officers, do read the psalm, line by line, before the singing thereof." The clerk not only had to read the words, but also in some cases to start the tune, and it was not always easy to find a man who had " either ear or understanding to set one of these tunes musically as it ought to be." [1] Added to these difficulties was the irreverence which manifested itself in many congregations. The nobility set a bad example. They ogled, and whispered, and took snuff and slumbered during the services. The people were unpunctual and ill-behaved, and if the sermon was not to their liking they showed their displeasure with clamorous talk such as " was not to be silenced but by the bells." [2] Burney, commenting on this state of affairs, declared that the singing excited contempt and ridicule among the more serious part of the congregation, " who disdained to join, though they were forced to hear the indecorous jargon." One of Addison's essays gives an amusing account of Sir Roger de Coverley's behaviour in church [3] :—

> As Sir Roger is landlord of the whole congregation, he keeps them in very good order and will suffer nobody to sleep in it besides himself ; for if by chance he has been surprised in a short nap at sermon, upon recovering out of it he stands up and looks about him, and if he sees anybody else nodding, either wakes them himself, or sends his servants to them. Several others of the old Knight's

[1] John Playford's Introduction to his *Psalter*, 1671.
[2] Stoughton's *Religion in England under Queen Anne*.
[3] See *The Spectator*, No. 112, July 9, 1711.

particularities break out upon these occasions. Sometimes he will lengthen out a verse in the singing psalms, half a minute after the rest have done with it . . . and sometimes stands up when everybody else is upon their knees, to count the congregation, or see if any of his tenants are missing.

It is evident that virtue had gone out of public worship, and its thorough revision and revitalizing was called for.

The man who, above all others, contributed to this great end was Isaac Watts (b. 1674). In the opening sentences of the Introduction to his *Hymns and Spiritual Songs* he drew a picture of the state of the psalmody of the time as he noted it :—

> While we sing the Praises of our God in His Church, we are employ'd in that part of worship which of all others is the nearest akin to Heaven, and 'tis pity that this of all others should be perform'd the worst upon Earth. . . . That very action which should elevate us to the most delightful and divine Sensations doth not only flat our Devotion, but too often awakens our Regret, and touches all the Springs of Uneasiness within us.

Watts, in making this protest, declared that one great cause of the evil arose from " the matter and words to which we all confine our songs." There he went right to the heart of the trouble. He clearly saw that the worship-song of the Christian Church must centre in Christ if it was to possess life and power. Having arrived at that standpoint—the reasonableness of which seems so obvious to us—he bent all his powers to its achievement.

In the three Essays with which he prefaced his *Horæ Lyricæ*, his *Hymns* and his *Paraphrases*, he explains his policy with lucidity, force and good humour. He laments that poesy has so often been enslaved to vice and profaneness ; that while it took its inspiration from heaven, it had so far forgotten itself as to be engaged in the interests of hell. Dryden and Otway,

Congreve and Dennis—all four his literary contemporaries—spent their time, he says, on trifling and childish figments, whilst neglecting divine themes. Yet there is no grander poetry known to man than that of the Bible : David has a nobler theme than Virgil. But David's songs are not suited to a Christian dispensation.

> Some Sentences of the *Psalmist* that are expressive of the Temper of our own Hearts, and the Circumstances of our Lives, may compose our Spirits to Seriousness, and allure us to a sweet Retirement within ourselves ; but we meet with a following Line which so peculiarly belongs but to one Action or Hour of the Life of *David* or of *Asaph*, that breaks off our Song in the midst ; our Consciences are affrighted, lest we should speak a Falsehood unto God : Thus the Powers of our Souls are shock'd on a sudden, and our Spirits ruffled before we have time to reflect, that this may be sung only as a History of ancient Saints : And perhaps, in some Instances that *Salvo* is hardly sufficient neither. Besides, it almost always spoils the Devotion by breaking the Uniform Thread of it. For while our Lips and our Hearts run on sweetly together, applying the Words to our own Case, there is something of Divine Delight in it : But at once we are forced to turn off the Application abruptly, and our Lips speak nothing but the Heart of *David* : Thus our own Hearts are as it were forbid the Pursuit of the Song, and then the Harmony and the Worship grow dull of meer necessity.[1]

Watts here urges, with a fervour equal to Fox, that we cannot take all David's words upon our lips without being insincere. We must express our own case, not David's :—

> Moses, Deborah and the Princes of Israel ; David, Asaph and Habakkuk . . . sing their own joys and

---

[1] Watts's Preface to his *Hymns and Spiritual Songs*.

victories, their own hopes and fears and deliverances ; and why must we, under the Gospel, sing nothing else but the joys and hopes and fears of Asaph and David ? As well have compelled David to sing the words of Moses, and nothing else all through his rejoicing days.

Watts's way out was " to make David speak like an English Christian of the eighteenth century," and this he proceeded to do. " It is necessary," he says, " to divest David and Asaph, etc., of every other character but that of a Psalmist and a Saint, and to make them always speak the common sense of a Christian." In attempting this task he anticipated the objection that he was departing from the letter of the Scriptures ; and he modestly claimed that he had sometimes voiced the true intent of the Spirit of God in his own verses " farther and clearer than David could ever discover." So he asked Christian people to put away their prejudices and to try whether his songs did not kindle in their hearts a fire of zeal and exalt them to a temper of love and peace.

But the mere achievement of making David speak like a Christian, that is to say, of re-writing the songs of Judaism so as to adapt them in some sort of fashion to Christian worship, could in the very nature of the case only provide a makeshift. Calvin, in imposing the paraphrases on the Reformed Churches, had trammelled and confined their praises within limits that were at last recognized to be intolerable. The canvas was not large enough. It had many deficiencies —as Watts said—of light and glory. The Gospels, the story of the life and work of Christ, furnished a theme for " nobler, sweeter songs " than any ever sung by the poets of Israel. The need was for a new type of congregational song, witnessing to, and expressive of, Christian experience, and voicing the feelings of men and women in the presence of God as revealed to them in Jesus Christ.

This, then, was the double task which Watts essayed, and in both he succeeded far beyond any of his predecessors. For,

as we have seen, he was not the first in the field. The congregational hymn was slowly evolving, and its true form had been
indicated by Ken. The re-writing of the metrical Psalms so
as to accommodate them to Christian use had been attempted
by Phineas Fletcher [1] and a few other writers before Watts
took it in hand. That there was a growing desire for some
such developments is obvious from Watts's own testimony :—

> Many Ministers and many private Christians have long
> groan'd under this inconvenience (i.e. the insufficiency
> of the Psalms for Christian worship) and have wish'd
> rather than attempted a Reformation ; At their importu-
> nate and repeated Requests I have for some Years past
> devoted many Hours of leisure to this Service.[2]

Watts pays a tribute to one of his predecessors in the field,
John Patrick, a Preacher to the Charter House, London,
whose paraphrases he highly esteemed, and from which he
freely helped himself to good lines.

Among others who directly influenced Watts were William
Barton and Joseph Stennett. Barton's paraphrases and hymns
are said by Benson to have been in use in the church at Southampton which Watts, as a young man, attended. He it is
of whom Watts's brother said, " Honest Barton chimes us
asleep." Stennett's hymns, as well as his sermons, were
admired by Watts, and he, like Patrick, enjoys the honour of
having supplied Watts with many happy phrases. His hymns
are extraordinarily faithful to Scripture ; it is claimed that
almost every line can be matched with a text. We can forgive
the sanguinary language of the following verses for the sake
of their ethical value :—

> What mighty Conqueror do we see,
>   Whose garments are distain'd with blood,
> Whose rich apparel seems to be
>   All tinctured in a crimson flood,—

[1] See p. 152.   [2] Introduction to the *Hymns*, 1707, p. vi.

Like one who has the wine-press trod,
  Whose clothes the grape has purpl'd o'er ?
'Tis the eternal Son of God,
  All full of wounds, all stain'd with gore.

A mighty Conqueror indeed,
  Who conquers by receiving blows !
To give wounds, is content to bleed,
  And by His death subdue His foes !

During Watts's lifetime several musicians were seeking to raise the standard of Church music. Conspicuous among them was Henry Playford, son of John Playford, the famous music publisher, whose shop was near the Temple Church, where for a time he acted as parish clerk. Henry not only succeeded to his father's business, but also to his zeal for the improvement of congregational singing. Henry Playford's *Divine Companion* (1701), besides several paraphrases, contained twelve hymns, by Austin, Herbert, Crashaw and others, and a number of anthems. In the preface, Playford lamented that while English Church music was admired at the Vatican, our own parish churches, though equally dedicated to God's glory, " have been altogether destitute of such necessary assistances to Praise their Maker by ; and when they have the same claim as Christians to the Hallelujahs above after this life, have not been made partakers of the Hosannas below in it."

The music of the *Divine Companion* was contributed by Blow, Jeremiah Clark, Croft and others of the leading composers of the time. Here is a tune by Clark, set to a morning hymn by Flatman, first published in 1674, and which, it has been suggested, inspired Ken. The original music was in two parts :—

Awake, my Soul, awake, my Eyes,
Awake, my drowsy faculties,
Awake and see the new-born light
Sprung from the darksome womb of Night.

Look up and see th' unweari'd Sun,
Already has his Race begun,
The pretty Lark is mounted high,
And sings his mattines in the Sky.

Arise, my Soul, and thou, my Voice,
In Songs of Praise early rejoyce ;
O great Creator, Heavenly King !
Thy praises let me ever Sing.

Thy pow'r has made, Thy Goodness kept,
This senseless body when I slept.
Yet one day more, hast Thou kept me,
From all the Pow're of darkness free.

O keep my soul from sin secure,
My life unblamable and pure.
That when the last of days shall come,
I cheerfully may meet my doom.

Watts, then, was not a solitary adventurer upon unknown seas. Other explorers had gone before him. It is not correct to speak of him as the inventor of the English hymn, nor even as the first of our great hymn-writers. He did perfectly what most of his predecessors had done indifferently, and only a few well. But, what is far more remarkable, he not only excelled all who went before him, but all who have come since. Charles Wesley alone can challenge with him the right to be called the greatest of English hymn-writers.

His brother Enoch deserves a meed of praise for his share in this great adventure. Enoch was only twenty-two years of age when he wrote a letter of encouragement, importuning his brother to publish his hymns.

" There is," he says, " a great need of a pen, vigorous and lively as yours, to quicken and revive the dying devotion of the age, to which nothing can afford such assistance as poetry, contrived on purpose to elevate us even above ourselves."

The story of the writing of Watts's first hymn has often been told. He was then twenty-two, and was living with his parents at Southampton. He felt the inadequacy of the psalmody at the chapel he attended on Sundays, and one day his father challenged him to write something better. Thereupon he composed the hymn which afterwards occupied pride of place in his *Hymns and Spiritual Songs* :—

> Behold the glories of the Lamb,
> Amidst His Father's throne,
> *Prepare new honours for His name*
> *And songs before unknown.*[1]

> Let elders worship at His feet,
> The Church adore around,
> With vials full of odours sweet,
> And harps of sweeter sound.

> Those are the prayers of the saints,
> And these the hymns they raise ;
> *Jesus is kind to our complaints,*
> He loves to hear our praise.

This hymn was quickly followed by others, until at length, some years after the Southampton incident, two volumes of hymns and poems were published, *Horæ Lyricæ* in 1706, and *Hymns and Spiritual Songs* in the following year. Later came the *Paraphrases of the Psalms*, the *Divine and Moral Songs for Children*,[2] and more hymns. It is difficult for us at this distance of time, and in our different circumstances, to imagine what must have been the effect of this sudden infusion of a new and vital type of worship-song into the church at Southampton. The lips of the worshippers were unsealed, and now they were enabled to raise their hearts in songs of

[1] The italics are mine. The hymn has eight verses.
[2] See p. 265.

grateful praise to their Saviour. Think of them, after being pinned down all their days to the hymn book of the Jews, at last uniting in such a song of Christian joy as this :—

> Come let us join our cheerful songs
> With angels round the throne ;
> Ten thousand thousand are their tongues,
> But all their joys are one.

> " Worthy the Lamb that died," they cry,
>   " To be exalted thus " :
> " Worthy the Lamb," our lips reply,
>   For He was slain for us.

> Jesus is worthy to receive
>   Honour and power divine ;
> And blessings, more than we can give,
>   Be, Lord, for ever Thine.

> Let all that dwell above the sky,
>   And air, and earth, and seas,
> Conspire to lift Thy glories high,
>   And speak Thine endless praise.

> The whole creation join in one
>   To bless the sacred name
> Of Him that sits upon the throne,
>   And to adore the Lamb.[1]

Or imagine the delight, the sense of immediacy and almost of personal proprietorship, with which they must have sung the lines that, according to tradition, were inspired by the view, so familiar to them, of the meadows of Netley, as their living green shimmered against the blue across Southampton Water :—

> There is a land of pure delight
>   Where saints immortal reign ;
> Infinite day excludes the night,
>   And pleasures banish pain.

---

[1] This hymn is No. 72, Book I, of the *Hymns*, and is headed " Christ Jesus the Lamb of God, worshipped by all the Creation ; Rev. v, verses 11, 12, 13."

> There everlasting spring abides,
> And never-withering flowers :
> Death, like a narrow sea, divides
> This heavenly land from ours.
>
> Sweet fields beyond the swelling flood
> Stand dress'd in living green :
> So to the Jews old Canaan stood,
> While Jordan roll'd between.

The fame of Watts's hymns quickly spread, and they won their way into the hearts of the common people. It was for them he wrote, and not for the learned and the high. For them he " clipt his wings," and studied a plain, straightforward style, and " sunk to the level of vulgar capacities." " If the verse appears so gentle and flowing as to incur the censure of feebleness," he says, " I may honestly affirm that sometimes it cost me labour to make it so : some of the beauties of poetry are neglected, and some wilfully defac'd." He was careful, in his anxious desire to help the average worshipper, to avoid that " unhappy mixture of reading and singing " which results, in the case of so many writers, from inattention to the obvious hymnic necessities of punctuation. " I have seldom permitted," he claims, " a stop in the middle of a line, and seldom left the end of a line without one." [1] This act of self-abnegation had its recompense. His friend Doddridge, writing to him many years after the publication of his *Hymns*, told how in a village chapel there were tears in the eyes of several of the people as they sang his hymns, and after the service was over some of them confessed that they were not able to sing at all, so deeply were their minds affected. Such a reward might well be coveted by the greatest of poets.

Watts's best-known hymns are in the 1707 book, but the earlier *Horæ* contains a few interesting ones which clearly denote a master-hand. It must be remembered, when reading the following verses from its pages, that they are the product of his early manhood ; the dew of youth is on them. One

[1] Introduction to the *Hymns*, pp. 8 and 9.

wonders who the Phyllis of the " unhallowed name " can have
been (if, indeed, he had any one specially in mind) : she can
scarcely have been Elizabeth Singer, who was the object of
his love, for he apparently did not meet Miss Singer until
a year after the *Horæ* was published.

MEDITATION IN A GROVE

Sweet Muse, descend and bless the Shade,
    And bless the Evening Grove ;
Business and Noise and Day are fled,
    And every Care but Love.

But hence, ye wanton Young and Fair,
    Mine is a purer Flame ;
No *Phillis* shall infect the Air
    With her unhallowed Name.

Jesus has all my Powers possest,
    My Hopes, my Fears, my Joys :
He, the dear Sovereign of my Breast,
    Shall still command my Voice.

Some of the fairest Choirs above
    Shall flock around my Song
With Joy to hear the Name they love
    Sound from a mortal Tongue.

His Charms shall make my Numbers flow,
    And hold the falling Floods,
While Silence sits on every Bough,
    And bends the list'ning Woods.

I'll carve our Passion on the Bark,
    And every wounded Tree
Shall drop and bear some mystick Mark
    That *Jesus* dy'd for me.

The Swains shall wonder when they read
    Inscrib'd on all the Grove,
That Heaven itself came down, and bled
    To win a Mortal's love.

The two best-known, and probably the two finest, of Watts's
hymns are " Our God, our help in ages past " and " When

I survey the wondrous Cross." [1] They both, in a superlative degree, reveal the characteristic features of his best work—its simple strength, its transparency, its hold upon the common mind, its straightforwardness, its accentual and punctuative perfection, and its faithfulness to Scripture. The first has become the great ceremonial hymn of the English nation, and if nothing else had come from his pen, it justifies its author's memorial in Westminster Abbey. The other is more personal and has more passion. In this respect, as has often been remarked, Watts is usually in striking contrast with Wesley. He lived for many years in a park, among people of refinement ; and his life, except for repeated illnesses, was calm and unruffled ; whereas Charles Wesley wrote in the market-place, amid the turmoil of the Revival, and with a heart set on fire by the stirring events in which he was called to share.

Wright gives an interesting example of the way in which Watts used the hymn to clinch the message of his sermons.[2] In the sermon he said :—

> The man of courage can despise the threatenings of the great, and the scoffs of the witty, conscious of his own integrity and truth. He can face the world with all its terrors and travel onwards in the paths of piety without fear. The righteous man is as bold as a lion.

Then followed the hymn :—

> Am I a soldier of the cross,
> A follower of the Lamb ?
> And shall I fear to own His cause,
> Or blush to speak His name ?

---

[1] The opening lines in the original ran :—

When I survey the wondrous Cross
Where the young Prince of Glory dy'd.

[2] Thomas Wright's *Life of Isaac Watts*, p. 167.

Must I be carried to the skies,
On flowery beds of ease ;
While others fought to win the prize,
And sailed through bloody seas ?

Are there no foes for me to face ?
Must I not stem the flood ?
Is this vile world a friend to grace,
To help me on to God ?

Sure I must fight if I would reign ;
Increase my courage, Lord !
I'll bear the toil, endure the pain,
Supported by Thy Word.

And here, finally, is a good example of Watts's dignified
manner : slightly pompous and eighteenth-century-fied, but
worth reams of the ultra-sentimentalism and introspectiveness
that mark so much of the hymnody of a century later. It is
a free paraphrase of certain passages in Psalms xix and
lxxiii :—

God of the Morning, at whose voice
The cheerful sun makes haste to rise,
And like a giant doth rejoice
To run his journey through the skies :

From the fair chambers of the east
The circuit of his race begins,
And without weariness or rest
Round the whole earth he flys and shines.

O like the sun may I fulfil
Th' appointed duties of the day,
With ready mind and active will
March on and keep my heavenly way.

But I shall rove and lose the race,
If God my Sun should disappear,
And leave me in this world's wild maze
To follow every wand'ring star.

Lord, Thy commands are clean and pure,
Inlightning our beclouded eyes,
Thy threat'nings just, Thy promise sure,
Thy gospel makes the simple wise.

> Give me Thy counsels for my guide,
> And then receive me to Thy bliss ;
> All my desires and hopes beside
> Are faint and cold, compar'd with this.

Watts's work was epoch-making. In him the two main streams of church-song meet—the Scripture paraphrase and the devotional lyric—and are directed into their final hymnic channel. If he was not the first to set the form of the congregational hymn, he definitely established it as the normal medium of public praise. He was the first effectively to initiate a new type of worship-song in the English tongue, with Christ as its central theme, and in so doing he placed our modern hymnody on right and firm foundations. Not the form only, but the content of the English hymn was at length determined. The number of his hymns in common use grows less and less with the years ; but everyone is entitled to be judged by his best work, and Watts at his best remains almost unrivalled ;

> And who could wake, with master-hand,
> Such music from the harp ?

His triumph, though striking enough, was only partial. He dominated certain branches of the Free Churches, but a long period was to elapse before the Anglicans took to hymn-singing.

Both Watts and his friend Doddridge have interesting links with the slowly expiring era of religious persecution. Watts's mother was descended from a Huguenot family who came to England to escape the fury of the St. Bartholomew massacre, and his father was more than once a prisoner in Southampton gaol during the persecutions that followed the revocation of the Declaration of Indulgence. Doddridge was the grandson, on his father's side, of one of the ministers ejected under the Commonwealth, and, on his mother's side, of a Lutheran pastor who had fled from Bohemia for conscience' sake, " with his little store of money bound up in his girdle, and Luther's Bible for all his heritage." [1] Both Watts and Doddridge,

[1] Mrs. Charles's *The Voice of Christian Life in Song.*

emulating the faithfulness of their forefathers, declined the offer of a University education for ordination in the Church of England, preferring to cast their lot with the Nonconformists. And both have this great consolation, that their songs of joy and trust are to-day sung alike by the children of the oppressors and of the oppressed.

Doddridge, through many years of his ministry at Northampton, followed Watts's custom of writing a hymn to be sung after the sermon. His hymns number about four hundred, and many of them (to quote Montgomery's estimate) " shine with the beauty of holiness." They include " O God of Bethel " (now much altered), " Hark the glad sound " and " See Israel's gentle Shepherd stand." A beautiful lyric " to be used when composing oneself to sleep " may be compared with Ken's on the same theme : [1] here are a few stanzas :—

> What though downy slumbers flee,
> Strangers to my couch and me ?
> Sleepless, well I know to rest,
> Lodged within my Father's breast.
>
> While the empress of the night
> Scatters mild her silver light,
> While the vivid planets stray
> Various through their mystic way,
>
> While the stars unnumbered roll
> Round the ever constant pole,
> Far above these spangled skies
> All my soul to God shall rise.
>
> *   *   *   *   *
>
> He in these serenest hours
> Guides my intellectual powers,
> And His Spirit doth diffuse,
> Sweeter far than midnight dews,
>
> Lifting all my thoughts above
> On the wings of faith and love ;
> Blest alternative to me,
> Thus to sleep, or wake with Thee !

See p. 174.

Doddridge is a less powerful hymn-writer than Watts. His hymns were not published until after his death in 1751, but they were written at intervals during his long ministry at Northampton, and they thus form a connecting-link between those of the two great masters of English hymnody, Isaac Watts and Charles Wesley.

CHAPTER XII

THE WESLEYS

THE condition of England during the opening decades of the eighteenth century has often been painted in dark colours by our national historians. The moral temperature was depressed. There were hardly any schools. Politics were corrupt. Literature was unclean. Sanitation was neglected. Intemperance was a fashionable weakness, and men were known to blush for being suspected of chastity. The prisons were full and unspeakably loathsome. Thousands attended the frequent public executions. Highwaymen infested the country roads. Labour was rewarded with starvation wages. Christian men carried on a trade in slaves. As for religion, Green estimates that it was never at a lower ebb. Puritanism had spent its force, and no dynamic faith possessed the souls of men. Nonconformity, worn out by its long struggle for existence, had lost its virility. Inside the churches fervour was frowned upon, and the preaching was frigid, formal and argumentative.

Into such a world, from the pure atmosphere of Epworth parsonage, John and Charles Wesley came with cleansing fire, and the religious Revival which they initiated, perhaps more than any other factor, saved the soul of England. The impact of the Revival, both directly and indirectly, upon our national life was immensely powerful. The country was hurrying on to one of the most critical periods in its history, and the shadows of the approaching industrial revolution were already darkening the people's life. The Revival furnished the nation with a moral backbone and a religious faith which enabled it to meet the crisis without enduring the agonies that overtook France. But more, it so raised the moral temperature of the nation that a whole range of reforms became possible. It " gave the first impulse to our popular education " [1] ; it hastened on sanitary reform, poor law reform, prison reform, the care of the sick, and the abolition of slavery. " For in the light of the new humanity, poverty, vagrancy, disease and vice had to be fought rather than endured." [2] As for the Churches, it pulled many of them out of their stagnation ; but it went beyond them, out beyond the respectability of the middle-class pews and into the highways and hedges, the market-places and village greens, the prisons, and even Tyburn itself, with a boundless enthusiasm and an illimitable love for men. And at the heart of it all was a hymn book.

John Wesley had learned the value of the hymn as an aid to the devout life from the Moravians. On the way out to Georgia their calm behaviour when a storm threatened to destroy them had deeply impressed him. He had commenced to study their hymns early on the voyage. The seas were rolling when he began to examine their " Gesang-Buch." The storm incident intensified his interest, and on his arrival in Georgia he translated the hymns for the use of his English Societies. Soon he was devoting some hours a day to selecting, translating and versifying ; his diary through 1736 contains constant references to the fact. He began this work on May 7th of that year. It was, Curnock remarks, " one of the momentous days in Wesley's life and in the history of English hymnology." [3] From early morning he was translating and writing, and then reciting and singing what he had written. It is profoundly interesting to look back, across an interval of wellnigh two hundred years, at the little groups of communicants who met with Wesley from time to time during his brief stay in those distant lands, for " singing, reading and conversation." He was not merely guiding a few simple folk into the way of life. Wider currents were flowing.

[1] J. R. Green.   [2] Newman's *Health of the State.*
[3] Curnock's edition of the *Journal*, vol. i, p. 212.

A would-be missionary, cut adrift from his old life, driven, against his will, into strange and not very congenial work ; little groups of men, women and young people, needing song for the uplifting of their religious life ; . . . a master in language-learning, with an hereditary and highly trained gift of picturesque expression and musical rhythm—these were the elementary and providential preparations.[1]

Formative influences were at work in the life, first of one man, and then in the hearts of a handful of unlettered converts, which were to influence the lives of millions in all corners of the earth.

In 1737 John Wesley published his *Charlestown Hymn Book*, the first of a series which he and his brother were destined to give to the world. It will be worth our while to look into this famous little book and notice the sources from which he gathered the hymns together. His own translations from the German—five in all—imparted peculiar interest to the collection. They reveal a master-hand. They are all the product of the Pietist school of German poets whose hymns have opened to English Christians a new treasury of sacred song. The remainder of the hymns are from English sources : one half are from Watts ; seven are from the saintly Roman Catholic poet, John Austin ; six are adapted from George Herbert, whom Susannah Wesley had taught her boy to love ; and there are two of Addison's which had appeared in the Saturday *Spectator* when Wesley was a child.[2] The Wesley family contributed fifteen. There are the five German translations : there is the father's Good Friday meditation, which had been rescued from the fire at Epworth in which John nearly lost his life, " Behold the Saviour of mankind," with four others of his ; and there are five by John's brother Samuel, a poet whose powers were praised by Addison and

---

[1] Curnock's edition of the *Journal*, vol. i, p. 229.
[2] " The spacious firmament " and " When all Thy mercies, O my God."

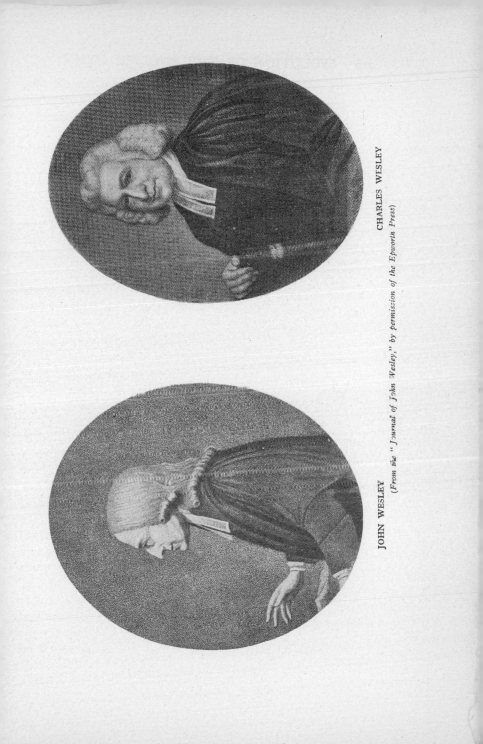

JOHN WESLEY   CHARLES WESLEY

(From the "Journal of John Wesley," by permission of the Epworth Press)

by Pope. Ken is not represented ; Wesley seems to have
had no great liking for him. As for Sternhold, we know that
Wesley looked on his verses as " miserable, scandalous
doggerel " that were " bawled out " by " raw, unawakened
striplings." There are no contributions from Charles, whose
time had not yet come.

Such was the slender hymnological outfit in this country
before Charles Wesley's muse awoke. Charles must have
imbibed a love of devotional poetry in the home circle. That
was indeed " a nest of singing birds." The father and three
of the sons were no mean poets : Mehetabel, the fair Hetty,
" the wittiest, cleverest, mirthfullest of them all," possessed
such exquisite poetical powers that some authorities believe
if she had written hymns she could have rivalled Charles.[1]
When the two brothers, John and Charles, were students at
Oxford, they used often to go for a walk in the meadows,
singing psalms together.[2] When they were still in early
manhood, Watts met them and they walked and sang together
with him.[3] There is scarcely any word that appears in John's
Journal so frequently as " singing." He is at it morning,
noon and night. As for Charles, from the day of his conversion almost to the day of his death he is writing, writing,
writing, until his hymns and short devotional lyrics number
more than six thousand, and range over the whole gamut of
his spiritual experiences.

It is not sufficiently realized, though it will be evident to
the reader, that John Wesley and not Charles stands at the
fountain-head of Methodist hymnody. He was the first in
the field, and his directing and controlling hand was never
withdrawn. He saw, more clearly than any man since Luther,
the propagandist value of song as an aid to the evangelist.
The acquaintance which he had made in Georgia with the
hymnody of the Moravians quickened his desire to know

---

[1] Dr. Overton's article in Julian's *Dictionary*, p. 1258, where a poem
of hers is given. See also Quiller-Couch's delightful novel *Hetty
Wesley.*
  [2] *Journal,* May 9, 1740.   [3] *Diary,* October 8, 1738.

more of them, and this was accentuated by the friendship which, on his return home, he formed with Peter Böhler. He determined to visit the Moravian colony at Herrnhut, " to see the place where the Christians live." [1] In his *Journal* he records that he attended their services and love-feasts, and heard them sing many of their hymns " with the voice of praise and thanksgiving." At night, the men " walked quite round the town singing praises with instruments of music " and pouring out their souls for those that slept, and by their hymns raising " the hearts of any who are awake to God." He does not say what these hymns of the night-time were, but one used at another place is on record : it is a cumulative numerical rhyme, and begins :—

> Hark, ye neighbours, and hear me tell,
> *One* has pealed on the belfry bell.
> One God alone, one Lord indeed,
> Who bears us forth in our hour of need.
> Human watch from harm can't ward us ;
> God will watch and God will guard us ;
> He, through His eternal might,
> Give us all a peaceful night !

At two o'clock the reference is to the two paths, the broad and the narrow, in which men choose to walk ; at three, it is the Trinity ; at four, the Evangelists, and so on to the twelve Apostles.[2] While on this journey Wesley met Zinzendorf and Rothe, whose hymns, in masterly translations, he introduced to his English Societies.

John Wesley's share in the voluminous output of hymns for which he and his brother are responsible has never been exactly determined.[3] It is generally thought that John, absorbed in the many tasks which the spread of the Revival cast upon him, contented himself with his German translations and left the writing of the English hymns to his brother,

[1] *Journal*, July 22, 1738.
[2] *The Book of Children's Rhymes*, by " The Daughter of a Clergyman."
[3] See *The Hymns of Methodism in their Literary Relations*, 1920 edition, where the author, the Rev. Hy. Bett, has made a patient study of the subject.

whom God had so evidently endowed for the gracious task ;
only never relaxing his kindly but critical oversight of all that
his brother wrote before it passed into public use. John
preached and organized, whilst Charles sang. It is a significant
fact that to-day the sermons are forgotten except by the select
few, while the hymns remain to bring daily inspiration, comfort
and refreshment to countless struggling souls.

It is impossible fully to appreciate Charles Wesley's hymns
unless they are related to the events which called them forth.
The Wesley hymn books constitute an extraordinarily interesting human document, palpitating with real life. Every
event of those wonderful years, every experience, public or
private, through which the singers passed, is mirrored in
some sweet song. But there is more in them than that.
They are a *Pilgrim's Progress* in verse. They trace the
religious life of every man as he travels from the City of
Destruction to the Celestial City. They unfold the spiritual
drama of the soul of man : his hopes and fears, his aspirations
and affections, his failures and victories ; each chequered
experience trembles into song, and scarcely a note is missing.
Springing from the heart of the eighteenth century, their music
seems to drown its licentiousness and frivolity in pæans of
praise. It must here suffice to place a few of them in their
original setting.

A hymn which Charles wrote immediately after the spiritual
crisis of May 1738, and which is said to have been sung " with
great joy " a few days later in his room in Little Britain,
after John, too, had " found peace," may be regarded as the
birth-song of the Revival. It constitutes a kind of encyclical
or proclamation of the lifework to which the brothers then
dedicated themselves. It voices the yearning love for the
people which consumed them ; and we read without surprise
that when, years afterwards, Charles invited the prisoners in
Cardiff gaol to join with him in singing it, to the plaintive
strains of the " Old Twenty-third," [1] many broke into tears

[1] Preface, *Methodist Hymn Book*, 1904.

as he identified himself with them among the lost—a slave, a brand, whom Jesus came to seek and save :—

> Where shall my wondering soul begin ?
> How shall I all to heaven aspire ?
> A slave redeemed from death and sin,
> A brand plucked from eternal fire,
> How shall I equal triumphs raise,
> Or sing my great Deliverer's praise ?
>
> *   *   *   *   *
>
> Outcasts of men, to you I call,
> Harlots, and publicans, and thieves !
> He spreads His arms to embrace you all ;
> Sinners alone His grace receives :
> No need of Him the righteous have ;
> He came the lost to seek and save.

A year later, on the anniversary of his conversion, he penned the hymn " O for a thousand tongues to sing," in which he gratefully recounted what the Saviour had done for him :—

> He breaks the power of cancelled sin,
> He sets the prisoner free ;
> His blood can make the foulest clean,
> His blood availed for me.

Some of his hymns were written to inspire the local preachers, or to sustain his own courage as he journeyed from place to place to preach to the crowds who flocked to hear him :—

> Inlarge, inflame, and fill my heart
> With boundless charity divine,
> So shall I all my strength exert
> And love them with a zeal like Thine,
> And lead them to Thine open side,
> The sheep for whom the Shepherd died.[1]

The persecutions to which the brothers and their helpers were subjected provoked many songs of joy. " Blessed are ye when men persecute you " their music seems to say. The splendid lines beginning " Ye servants of God, your Master proclaim, " were written " to be sung in a tumult "—which is

---

[1] *Hymns and Sacred Poems*, Part I, No. 188.

quite a different proposition from the calm backwater of a chapel-pew :—

> The waves of the sea have lift up their voice,
> Sore troubled that we in Jesus rejoice ;
> The floods they are roaring, but Jesus is here ;
> While we are adoring, He always is near.

" Soldiers of Christ, arise " was also written in times of persecution. In it you can hear the shout of victory above the noise of the battle. Goaded, perhaps, by the fury of his persecutors (who sometimes threatened his life and that of his colleagues),[1] he occasionally laid about him in powerful fashion :—

> Jesus, the growing work is Thine,
>   And who shall hinder its success ?
> In vain the alien armies join,
>   Thy glorious Gospel to suppress,
> And now, with Satan's aid, to o'erthrow
> The work Thy grace revives below.
>
> The wary world, as Julian [1] wise,
>   Wise with the wisdom from beneath,
> A-while its milder malice tries,
>   And lets these mad enthusiasts breathe,
> Breathe to infect their purest air,
> And spread the plague of virtue there.
>
> Wond'ring the calm despisers stand,
>   And dream that *they* the respite give,
> Restrain'd by Thine o'erruling hand,
>   They kindly suffer us to live,
> Live to defy their master's frown,
> And turn his kingdom upside down.
>
> Still the old dragon bites his chain,
>   Not yet commission'd from on high,
> Rage the fierce Pharisees in vain,
>   " Away with them " the zealots cry,
> And hoary Caiaphas exclaims,
> And Bonner [3] dooms us to the flames.

---

[1] Telford's *Life of Charles Wesley*, chap. vi.
[2] Julian the Apostate, the fourth-century Roman Emperor who abjured Christianity.
[3] Bishop Bonner, who under Queen Mary persecuted the Protestants.

But our great God, who reigns on high,
  Shall laugh their haughty rage to scorn,
Scatter their evil with His eye,
  Or to His praise their fierceness turn ;
While all their efforts to remove
His Church, shall stablish her in love.

The Wesleys always showed a fine contempt for wealth
and honours. John's sermon on " The Use of Money "
calls on Christian people to " cut off every expense which
fashion, caprice, or flesh and blood demand." " No more
covetousness," he says, " but employ whatever God has
entrusted you with in doing good, all possible good, in every
possible kind and degree, to the household of faith, to all
men." He has been criticized for laying down the rule
" Gain all you can," but the qualification that follows, " We
ought not to gain money at the expense of life," is far-reaching
enough. As for Charles, did he not in his youth decline the
heirship to a fortune ? He preferred not to be rich. Here is
his declaration (written on the occasion of an earthquake) :—

No foot of land do I possess,
No cottage in this wilderness ;
  A poor, wayfaring man,
I lodge awhile in tents below,
Or gladly wander to and fro
  Till I my Canaan gain :

*   *   *   *   *

There is my house and portion fair,
My treasure and my heart are there,
  And my abiding home.

The Revival involved the Wesleys more than once in theological controversies. A rigid Calvinistic doctrine obviously
cut at the very roots of their life-work. How could the
hopes raised in that first hymn at Little Britain ever be
realized if the " harlots and publicans and thieves " of whom
it spoke were predestined to be lost ? If Wesley ever heard
Swift's sneer at the Calvinists he must have enjoyed its biting
sarcasm :—

> We are God's chosen few,
>   All others will be damned ;
> There is no place in heaven for you,
>   We can't have heaven crammed !

So he set about combating the doctrine with song, and
surely never since the days of Arius had its value as an aid to
the teacher been more strikingly exemplified. Hymn after
hymn was poured out to teach that salvation is free ; that no
man, however far he may have fallen, has sunk deeper than
God's love can reach. The *Hymns on God's Everlasting
Love* played a great part in the controversy :—

> Sinners, believe the Gospel word,
>   Jesus is come your souls to save !
> Jesus is come, your common Lord ;
>   Pardon ye all through Him may have,
> May now be saved, whoever will ;
> This Man receiveth sinners still.

With touching humility he cites his own case. " If God
can save me," in effect he says, " He can save anyone " ;
and so in a moving outburst he cries :—

> O let me kiss Thy bleeding feet,
>   And bathe and wash them with my tears !
> The story of Thy love repeat
>   In every drooping sinner's ears,
> That all may hear the quickening sound,
> *Since I, even I, have mercy found !* [1]

And again, writing of the grace of God, he says :—

> Throughout the world its breadth is known,
>   Wide as infinity !
> *So wide, it never passed by one,*
>   *Or it had passed by me.*

Another troublesome controversy concerned the doctrine
of entire sanctification. Can a man be perfectly holy ? Here
John Wesley and Toplady were the protagonists, and the

---

[1] This and the previous stanzas are from the *Hymns on God's Everlasting
Love*, No. X, beginning, " Would Jesus have the sinner die ? " Extracts
from it are in the *Methodist Hymn Book*, 1904, Nos. 159 and 283.

strong language which was indulged in by both sides at least shows how difficult it is for the best of men to attain perfection. In his hymns Charles Wesley supports his brother, and constantly propounds what one may speak of as the doctrine of progressive perfection. He will not limit the influence of the Divine Spirit upon life. It is worth while recalling John's declared meaning. " By perfection," he said, " I mean the humble, gentle, patient love of God and our neighbour ruling our words and actions." And again, when visiting Wells in Somerset, in company with Charles, he summed up " what he had said many times, from the beginning, of faith, holiness and good works as the root, the tree, and the fruit, which God had joined and man ought not to put asunder." [1] Charles's hymn based on Isaiah xxvi, which stands first in the *Hymns and Sacred Poems*, deals with the subject :—

> This is the triumph of the just,
> Whoe'er on Thee their spirit stay,
> Shall find the God in whom they trust ;
> PERFECTION is their shining way.

Gregory quotes, as setting forth the Wesleyan doctrine of Christian perfection with great simplicity, the hymn, " The thing my God doth hate," [2] the first verses of which run :—

> The thing my God doth hate,
> That I no more may do ;
> Thy creature, Lord, again create,
> And all my soul renew ;
>
> My soul shall then, like Thine,
> Abhor the thing unclean,
> And, sanctified by love divine,
> For ever cease from sin.

This kind of teaching roused the Calvinists. Toplady would have none of it. In a magazine of which he was editor he drew a fantastic picture of a man's potential capacity of

---

[1] *Journal*, August 30, 1739.
[2] *The Hymn Book of the Modern Church*, by A. E. Gregory. The hymn is No. 527 in the *Methodist Hymn Book*, 1904.

sinning. Assuming that a man never "rises to the mark of legal sanctity," and therefore breaks the law "every second of our sublunary durations" (and he allowed nothing for the years of babyhood or the hours of sleep), he arrived at the mathematical conclusion that at eighty the man is chargeable with many millions of sins. That is a debt he can never hope to pay ; but he need not despair, for Christ has redeemed him, and this will "infinitely overbalance ALL the sins of the WHOLE believing world." The article closed with the hymn "Rock of Ages," headed, "A Living and Dying Prayer for the Holiest Believer in the World."

> Not the labours of my hands
> Can fulfil Thy laws demands.
> Could my zeal no respite know,
> Could my tears for ever flow,
> All for sin could not atone,
> Thou must save, and Thou alone.

In spite of some confusing figures of speech, this famous hymn has great power. It will retain its hold because it voices a universal need. We all are conscious of a stain within that mars our life. "Create in me a clean heart, O God !" is the cry of every man who has tried to know himself.

But it was not all conflict with the Wesleys. There were triumphs to record. A rich spiritual harvest was being reaped in the land. At Kingswood, the colliers who gathered in their thousands to hear Wesley and Whitefield preach, instead of cursing and swearing, made the woods resound with hymns.[1] At Builth the people "made the mountains echo while they sang" :—

> Ye mountains and vales, in praises abound,
> Ye hills and ye dales, continue the sound ;
> Break forth into singing, ye trees of the wood,
> For Jesus is bringing lost sinners to God.

Again and again the crowds of listeners, in a fervour of emotion, "burst out, as with one consent, into loud praise

[1] Whitefield's *Journal*, July 10, 1739.

P

and thanksgiving," [1] until it almost seemed that heaven had
come down to earth.[2]   The unique suitability of many of the
hymns for the open-air gatherings which formed so conspicuous
a feature of the Revival has often been remarked upon. The
crowds were swayed by the passionate words of the preacher ;
and the exuberance, the lilt, the simple directness of the
" hymns of invitation " exactly suited their need. Here is
one sung on a cold winter's day in the streets of Newcastle,
after Charles Wesley had preached to a crowd of colliers and
had " called the poor, the lame, the halt, the blind, with that
precious promise ' Him that cometh to Me I will in no wise
cast out ' " [3] :—

> Ye neighbours and friends, to Jesus draw near :
> His love condescends by titles so dear
> To call and invite you His triumph to prove,
> And freely delight you in Jesus's love.
>
> The blind are restored through Jesus's name,
> They see their dear Lord, and follow the Lamb ;
> The halt they are walking, and running their race ;
> The dumb they are talking of Jesus's grace.
>
> The deaf hear His voice and comforting word,
> It bids them rejoice in Jesus their Lord,—
> Thy sins are forgiven, accepted thou art ;
> They listen, and heaven springs up in their heart.

One further quotation must be given, for it is too apposite
to the theme of this book to be omitted.   It is from the verses
on " The True Use of Music," a hymn which " makes wholesome reading for all singers in church " [4] :

> Jesus, Thou soul of all our joys,
> For whom we now lift up our voice,
> And all our strength exert,

---

[1] See, e.g., John Wesley's *Journal*, June 16, 1739.
[2] Telford's *Life of Charles Wesley*, p. 97.
[3] John Telford's note to the hymn, No. 284 in *The Methodist Hymn Book
Illustrated.* The original has twelve verses.
[4] Curwen's *Studies in Worship Music*, vol. i, p. 74.

Vouchsafe the grace we humbly claim,
Compose into a thankful frame,
    And tune Thy people's heart.

    *   *   *   *   *

Still let us on our guard be found,
And watch against the power of sound,
    With sacred jealousy;
Lest haply sense should damp our zeal,
And music's charms bewitch and steal
    Our hearts away from Thee.

That hurrying strife far off remove,
That noisy burst of selfish love,
    Which swells the formal song;
The joy from out our heart arise,
And speak and sparkle in our eyes,
    And vibrate on our tongue.

    *   *   *   *   *

With calmly reverential joy,
We then shall all our lives employ
    In setting forth Thy love,
And raise in death our triumph higher,
And sing with all the heavenly choir
    That endless song above.

Enough has been quoted to show how intimately the hymns were linked to the daily events of those stirring years. Nothing escaped the poet's notice; there were hymns on the earthquake, the Battle of Culloden, the Gordon Riots, the rumoured French invasion; hymns commemorating his many friends; hymns for every phase of the Christian life; and the wonderful series was brought to a close by the pathetic lines dictated to his wife a few days before his death, " In age and feebleness extreme." He wrote far too much; yet no other writer has so often or so surely struck the *inevitable* note. The reason why there is a growing hesitation to use in public worship so many of the hundreds that still find a place in Methodist hymn books is that they spring out of an extraordinary experience that is not ours, and are foreign to our present-day mentality and modes of speech. But when we have given up the ephemeral and transitory, there remain a series of masterly productions which have secured for Charles Wesley a leading, if not the premier, place in the hymnody of English-speaking Christendom. "Jesu, Lover of my soul," and "Come, O Thou Traveller unknown," are among the masterpieces of devotional poetry, and there are others that will retain a sure place in English hymn books for many generations yet to come. In certain respects, as has already been hinted,[1] Wesley leaves Watts far behind. Watts is reserved : Wesley is passionate. Watts seldom reaches the masses of the people : Wesley puts exuberant songs in their mouth. But between them the two men opened a new fountain of joyous praise among the people, which was destined "to change the face of public devotion throughout England."[2]

So completely did Charles Wesley dominate his age that his few contemporary hymn-writers are altogether dwarfed beside him. Whitefield, after his breach with the Wesleys, published a collection of hymns, largely by Watts and Wesley, but altered to suit his own theological views ; and the Countess of Huntingdon also had her own collection.

Cennick, who was one of Wesley's earliest lay-preachers, is the most conspicuous of the lesser lights. He was partly of Quaker and partly of Moravian descent, but was somewhat vacillating, for, after following both Wesley and Whitefield, he ended up as a deacon in the Moravian Church. He was responsible for a queer collection of "dialogue" hymns, where questions and answers are exchanged between the men and women worshippers, thus :—

MEN :   Tell us, O Women, we would know
            Whither so fast ye move ?

WOMEN :   *We, called to leave the world below,*
            Are seeking one above.

MEN :   Is not your native country here,
            The place of your abode ?

WOMEN :   *We seek a better country far,*
            A city built by God.

[1] See p. 209.
[2] The quotation is from J. R. Green's *Short History of the English People*.

But Cennick could do better than that. He is the author of the two well-known graces, " Be present at our table, Lord," and " We thank Thee, Lord, for this our food." Perhaps his most pleasing hymn is " Children of the heavenly King." It is full of joy and trust.

Thomas Olivers was another of Wesley's preachers. It is astonishing to read that the author of so majestic a lyric as " The God of Abraham praise " was brought up in a dissolute circle, and for twenty years or more was reckoned the worst lad in the neighbourhood. Poor, wretched, ill-educated, his life was completely changed when hearing Whitefield preach from the words, " Is not this a brand plucked from the burning ? " His great hymn represents an attempt to Christianize the articles of the Jewish creed.

Edward Perronet, yet another of the preachers, and a companion of Charles Wesley in many persecutions, wrote " All hail the power of Jesu's name," a hymn which owes not a little to the tunes " Miles Lane " and " Diadem," which have carried it far and wide.

Truth to tell, John Wesley apparently did not greatly encourage any of his helpers, excepting his brother, to write hymns. He knew well how difficult a task it is. " Were we to encourage little poets," he said, " we should soon be over-run." [1] Charles's hymns seemed to him to reach perfection. In his famous Preface he claimed almost as much, and to those " gentlemen " who had attempted to improve them he said : " They really are not able. None of them is able to mend either the sense or the verse. Therefore I must beg of them one of these two favours : either to let them stand as they are, to take them for better for worse ; or to add the true reading in the margin, or at the bottom of the page, that we may no longer be accountable either for the nonsense or for the doggerel of other men."

One other hymn-writer, of peculiar attractiveness, who was intimately associated, though not as a preacher, with the

---

[1] See his letter to Thos. Wride, 1774.

Wesleys, was John Byrom. He occasionally took coffee with the Wesleys, when they discussed William Law and Tauler and mysticism in general. John admired his poems, and remarked upon their wit and humour, and their serious vein of piety,[1] so that when he received from Byrom two hymns of Madame Bourignon (who was Byrom's "supreme saint" until he discovered William Law), he gladly inserted them in *Hymns and Sacred Poems*,[2] and one has survived in the *Methodist Hymn Book* of 1904.[3] But more interesting than the hymns of the French mystic are those of Byrom himself. Many of them are tedious and preachy, but there are a few gems, and one that is among the most dearly loved in the language. Here is a verse from the "Divine Pastoral," founded upon Psalm xxiii—a poem which Ward praises for its freshness and felicity :—

> The Lord is my Shepherd,—what then shall I fear ?
> What danger can frighten me, whilst He is near ?
> Not, when the time calls me to walk through the vale
> Of the shadow of death, shall my heart ever fail ;
> Though afraid, of myself, to pursue the dark way,
> Thy rod and Thy staff be my comfort and stay ;
> For I know, by Thy guidance, when once it is pass'd,
> To a fountain of Life it will bring me at last.

His Christmas hymn, known the world over, was written as a gift for his daughter "Dolly." Here is the original version :—

> Christians, awake, salute the happy morn
> Whereon the Saviour of the World was born ;
> Rise to adore the Mystery of Love
> Which Hosts of Angels chanted from above ;
> With them the joyful Tidings first begun
> Of God incarnate and the Virgin's Son.
> Then to the watchful Shepherds it was told
> Who heard th' Angelic Herald's Voice : " Behold !
> I bring good Tidings of a Saviour's Birth
> To you and all the Nations of the Earth ;

[1] *Journal*, July 12, 1773.
[2] *The Poems of John Byrom*, edited by A. W. Ward, vol. ii.
[3] It is No. 526 : a translation of " Venez, Jesus, mon salutaire.'

This day hath God fulfill'd his promis'd Word ;
This day is born a Saviour, Christ the Lord.
In David city, Shepherds, ye shall find
The long-foretold redeemer of Mankind ;
Wrapt up in swaddling cloaths, be this the Sign
A cratch contains the holy Babe divine."

He spake, and straightway the celestial Quire
In Hymns of Joy, unknown before, conspire ;
The Praises of redeeming Love they sung,
And Heav'n's whole Orb with Hallelujahs rung.
God's Highest Glory was their anthem still,
Peace upon Earth and mutual Goodwill !
To Bethlehem straight th' enlightened Shepherds ran
To see the Wonder God had wrought for Man ;
They saw their Saviour, as the Angel said,
The swaddled Infant in a Manger laid.
Joseph and Mary, a distressèd Pair,
Guard the sole Object of th' Almighty's Care ;
To human Eyes none present but they two,
Where Heav'n was pointing its concentred View.
Amaz'd, the wondrous story they proclaim,
The first Apostles of his Infant Fame,
But Mary kept and pondered in her Heart
The heav'nly Vision which the Swains impart.
They to their Flocks, and praising God, return
With Hearts, no doubt, that did within them burn.

Let us, like these good Shepherds, then, employ
Our grateful Voices to proclaim the Joy ;
Like Mary, let us ponder in our Mind
God's wondrous Love in saving lost Mankind.
Artless and watchful as these favour'd Swains,
While Virgin Meekness in the Heart remains,
Trace we the Babe, who has retriev'd our Loss,
From his poor Manger to his bitter Cross ;
Follow we him who has our Cause maintain'd
And Man's first heav'nly State shall be regain'd.
Then, may we hope, th' Angelic Thrones among,
To sing, redeem'd, a glad Triumphal Song.
He That was born upon this joyfull Day
Around us all his Glory shall display ;
Sav'd by his Love, incessant we shall sing
Of Angels and of Angel-men the King.

CHAPTER XIII

THE MODERN ERA

OUR story is now almost told. The foundations of the
English hymn of the present day are deeply embedded in
the past, and the material has been brought from many lands
and many Christian communities. And yet, in spite of the
wealth of treasure which has accumulated through the ages,
the strange fact confronts us that two hundred years ago
only a fraction of the congregations of this country included
hymn-singing in their worship. Watts and the Wesleys cap-
tured the Nonconformist Churches ; but the Church of
England held coldly aloof, and the protestations of John and
Charles Wesley that they lived and died in her communion
did not affect the immediate situation. The Anglican view
was that the practice was unscriptural, schismatical, and
doctrinally dangerous, and this view was widely persisted in
well into the nineteenth century. Thus Romaine in 1778
asked why Watts, or any other hymn-writer, should " not
only take precedence of the Holy Ghost, but also thrust Him
entirely out of the Church ? " ; and as lately as 1854 a Bishop
objected to the singing of the Passiontide hymn " Jesu, meek
and lowly " as " contrary to the spirit of the Book of Common
Prayer." But as the eighteenth century drew to a close the
new leaven was seen to be at work, and Anglican prejudices
gradually gave way, until at length every branch of the
Christian Church in this country, with the notable exception
of the Society of Friends, had adopted hymn-singing as a
normal part of public worship. It is the purpose of this
chapter to trace the steps by which this result was attained.

It was primarily due to the constructive work of a few
Churchmen of outstanding ability and initiative. Newton and
Cowper, Cotterill and Heber, followed by the singers of the

Oxford Movement and the translators of the treasures of the past—these were the men and women who pointed the line of march, while a whole host of minor singers came after them. At first, here and there, a few clergymen, realizing the significance of the events of the Wesleyan Revival, and especially the power of its poetry over the hearts of the people, began making collections for private use and then for adoption in their churches.

The Olney Hymns gave a great stimulus to this movement. They were the joint work of John Newton, a leader of the evangelical party within the Anglican Church, and his friend and lay-reader, William Cowper. Cowper was proud to claim Donne among his ancestors. " There is in me," he said, " more of the Donne than the Cowper." He went to live at Olney so as to be near Newton, who was curate there, and whose evangelical interests he shared. Whether Newton's influence upon his sensitive friend's life was good or bad is one of those debatable questions upon which literary critics are likely to continue to differ. Goldwin Smith believes it was an " unhappy " influence [1] ; W. M. Rossetti, on the other hand, thinks that when the intercourse of the two friends was broken by Newton's removal to London, " one of the mainstays of the poet's activity and cheerfulness " was removed.[2] One thing is certain : Cowper's mental trouble began many years before he had met Newton, and continued long after they were separated.

The Olney Hymns, published in 1779, were written with a double purpose : firstly to promote " the faith and comfort of sincere Christians," and secondly " as a monument to perpetuate the remembrance of an intimate and endearing friendship." The intention was to provide a hymn book " for the use of plain people," that is to say, the village congregation that gathered week by week in the parish church, or in the " Great House " which did duty as a parish room,

[1] *Cowper*, " English Men of Letters " Series, by Goldwin Smith.
[2] *Lives of Famous Poets*, by W. M. Rossetti.

for prayer and praise. To them the collection was dedicated and to meet their needs " perspicuity, simplicity and ease " were studied by the poets when engaged upon their work.[1] Newton contributed by far the larger number of hymns, and his best are almost equal in quality to Cowper's. There is a touch of engaging intimacy and sincerity about them that ensures our sympathy with their very human author, " once an infidel and libertine, a servant of slaves in Africa." Here is a chapter from real life :—

> In evil long I took delight,
> Unaw'd by shame or fear,
> Till a new object struck my sight
> And stopped my wild career.

> I saw One hanging on a tree
> In agonies and blood,
> Who fix'd His languid eyes on me,
> As near His cross I stood.

> Sure never till my latest breath
> Can I forget that look ;
> It seemed to charge me with His death,
> Though not a word He spoke.

The lines are pathetic in their intensity. Palgrave suggests they are of such power that Bunyan might have been proud, or thankful, to own them. In his well-known hymns, "How sweet the name of Jesus sounds," and " One there is, above all others," we can trace Newton's simple and unaffected devotion to the Saviour who had rescued him from the degradations of his youthful years.

Cowper strikes a deeper, tenderer note. His hymns are poured out from his inmost soul : " they seem to break out of his heart with a cry." [2] Their self-conscious and over-wrought fervour makes them, as a rule, unsuitable for congregational singing. Cowper's poetry, it has often been

---

[1] See the Preface by John Newton.
[2] Stopford Brooke's *Theology of the English Poets.*

remarked, is in striking contrast with Pope's and the formal Georgian writings of that age. The contrast with Watts is less pronounced, but is quite obvious. Both lift us into the pure and serene atmosphere of worship, but the dignity and reserve of the one have yielded to the spiritual abandon of the other.

There are moments when Cowper's introspectiveness passes into morbidity and even terror. In "The Waiting Soul," for instance, he cries :—

> I seem forsaken and alone,
>   I hear the lion roar ;
> And every door is shut but one,
>   And that is Mercy's door.

And again in the following lines he seems to be clinging to a last spar amid the wreckage of life, for ever fearful that he will be lost in the stormy seas :—

> The billows swell, the winds are high,
> Clouds overcast my wintry sky ;
> Out of the depths to Thee I call,
> My fears are great, my strength is small.
>
> O Lord, the pilot's part perform,
> And guide and guard me through the storm ;
> Defend me from each threatening ill,
> Control the waves, say, " Peace, be still."
>
> Amidst the roarings of the sea
> My soul still hangs her hopes on Thee ;
> Thy constant love, Thy faithful care
> Is all that saves me from despair.

It is from the midst of such devastating emotions that the weary sufferer steadies himself in that hymn of trust, "God moves in a mysterious way." His verses "Ere God had built the mountains" show that he had learned in the school of Watts how to accommodate Old Testament poetry to Christian use. They are an amplification of Proverbs viii. 22–31 :—

Ere God had built the mountains,
Or rais'd the fruitful hills ;
Before He fill'd the fountains
That feed the running rills ;
In me from everlasting,
The wonderful I AM
Found pleasures never wasting,
And wisdom is my name.

When, like a tent to dwell in,
He spread the skies abroad,
And swath'd about the swelling
Of ocean's mighty flood ;
He wrought by weight and measure ;
And I was with Him then :
Myself the Father's pleasure,
And mine the sons of men.

Thus wisdom's words discover
Thy glory and Thy grace,
Thou everlasting Lover
Of our unworthy race !
Thy gracious eye survey'd us
Ere stars were seen above :
In wisdom Thou hast made us,
And died for us in love.

And couldst Thou be delighted
With creatures such as we !
Who, when we saw Thee, slighted
And nail'd Thee to a tree ?
Unfathomable wonder,
And mystery divine !
The voice that speaks in thunder,
Says, " Sinner, I am thine ! "

It is delightful to remember that the Olney Hymns, which
have gone all over the world and carried with them a message
of calm trust to countless waiting souls, were written for a
little village congregation. It was for the opening of a room
for " social prayer " that Cowper penned the beautiful lines :—

Jesus, where'er Thy people meet,
There they behold Thy mercy-seat ;
Where'er they seek Thee Thou art found,
And every place is hallowed ground.

The poet's favourite retreat was a rose-embowered summer-house, where many happy hours were passed in company with Newton and with his women friends :—

> The calm retreat, the silent shade,
>   With prayer and praise agree ;
> And seem by Thy sweet bounty made
>   For those who follow Thee.
>
> There, if Thy Spirit touch the soul,
>   And grace her mean abode,
> O with what peace, and joy, and love,
>   She communes with her God !
>
> There like the nightingale she pours
>   Her solitary lays ;
> Nor asks a witness of her song,
>   Nor thirsts for human praise.

Later in life, Cowper, at the suggestion of his friend William Bull, undertook the translation of some of Mme Guyon's hymns from the French. The poet " reverenced her piety and admired her genius." [1] Some regard her as an hysterical degenerate. Others look upon her as a saint, who lived in that atmosphere of inner calm which they alone know whose wills are yielded to the will of God and whose hearts are the passive recipients of Divine grace. It is obvious that a woman who won the devotion of the accomplished Fénelon, who cast a spell over the court of Mme de Maintenon, and whose writings could enlist the interest of Cowper, must have been possessed of no ordinary gifts. Her hymns reflect her temperament, and it is not difficult to see why they appealed to Cowper. The best-known of them, entitled " The soul that loves God finds Him everywhere," is thought to have been written soon after she had left her home and children to embark upon her " apostolic life " of wanderings, exile and imprisonments. Here are its opening verses :—

---

[1] Bull's Preface to Cowper's Translations.

O Thou by long experience tried,
Near whom no grief can long abide ;
My Love ! how full of sweet content
I pass my years of banishment !

All scenes alike engaging prove,
To souls impress'd with sacred love ;
Where'er they dwell, they dwell in Thee ;
In heav'n, in earth, or on the sea.

To me remains nor place nor time ;
My country is in ev'ry clime ;
I can be calm and free from care
On any shore, since God is there.

And here are some lines, written in her prison cell at St.
Marie, which recall Lovelace :—

My cage confines me round ;
    Abroad I cannot fly ;
But though my wing is closely bound,
    My heart's at liberty.
My prison walls cannot control
The flight, the freedom of the soul.

In the early years of the nineteenth century, a Sheffield
clergyman, Thomas Cotterill, stands out as a conspicuous
figure in our story. He, more than most men, undermined
the stubborn Anglican conservatism which prevented the use
of Watts's and Wesley's hymns in church. When he was a
young curate in Staffordshire he had assisted in the compila-
tion of one or two hymnals which included selections from
Watts, Cowper and Newton. On his removal to Sheffield
he introduced these hymns into use in St. Paul's Church,
and soon found himself in trouble with his congregation,
some of whom objected that such singing was unauthorized
and irregular, and insisted on carrying their complaint to the
Consistory Court at York, averring in their indictment that
they pressed the case " for the health of Thomas Cotterill's
soul and the lawful correction and reformation of his manners

and excesses." [1] The issue, thanks to the diplomatic intervention of Archbishop Harcourt, narrowed itself down to the revision of the hymnal. Cotterill went back to Sheffield encouraged to try again, and was wise enough to enlist the help of his friend James Montgomery. Between them they "clipped, underlined and remodelled" the old book, and Montgomery wrote a number of hymns for the new one. When the Archbishop saw the revised volume he gave permission for it to be dedicated to him, thus implicitly allowing its use in St. Paul's Church. The action of the Archbishop is of great importance in the long story of the introduction of hymn-singing into the Anglican Church. It signified the end of an epoch. It effectively broke down the opposition which had persisted ever since the days of John Calvin. Clergymen all over the country noted Harcourt's attitude and accepted it—as doubtless was intended—as authorizing them to introduce hymns into their services, with the result that a great increase in the number of parochial hymn books followed. [2]

Montgomery is of interest, not only because he stands among the first dozen of great English hymn-writers, but also because he was one of the first to make a serious study of hymnology. Like the Wesleys, he owed his first impulse towards hymn-writing to the Moravians. At their School at Fulneck, where he received his early education, the Moravian hymns delighted him, and he records that as soon as he could write and spell he imitated them. He admired Cowper, but declared with boyish confidence, "I could write better verses myself," and this he followed up by averring, at the age of fourteen, that he intended to outdo Milton! In later life he was in the running for the Laureateship, and his poetical powers were admired by Wordsworth, Southey, Byron and Moore. His hymns constitute his most abiding monument.

---

[1] The same complaint had involved Wesley in a trial before the magistrates in Georgia.
[2] The legal documents of the Cotterill case can be consulted at York Minster.

Virile in thought, graceful and dignified in expression, and free from unhealthy introspectiveness, they will carry their gracious message through many centuries ; and the best of all is that they and their writer make one music. His " Sabbath Hymn for a Sick Chamber "—not to be found in many present-day collections—is full of quiet confidence in God's overruling care :—

Thousands, O Lord of Hosts ! this day
  Around Thine altar meet ;
And tens of thousands throng to pay
  Their homage at Thy feet.

They see Thy power and glory there,
  As I have seen them too ;
They read, they hear, they join in prayer,
  As I was wont to do.

They sing Thy deeds, as I have sung,
  In sweet and solemn lays ;
Were I among them, my glad tongue
  Might learn new themes of praise.

For Thou art in their midst, to teach,
  When on Thy name they call ;
And Thou hast blessings, Lord, for each,
  Hast blessings, Lord, for all.

I, of such fellowship bereft,
  In spirit turn to Thee ;
O hast Thou not a blessing left,
  A blessing, Lord, for me ?

The dew lies thick on all the ground,
  Shall my poor fleece be dry ?
The manna rains from heaven around,
  Shall I of hunger die ?

Behold thy prisoner ;—loose my bands,
  If 'tis Thy gracious will ;
If not,—contented in Thine hands,
  Behold Thy prisoner still !

I may not to Thy courts repair,
  Yet here Thou surely art ;
Lord, consecrate a house of prayer
  In my surrender'd heart.

To faith reveal the things unseen,
    To hope, the joys untold ;
Let love, without a veil between,
    Thy glory now behold.

Oh ! make Thy face on me to shine,
    That doubt and fear may cease ;
Lift up Thy countenance benign
    On me,—and give me peace.

The next representative figure in our unfolding story is
Reginald Heber. What a great idea that was of enlisting
Scott and Southey and Milman in the task of compiling a
worthy hymnal for the National Church ! The scheme never
matured, but Heber managed, before his untimely death in
India, to gather together a collection of about one hundred
hymns, of which more than half were his own, and twelve
from Milman's pen, and which were published posthumously
in 1827. Three distinguishing features characterize this book,
each marking an important stage in the evolution of the English
hymn. The hymns were arranged to follow the order of the
ecclesiastical year ; they were impersonal and sober in feeling,
and they brought our hymnody into line with the Romantic
revival which was then imparting a new charm and appeal
to English poetry. The arch-Romanticist of his day, Sir
Walter Scott, had written some lyrical devotional poetry, and
so had Wordsworth and Coleridge, but it was Heber above
all who heralded the literary hymn. At one step, his little
volume added several treasures to the worship-song of
Christendom. Milman's " When our heads are bowed with
woe," and his own " Holy, holy, holy, Lord God Almighty "
and " The Son of God goes forth to war," typified a new order
of praise.

Almost simultaneously with Heber's little volume Keble's
Christian Year was published, and the literary hymn firmly
established itself in Anglican circles. It was Pusey's opinion
that *The Christian Year* was the real source of the Oxford
Movement. Keble and Newman and the other outstanding

leaders of the Movement felt that the clean cut with the past which the Reformation had seemed to effect had involved the loss to the English Church of many valuable aids to worship. With their belief in the power of historical association and liturgical continuity to enable the worshipper to feel himself one with the adoring ages, it was only to be expected that they would try to recover some of the lost treasures of the Breviaries and Service Books of the ancient Greek and Latin Churches. Newman is one of the greatest restorers of Latin hymnody. His disciple at Edgbaston, Edward Caswall, rediscovered such gems as " Jesu, the very thought of Thee," " Hark, an awful Voice is sounding," and " At the cross her station keeping." Isaac Williams, Trench and Chandler are of the same circle. Neale stands somewhat apart, but he is the most prolific and in some respects the ablest of them all. He is the first translator of Greek hymns into our tongue. To him we owe the translations and adaptations " Art thou weary ? ", " 'Tis the day of resurrection," " The day is past and over," and several others, as well as that masterly translation from the Latin, " Jerusalem the Golden." He also has given us the charming carol " Good King Wenceslas." The work of these men and others who have followed them has brought into our English Churches many songs of devotion and love which refreshed the hearts of the Christian communities of the early and mediæval Church. The barriers of time are broken down ; the venerable Ambrose steps out from the fourth century ; the monks of Mar Saba from the eighth ; Notker the Stammerer from the tenth; and Abélard and Adam of St. Victor from the twelfth, once again to lead God's people in their songs of purest praise.

The original English hymns of the Oxford writers are of singular beauty. Never since the time of George Herbert and his satellites had there been such a rich lyrical harvest of devotion. Keble stands at their head. He learned from Wordsworth to find " authentic tidings of invisible things " in the quiet beauty of the English countryside. *The*

Christian Year is rich in nature mysticism. Unhappily, the
hymns which have been taken from its pages suffer by being
torn from their context. Thus the opening stanzas of the
Evening Hymn picture the fading light and the benighted
traveller, and so prepare the way for a fervent prayer to Him
who is the Light of life :—

> 'Tis gone, that bright and orbéd blaze,
> Fast fading from our wistful gaze ;
> Yon mantling cloud has hid from sight
> The last faint pulse of quivering light.

> In darkness and in weariness
> The traveller on his way must press,
> No gleam to watch on tree or tower,
> Whiling away the lonesome hour.

> Sun of my soul ! Thou Saviour dear,
> It is not night if Thou be near ;
> O may no earth-born cloud arise
> To hide Thee from Thy servant's eyes.

> When round Thy wondrous works below
> My searching rapturous glance I throw,
> Tracing out Wisdom, Power and Love,
> In earth or sky, in stream or grove ;

> When with dear friends sweet talk I hold,
> And all the flowers of life unfold ;
> Let not my heart within me burn,
> Except in all I Thee discern.

Every page of *The Christian Year* bespeaks the saint-
liness of its author's life : everything there is lovely and of
good report. Not mere literary skill, but a trustful, childlike
spirit, is revealed in such verses as these :—

> " Father to me thou art and mother dear,
>   And brother too, kind husband of my heart "—
> So speaks Andromache in boding fear,
>   Ere from her last embrace her hero part :
> So evermore, by Faith's undying glow,
> We own the Crucified in weal or woe.

> Strange to our ears the church-bells of our home ;
>   The fragrance of our old paternal fields
> May be forgotten ; and the time may come
>   When the babe's kiss no sense of pleasure yields
> Even to the doting mother ; but Thine own
> Thou never canst forget, nor leave alone.

> There are who sigh that no fond heart is theirs,
>   None loves them best—O vain and selfish sigh !
> Out of the bosom of His love He spares—
>   The Father spares the Son for thee to die :
> For thee He died—for thee He lives again :
> O'er thee He watches in His boundless reign.

And here is a beautiful prayer, which surely was abundantly answered in its author's own life :—

> Lord, make my heart a place where angels sing !
>   For surely thoughts low-breathed by Thee
> Are angels gliding near on noiseless wing ;
>   And where a home they see
> Swept clean, and garnished with adoring joy,
>   They enter it and dwell,
>   And teach that heart to swell
> With heavenly melody, their own untired employ.

Newman's best-known hymns are "Lead, kindly Light"—a poem wrung from his heart in hours of agony—and some verses from "The Dream of Gerontius." It is to be regretted that others from his pen are not in wider use, for they have a vigour about them that is none too often met with in nineteenth-century hymn books. The following "Thanksgiving" is clearly autobiographical :—

> Lord, in this dust Thy sovereign voice
>   First quicken'd love divine ;
> I am all Thine, Thy care and choice,
>   My very praise is Thine.

> I praise Thee, while Thy providence
>   In childhood frail I trace,
> For blessings given, ere dawning sense
>   Could seek or scan Thy grace ;

Blessings in boyhood's marvelling hour,
 Bright dreams, and fancyings strange ;
Blessings, when reason's awful power
 Gave thought a bolder range ;

Blessings of friends, which to my door
 Unask'd, unhoped, have come ;
And, choicer still, a countless store
 Of eager smiles at home.

Yet, Lord, in memory's fondest place
 I shrine those seasons sad,
When, looking up, I saw Thy face
 In kind austereness clad.

I would not miss one sigh or tear,
 Heart-pang, or throbbing brow ;
Sweet was the chastisement severe,
 And sweet its memory now.

Yes ! let the fragrant scars abide,
 Love-tokens in Thy stead,
Faint shadows of the spear-pierced side
 And thorn-encompass'd head.

To Newman the danger of insincerity in worship-song was
no less imminent than to Augustine or George Fox. Beautiful
words without deeds are as flowers without fruit.

Prune thou thy words, the thoughts control
 That o'er thee swell and throng ;
They will condense within thy soul,
 And change to purpose strong.

But he who lets his feelings run
 In soft luxurious flow,
Shrinks when hard service must be done,
 And faints at every woe.

Faith's meanest deed more favour bears,
 Where hearts and wills are weigh'd,
Than brightest transports, choicest prayers,
 Which bloom their hour and fade.[1]

[1] The two selections from Newman are taken from his *Lyra Apostolica*.

Newman had no more attractive disciple than Faber. Faber was a born poet, as no less a judge than Wordsworth has testified. As a hymnist, he did for Roman Catholicism in this country what Watts did for Nonconformity and Heber for Anglicanism. When he preached his last sermon in an Anglican church he flung his surplice on the vestry floor to show that he had divested himself of his past life ; but he could not divest himself of the memories of his youth. The Olney Hymns especially had exercised their spell over him for years,[1] and it can hardly be doubted that they had their share in influencing him to undertake the writing of a series for use in the Oratory in London. There were scarcely any vernacular hymns in use there when he joined the community, and when he introduced his own the Catholics of London looked upon them with suspicion. But the objections were short-lived, and the hymns rapidly won their way into our Churches, and to-day occupy the same position of pre-eminence among English Catholics as Wesley's do in Protestant circles. Yet they are marred by one great weakness. The softness of Italy seemed to have entered into Faber's veins. " He saturated himself with all that was warm and full of sweetness " in its worship, and believed that Italian practices and devotion could minister to our colder English temperament.[2] This it is that accounts for the overwrought emotionalism and intensity of his hymns. They are made out of the fine material of his own soft and affectionate nature. This is how he portrays the spiritual experiences of his boyhood :—

> O God ! who wert my childhood's love,
>   My boyhood's pure delight,
> A presence felt the livelong day,
>   A welcome fear at night ;—

*　　*　　*　　*　　*

[1] See the Preface to his *Hymns*, 1861 edition.
[2] *Father Faber*, by M. S. B. Malins ; Catholic Truth Society's Tract.

At school Thou wert a kindly face
Which I could almost see ;
But home and holyday appeared
Somehow more full of Thee.

I could not sleep unless Thy hand
Were underneath my head,
That I might kiss it, if I lay
Wakeful upon my bed.

And quite alone I never felt,—
I knew that Thou wert near,
A silence tingling in the room,
A strangely pleasant fear.

It is a strange note to come from the heart of a boy ! In
some later verses of the same hymn, where he seems to be
looking back upon his boyhood, the grown man adds :—

Father ! what hast Thou grown to now ?
A joy all joys above,
Something more sacred than a fear,
More tender than a love !

With gentle swiftness lead me on,
Dear God ! to see Thy face ;
And meanwhile in my narrow heart
O make Thyself more space.

Faber is better than his creed. He knows that

We make His love too narrow
By false limits of our own ;

and that God dwells not in temples but in the heart :—

God is never so far off
As even to be near ;
He is within ; our spirit is
The home He holds most dear.

And again :—

Thy home is with the humble, Lord !
The simple are Thy rest ;
Thy lodging is in childlike hearts ;
Thou makest there Thy nest.

Dear Comforter ! Eternal Love !
If Thou wilt stay with me,
Of lowly thoughts and simple ways
I'll build a nest for Thee.

Who made this beating heart of mine,
But Thou, my heavenly Guest ?
Let no one have it then but Thee,
And let it be Thy nest.[1]

Among Caswall's vernacular hymns none is more affecting
than the one entitled " The Good Shepherd." Its realistic
note, its tendency to play in poetic fashion around the wounds
of Christ, is characteristic of English Roman Catholic hymnody ;
but it is full of devotional fervour :—

I met the good Shepherd,
But now on the plain,
As homeward He carried
His lost one again.
I marvell'd how gently
His burden He bore ;
And, as He pass'd by me,
I knelt to adore.

O Shepherd, good Shepherd,
Thy wounds they are deep ;
The wolves have sore hurt Thee,
In saving Thy sheep ;
Thy raiment all over
With crimson is dyed ;
And what is this rent
They have made in Thy side ?

Ah, me ! how the thorns
Have entangled Thy hair,
And cruelly riven
That forehead so fair !
How feebly Thou drawest
Thy faltering breath !
And, lo, on Thy face
Is the shadow of death !

[1] From the hymn " Sweetness in Prayer."

REGINALD HEBER

J. M. NEALE

F. W. FABER

JOHN JULIAN

O Shepherd, good Shepherd !
    And is it for me
This grievous affliction
    Has fallen on Thee ?
Ah, then let me strive,
    For the love Thou hast borne,
To give Thee no longer
    Occasion to mourn !

Among other legacies of the Oxford Movement are the hymns of Mrs. Alexander [1] and F. T. Palgrave. Palgrave is uniformly excellent, though the thrill and certainty of a Wesley are not there. He wistfully voices a lament that the day of the incarnate Christ seems so remote :—

So long since Thou wast here, that to our seeming
Thou art like some fair vision seen in dreaming ;
With glare and glow and turmoil, sign and shout,
The world rolls on, and seems to bar Thee out.

The same note is struck in *Faith and Sight* :—

Dim tracts of time divide
    Those golden days from me :
Thy voice comes strange o'er years of change ;
    How can I follow Thee ?

Comes faint and far Thy voice
    From vales of Galilee ;
Thy vision fades in ancient shades ;
    How should we follow Thee ?

Unchanging law binds all,
    And Nature all we see ;
Thou art a Star, far off, too far,
    Too far to follow Thee !

Yet the poet sees with the eye of faith through matter to spirit. He cannot see the Lord, but he knows Him to be the indwelling Guest of the humble-hearted :—

Set up Thy throne within Thine own ;—
    Go, Lord : we follow Thee.

[1] See p. 276.

At the end of his little volume, Palgrave includes a curious poem, " The Reign of Law." It is unique of its kind—a poet's musings on the relation of science to religion and the long evolutionary process which ends in the complete apprehension of God as " the Whence and Whither " : not exactly a hymn, though the poet describes it as such. Here are three verses :—

> We may not hope to read
>   Nor comprehend the whole
> Or of the law of things
>   Or of the law of soul :
> E'en in the eternal stars
>   Dim perturbations rise,
> And all the searchers' search
>   Does not exhaust the skies ;
> He who has framed and brought us hither
> Holds in His hands the whence and whither.

> He in His science plans
>   What no known laws foretell ;
> The wandering fires and fix'd
>   Alike are miracle ;
> The common death of all,
>   The life renew'd above,
> Are both within the scheme
>   Of that all-circling love ;
> The seeming chance that cast us hither
> Accomplishes His whence and whither.

> Then though the sun go up
>   His beaten azure way,
> God may fulfil His thought
>   And bless His world to-day
> Beside the law of things
>   The law of mind enthrone,
> And, for the hope of all,
>   Reveal Himself in One ;
> Himself the way that leads us thither,
> The All-in-all, the Whence and Whither.

With the Oxford Movement not only did Anglican prejudices against hymn-singing almost entirely disappear, but the leadership in the production of congregational hymns passed over from Nonconformist to Anglican circles. The pioneer English writers, as we have seen, were in practice Dissenters : but the leading hymnists of the mid-nineteenth century, when the art " burst into almost tropical luxuriance," were for the most part Churchmen, who produced a succession of hymnals chiefly for parochial use. Towards the sixties a great attempt was made to compile a book for the Church of England which would command general confidence, and an appeal was made to the clergy at large to withdraw their individual collections in favour of a unified effort. The appeal met with so wide-spread a response that the production, in 1861, of a representative book, under the title of *Hymns Ancient and Modern,* became possible. The editors had at their disposal the spoils of eighteen centuries of Christian song as well as the original hymns of many talented contemporary authors. Their success was immediate and indeed overwhelming : far more so than the merits of the book would seem to warrant. But *Ancient and Modern* met a great need, and with its appearance hymn-singing came to occupy a place of first importance in English religious worship ; and the blending of old and new, the songs of long ago with the songs of modern times, set a standard to which all later responsible hymnals have more or less closely conformed.

At length, then, we have reached the culminating point of the story we set out to tell. So voluminous has been the production of new hymns since *Hymns Ancient and Modern* appeared that a separate volume would be required adequately to review them. Thousands of them have had but an ephemeral life, and many others that timid editors perpetuate have long outlived their usefulness. But after the winnowing fan of criticism has swept away plentiful supplies of chaff, a good wholesome measure of wheat survives in our garner. Lyte's " Abide with me," Lynch's " Gracious Spirit, dwell with me," Baring-Gould's " Now the day is over," Ellerton's

" Saviour, again to Thy dear Name," Bonar's " He liveth long
who liveth well," Matheson's " O Love, that wilt not let me
go," Hatch's " Breathe on me, Breath of God," Anna Waring's
" In heavenly love abiding," Thring's " Fierce raged the
tempest," and a few others of equal beauty, have taken their
place among the classics of devotion.[1]

But although no detailed consideration of the hymnody of
recent decades can here be attempted, some outstanding
characteristics may be noticed.

1. *There has been a notable addition of German and Greek
translations.* We have already seen how both John Wesley
and James Montgomery owed their inspiration to the Moravians.
The fine work John Wesley accomplished as a translator has
been ably seconded by a band of women writers, including
Mrs. Rundle-Charles, Elizabeth Winkworth, the Borthwick
sisters and Frances Cox. Neale's work upon the ancient
Greek Service Books has been admirably supplemented by
Dr. Brownlie and others.

2. *An invaluable contribution has reached us from America.*
Most of the leading American poets have been hymn-writers,
including Bryant, Longfellow, Holmes, Lowell, Whittier and
Van Dyke. Whittier's work has been dealt with elsewhere.[2]
He is by far the most important American hymn-writer. Two
literary partnerships have resulted in an enrichment of our
worship-song where it was weak, that is, in the expression
of the social and communal mission of the Church of Christ
—the one between Samuel Johnson and Samuel Longfellow,
and the other between F. L. Hosmer and Wm. C. Gannett.
All four of these writers belong to a liberal and spiritual
type of Unitarian faith, and their publications have been
fruitful " source-books " for the hymnals of many Churches
besides their own.

Of the Sankey type of American hymn there is little need
to write. It cannot be questioned that it has helped the

---

[1] One or two of the hymns enumerated were written before 1861, but
have only come into general use since then.   [2] See p. 194.

inner life of many people, though it is equally certain that it has hindered others. Historically it is of little count.

3. *The Liturgical tendency is becoming more pronounced.* Anglican hymn books are being arranged more elaborately to fit in with the order of the Church Year and the sequence of Festivals and Saints' Days. The advantages of such an arrangement are obvious, but in effecting it a considerable measure of unreality is sometimes arrived at. Special hymns are assigned to several of the " Saints." For example :—

> For David, prince of Cambrian saints,
> We praise Thee, holy Lord.

And again, St. Anne is apostrophized as the—

> Stem, with honey laden,
> Whence came Mary maiden.

Even the mythical figure of St. George has his niche :—

> To George our Saint Thou gavest grace
> Without one fear all foes to face,
> And to confess by faithful death
> That Word of Life which was his breath.
> O help us, Helper of St. George,
> To fear no bonds that man can forge :
> Arm us like him, who in Thy trust
> Beat down the dragon to the dust.[1]

It is difficult to believe that worshipping hearts can be greatly stirred by hymns of this kind.

4. *A new type of hymn, concerned with the humanitarian and social implications of the Gospel, is emerging.* Its concern is not greatly with the next world ; rather it seeks to keep in touch with this life and all its " crowded ways." There are plentiful signs of the times that the Church is being called upon to relate its worship more closely to the ideals of social democracy.[2] Such a demand is sure to grow, and along with it a new type of social hymnody will be created. Some such

---

[1] These three extracts are taken from *The English Hymnal* and *Songs of Syon*.　　[2] See Benson's *The English Hymn*, p. 587.

attempt was made in " the hungry forties " by Thomas Cooper
and his fellow Chartist poets. They produced *The Shake-
spearian Chartists' Hymnal*—a book which struck a very
human note. Such ideas as these pervade Cooper's volume :—

> God of the earth and sea and sky,
> To Thee Thy mournful children cry ;
> Did'st Thou the blue that bends o'er all
> Spread for a general funeral pall ?
>
> Father, why did'st Thou form the flowers ?
> They blossom not for us or ours :
> Why did'st Thou clothe the fields with corn ?
> Robbers from us our share have torn.
>
> Father, our frames are sinking fast ;
> Hast Thou our names behind Thee cast ?
> Our sinless babes with hunger die ;
> Our hearts are hardening. Hear our cry !

Cooper's lines may not be great poetry, and it may be
objected that they were political in intent : but they at least
throb with life, and must have made a deep appeal to the
Leicester stockingers who could barely command a wage of
five shillings a week. Coming to our own time, here are some
recent lines, quite obviously suggested to their author, Dr.
North of New York, by the " underworld " of a great city,
with all its sin and wretchedness :—

> Where cross the crowded ways of life,
>   Where sound the cries of race and clan,
> Above the noise of selfish strife,
>   We hear Thy voice, O Son of Man.
>
> In haunts of wretchedness and need,
>   On shadowed thresholds dark with fears,
> From paths where hide the lures of greed,
>   We catch the vision of Thy tears.
>
> From tender childhood's helplessness,
>   From woman's grief, man's burdened toil,
> From famished souls, from sorrow's stress,
>   Thy heart has never known recoil.

The cup of water giv'n for Thee
   Still holds the freshness of Thy grace;
Yet long these multitudes to see
   The sweet compassion of Thy face.

O Master, from the mountain side,
   Make haste to heal these hearts of pain;
Among these restless throngs abide,
   O tread the city's streets again;

Till sons of men shall learn Thy love,
   And follow where Thy feet have trod;
Till glorious from Thy heaven above,
   Shall come the City of our God.

The following " Hymn of the Industrial Christian Fellowship," by G. A. Studdert-Kennedy, is a pioneer experiment
of a somewhat similar character :—

When through the whirl of wheels, and engines humming,
   Patiently powerful for the sons of men,
Peals like a trumpet promise of His coming
   Who in the clouds is pledged to come again;

When through the night the furnace-fires flaring,
   Shooting out tongues of flame like leaping blood,
Speak to the heart of Love, alive and daring,
   Sing of the boundless energy of God;

When in the depths the patient miner striving,
   Feels in his arms the vigour of the Lord,
Strikes for a Kingdom and his King's arriving,
   Holding his pick more splendid than the sword;

When on the sweat of labour and its sorrow,
   Toiling in twilight flickering and dim,
Flames out the sunshine of the great to-morrow,
   When all the world looks up because of Him :—

Then will He come with meekness for His glory,
   God in a workman's jacket as before,
Living again the eternal gospel story,
   Sweeping the shavings from His workshop floor.

Of recent collections, *The Fellowship Hymn Book*
perhaps comes nearest to meeting the need for " social hymns,"

and in many other twentieth-century books a special section is devoted to them.[1] In this connection it is of special interest to note the wide use now being made of Blake's " Jerusalem," beginning " And did those feet in ancient time." Thanks largely to Parry's setting, these verses promise almost to attain the dignity of a national anthem.

5. *A high literary standard is increasingly being demanded.* No man has done more towards this end than Dr. Bridges. His *Yattendon Hymnal* (1899) shows that poetry and hymnody can be successfully wedded together. *The English Hymnal* (1906), which is representative of the high Anglican school of thought, reveals the admirable literary and musical taste of its editors, and its influence has been pronounced. These verses, by Bridges, are marked by an Ambrosian strength and simplicity [2] :—

> Rejoice, O land, in God thy might,
> His will obey, Him serve aright ;
> For thee the Saints uplift their voice :
> Fear not, O land, in God rejoice.
>
> Glad shalt thou be, with blessing crowned,
> With joy and peace thou shalt abound ;
> Yea, love with thee shall make his home
> Until thou see God's kingdom come.
>
> He shall forgive thy sins untold :
> Remember thou His love of old ;
> Walk in His way, His word adore,
> And keep His truth for evermore.

The literary movement has in recent times been greatly helped by the tendency among many of our leading authors to write hymns. Christina Rossetti ranks with George Herbert as a devotional poet of the first order : and we may take heart for the future as we find among the contributors to our modern hymnals such gifted writers as Charles Kingsley and George Macdonald ; Jean Ingelow and Adelaide Procter ;

[1] *Songs of Praise*, 1925, edited by Percy Dearmer and others, has a strong section of such hymns.   [2] See p. 54.

Stopford Brooke and Arthur C. Benson; William Canton and Rudyard Kipling; Laurence Housman and G. K. Chesterton, as well as other poets whose work has already been reviewed.

Here is a lovely poem by Christina Rossetti :—

> Thy lilies drink the dew,
> Thy lambs the rill, and I will drink them too;
>   For those in purity
> And innocence are types, dear Lord, of Thee.
>   The fragrant lily flower
> Bows and fulfils Thy will its lifelong hour;
>   The lamb at rest and play
> Fulfils Thy will in gladness all the day;
>   They leave to-morrow's cares
> Until the morrow, what it brings it bears.
>   And I, Lord, would be such;
> Not high or great or anxious overmuch,
>   But pure and temperate,
> Earnest to do Thy will betimes and late,
>   Fragrant with love and praise
> And innocence through all my appointed days;
>   Thy lily I would be,
> Spotless and sweet, Thy lamb to follow Thee.

Her verses " None other lamb " and the following carol have found a place in several recent hymnals :—

> Love came down at Christmas,
>   Love all lovely, Love Divine;
> Love was born at Christmas,
>   Star and Angels gave the sign.
>
> Worship we the Godhead,
>   Love Incarnate, Love Divine;
> Worship we our Jesus:
>   But wherewith for sacred sign?
>
> Love shall be our token,
>   Love be yours and love be mine,
> Love to God and all men,
>   Love for plea and gift and sign.

The following, on the same theme, is by Laurence Housman :—

The Maker of the sun and moon,
　　The Maker of our earth,
Lo ! late in time, a fairer boon,
　　Himself is brought to birth !

How blest was all creation then,
　　When God so gave increase ;
And Christ, to heal the hearts of men,
　　Brought righteousness and peace !

No star in all the heights of heaven
　　But burned to see Him go ;
Yet unto earth alone was given
　　His human form to know.

His human form, by man denied,
　　Took death for human sin :
His endless love, through faith descried,
　　Still lives the world to win.

O perfect Love, outpassing sight,
　　O Light beyond our ken,
Come down through all the world to-night,
　　And heal the hearts of men ! [1]

Such poems as these have literary grace, but they only imperfectly meet the conditions requisite for congregational praise. They are touched with sincere religious feeling, but they are lacking in that simple directness which gave such power to the hymns of Luther and Wesley. These poets fly too high. If, like Watts, they would be content to clip their wings, they could lift the common heart into a heaven of praise.

It. only remains to be added that recent hymnological developments have been guided and stimulated by Dr. Julian's monumental *Dictionary of Hymnology*. First published in 1892, that great work has brought a wealth of scholarship to bear upon the origins and history of Christian hymnody of all ages and nations.

---

[1] From *Songs of Praise*, by permission of the Oxford University Press.

CHAPTER XIV

HYMNS OF CHILDHOOD

A TRAVELLER exploring the sources of some great river is often tempted to turn aside to wander in the green meadows and shaded valleys through which the smaller rivulets wend their way to the parent stream. So we will turn aside for a while to explore one or two delightful by-paths before our journey comes to an end.

A child literally lives in an enchanted world. It is almost as natural for him, as for the birds, to sing. All the joy of childhood, its sweet abandon and innocence, its sense of wonder, its vivid imagination, are the very stuff of which music is made. The difficulty among grown-up people of entering into the mind of children is pathetically reflected in the reams of " moral " literature which we have inflicted upon them. We have been too anxious to " rub it in," forgetful that every hour of the normal child's day is full of experiences which are teaching him to discriminate between good and evil. It is bad psychology to put labels on everything the child sees and experiences, " This will do you good " or " This will do you harm."

In the realm of children's hymnody we have " offended against these little ones " with a positively alarming didactical ineptitude. The hymnody of the early and mid-nineteenth century, especially, takes us into a weary wilderness of smug morality, out of which every healthily minded boy and girl might well have prayed to be delivered. Either the poor child was warned that he was " conceived in sin " and that the devil and hell-fire were waiting for him if he dared to be naughty ; or, if he were good (ah ! how wearisome the species !), he was promised a series of rewards, such as golden crowns and silver wings and palms of victory, which he did not want, but which he was doomed to wear for ever and ever in an unreal other-world " above the bright blue sky." All this had little relation to the child's actual experiences or aspirations, and one wonders how it affected his conception of God and of the religious life.

The issues are of such first-class importance that it is surprising that the Christian Church has given so little thought to the provision of a worthy hymnal for her children.

The first Christian hymn still in use in this country was written by Clement, for the scholars of the Catechetical School at Alexandria, under circumstances that have already been described.[1]

From the days of Clement to those of Luther scarcely any children's hymns were written ; or if they were, they have long since been lost. A few flowers only blossom in the wilderness. Prudentius, the Spaniard-poet of the fourth century, has bequeathed to us some tender verses about the child martyrs of early Christian times, which have been incorporated in the Roman Breviary for the Feast of Holy Innocents :—

> Little flowers of martyrdom,
>   Whom the cruel sword hath torn,
> (On the threshold of the morn—)
>   Rosebuds by the whirlwind shorn !
>
> All regardless of their doom,
>   'Neath the altar where they lay,
> With their palms and chaplets gay—
>   Little simple ones ! they play ![2]

A grand ninth-century hymn, " Gloria, laus et honor," introduces us to a delightful picture, which could be seen for many generations on Palm Sundays in old cathedral cities like York and Hereford, Rouen and Tours. At York a gallery was specially constructed above the door of the Minster, from which seven chorister boys, in their white robes, sang three

---

[1] See p. 43.
[2] Translated by Isaac Williams, from *The Parisian Breviary*.

stanzas, whilst the others, kneeling on the steps below, joined
in the glad refrain. At Hereford the hymn was sung from
the city gates.

> All glory, laud and honour
>   To Thee, Redeemer, King,
> To whom the lips of children
>   Made sweet Hosannas ring.
>
> Thou art the King of Israel,
>   Thou David's royal Son,
> Who in the Lord's name comest,
>   The King and Blessed One.
>
> The company of Angels
>   Are praising Thee on high,
> And mortal men, and all things
>   Created, make reply.

A further quaint verse, which it is said was usually sung
till the seventeenth century, ran :—

> Be Thou, O Lord, the Rider,
>   And we the little ass ;
> That to God's holy city
>   Together we may pass.

Taking a leap over several centuries, it is pleasant to find
Martin Luther amongst the children's-hymn writers. In his
own youth he sang from door to door, and so sweetly as to
make for himself a home in a cultured family circle, and to
earn among his boy companions the name of " the Musician."
When at length he had a home of his own, many were the
delightful musical reunions in company with his friends with
which he beguiled the strain of his public anxieties. One
Christmas when the whole family were gathered together
round the Christmas-tree, he taught them to sing a charming
child's-song which he had especially written for his little
boy Hans, and which has now found its way all over the
world.[1] The simple ceremony began with the appearance of
a member of the family circle dressed as an angel and

[1] I have been unable to trace any connection between Luther and the
lines beginning " Away in a manger," which are attributed to him in some
modern hymn books.

announcing the coming of the Christ Child, and then the
whole circle broke out into a glad song of welcome :—

> Welcome to earth, Thou noble guest,
> Through whom e'en wicked men are blest !
> Thou com'st to share our misery,
> What can we render, Lord, to Thee ?

> *   *   *   *   *

> Ah ! dearest Jesus, Holy Child,
> Make Thee a bed, soft, undefiled,
> Within my heart, that it may be
> A quiet chamber kept for Thee.

> My heart for very joy doth leap,
> My lips no more can silence keep ;
> I too must sing with joyful tongue
> That sweetest ancient cradle-song—

> Glory to God in highest Heaven,
> Who unto man His Son hath given !
> While angels sing with pious mirth
> A glad New Year to all the earth.[1]

Hawkins, in his *History of Music*, mentions a queer little
prayer from the monastic period for the use of school-children
when learning the alphabet. The prayer was known as the
Criss-Cross, because a Cross was usually placed before the
letter " a " to remind the scholar to cross himself before
beginning his lesson. The earliest versions began with an
invocation to St. Nicholas, the patron-saint of children—the
Santa Claus of Christmastide—" St. Nicholas be my speed " ;
but Hawkins says that the Reformers of Elizabeth's time, in
their efforts to " protestantize " the song, dropped the saint !

> Christie's Cross by my speed
> In all virtue to proceed,
> A b c d e f g h i j k l m n o p, q, r, s and t
> Double-u, v, x with y ezod,
> And per se con per se title title, Amen.
> When you have done, begin againe, begin againe ;
>   Christie's Cross be my speed
>   In all virtue to proceed.

[1] Translated by Miss Winkworth in *Lyra Germanica*.

Now let us glance at some of the " moral " literature for children upon which our forefathers for many generations relied for their virtuous and religious instruction. As we proceed, the subject will be found to be relevant to our main theme, as it quite naturally prepares the ground for the children's hymnody of to-day.

In a delightful volume dating from 1480, *The Babee's Book*, there is a section entitled " The Lytylle Childrenes Lytil Boke." The " boke " is intended for the instruction of noblemen's and rich men's children, and in its directions for behaviour in the minutest details of life it recalls Clement of Alexandria's *Pedagogus* of thirteen centuries earlier. Particularly entertaining is its advice upon behaviour at meals. The child is exhorted to see that his hands are clean ; he must not begin till grace has been said ; he must not eat quickly, nor put any food in his pockets, nor his fingers in the dish, nor his meat in the salt-cellar ; he must not " cram," nor drink when his mouth is full, nor put his arms on the table, nor " belch as if he had a bean in his throat." When he has finished, he should rise quickly and thank his host ; and people then will say, " A gentleman was here." The children so exhorted are expected to be grateful to the author of the " boke " :—

> Chyldren, for charyte,
> Love this boke, though it little be,
> And pray for him that made it thus.

A somewhat similar production, to be seen in the Bodleian Library, is Symons's *Lesson of Wysdom for all Maner Chyldryn*. Here the advice is prefaced with a warning : " *Children, attend ! You had better be unborn than untaught* " ; followed by a Polonius-like budget of counsel. Don't always expect your own way : keep your face and hands washed : don't throw stones at dogs or hogs : eat what is given you, and don't ask for this or that : don't go birds'-nesting, stealing fruit or throwing stones at windows : keep away from the

edge of brooks and wells : don't make faces at any man :
be early at school : honour your parents and kneel for their
blessing : don't chatter in church : " be meek to clerks."
" If you want to be a bishop you must diligently attend to all
these precepts." And finally, it will do you good to have a
little birching now and then : " Al chyldryn chastysd shold
be." If you are a good child, the chastising shall not be very
hard. " So may God keep you good."

It will be seen that these entertaining books of manners are
not far removed from the moral and religious verses which
were addressed, with all due solemnity, in a later period, to
the childhood of England by Bunyan and Watts and the ever-
delightful Jane and Ann Taylor, to say nothing of a host of
colourless imitators.

Bunyan's *Divine Emblems*, or, to give its fuller title,
*Divine Emblems : or Temporal Things Spiritualized ;
calculated for the Use of Young People*, is the forerunner
of many similar attempts to find spiritual laws in the natural
world for the improvement of the mind of youth. As Darton
truly says, Bunyan's poetry is bad, but his morality is sound.
But then Bunyan's aim was didactic rather than artistic.

> I do 't to show them how each fingle-fangle
> On which they doting are, their souls entangle,
> As with a web, a trap, a gin, a snare,
> And will destroy them, have they not a care.

Here is an example of Bunyan's method of teaching :—

ON THE CACKLING OF A HEN

> The Hen, so soon as she an egg doth lay,
> Spreads the fame of her doing what she may :
> About the yard a-cackling she doth go,
> To tell what 'twas she at her nest did do.
> Just thus it is with some professing men
> If they do ought that's good ; they, like our hen,
> Cannot but cackle out where e'er they go,
> And what their right hand does, their left must know.

At the time that Bunyan was imprisoned in Bedford Gaol for the offence of preaching the Gospel, Thomas Ken was enjoying a tranquil life at Winchester, where he was engaged in writing his *Manual of Prayers* for the boys of the famous School, and possibly also the two hymns which have made his name famous all over the English-speaking world.[1] Ken's hymns are not exactly children's hymns, but they were written for schoolboys, and were sung each morning and evening in the School. The importance of Ken's contribution to the evolution of the English hymn has been referred to elsewhere in these pages.[2] Not the least debt which we owe to him is that he stands first in order of time in the long roll of English hymn-writers for children.

Isaac Watts bridges the years between Ken and Charles Wesley. A scholar and logician, Watts learned at his mother's knee the art of rhyming. The careful mother offered a prize of a farthing to the child who brought her the best verse ; but little Isaac somewhat haughtily declined the prize, declaring

> I write not for a farthing, but to try
> How I your farthing writers can outvie !

Watts's *Divine and Moral Songs for Children* were composed, at the request of a friend, for school use.

Their author followed Bunyan's method, though perhaps not consciously so : for he was no mere imitator. They had a great run. " Faded Immortelles " they may be, but they took a long time to fade, whilst some few of them will continue to delight many generations of children. Here are the well-known lines " Against Idleness and Mischief " :—

> How doth the little busy bee
> Improve each shining hour,
> And gather honey all the day
> From ev'ry opening flower.

---

[1] Plumptre's *Life of Ken*, vol. i, p. 92.   [2] See p. 173.

How skilfully she builds her cell !
How neat she spreads her wax !
And labours hard to store it well
With the sweet food she makes.

In works of labour and of skill
I would be busy, too ;
For Satan finds some mischief still
For idle hands to do.

Again, we meet with this :—

Let dogs delight to bark and bite,
For God hath made them so ;
Let bears and lions growl and fight,
For 'tis their nature, too.

But children, you should never let
Such angry passions rise ;
Your little hands were never made
To tear each others' eyes.

Let love through all your actions run,
And all your words be mild,
Live like the blessed Virgin's Son,
That sweet and lovely child.

Verses follow on " The Ant," " The Rose," " The
Sluggard," and so forth, each with its moral tag.

As we should expect, Watts finds hell and the judgment
to come salutary weapons for the spiritual education of childhood. It is futile to condemn him for this : he must be
judged in relation to the theological enlightenment, or rather
darkness, of his age. This is how he tells the story of Elisha
and the bears :—

When children in their wanton play
Served old Elisha so,
And bade the prophet go his way,
" Go up, thou bald-head, go " ;

God quickly stop'd their wicked breath
And sent two raging bears,
That tore them limb from limb to death,
With blood and groans and tears !

It is this God who has prepared for sinful children

> A dreadful hell
> And everlasting pains,
> Where sinners must with devils dwell
> In darkness, fire and chains.

With what relief we turn from such horrors to greet his charming " Cradle Song," with its air of innocence and peace :—

> Hush, my babe, lie still and slumber,
>   Holy angels guard thy bed !
> Heavenly blessings without number
>   Gently falling on thy head.

> Sleep, my babe ; thy food and raiment,
>   House and home, thy friends provide ;
> All without thy care or payment,
>   All thy wants are well supplied.

> How much better thou'rt attended
>   Than the Son of God could be,
> When from heaven He descended,
>   And became a child like thee !

> Soft and easy is thy cradle :
>   Coarse and hard thy Saviour lay :
> When His birthplace was a stable,
>   And His softest bed was hay.

> See the kinder shepherds round Him,
>   Telling wonders from the sky !
> Where they sought Him, there they found Him,
>   With His Virgin-Mother by.

> Lo, He slumbers in His manger,
>   Where the hornéd oxen fed ;
> —Peace, my darling, here's no danger ;
>   Here's no ox a-near thy bed !

> May'st thou live to know and fear Him,
>   Trust and love Him all thy days ;
> Then go dwell for ever near Him,
>   See His face, and sing His praise !

John and Charles Wesley tried their hands at children's hymnody. John declared, with a touch of that self-satisfaction which ran away with him when he came to write the Preface to his general collection, that while Watts let himself down to the level of the children, he and his brother lifted them up to their own. He added that their *Hymns for Children* contained " strong and manly sense, yet expressed in such plain and easy language as even children may understand. *But, when they do understand them, they will be children no longer.*" It is difficult to imagine any child of to-day singing these heavy, grandiloquent theological verses. Hell, as in Watts, figures luridly in Wesley, the fires, if possible, having been given an extra stoking :—

> Dark and bottomless the pit
>   Which on them its mouth shall close ;
> Never shall they 'scape from it ;
>   There they shall in endless woes
> Weep and wail and gnash their teeth,
>   Die an everlasting death.

But again, as with Watts, we turn from Charles Wesley at his worst to listen to those lines which recall to thousands, more vividly perhaps than any others in the English tongue, the days of angel-innocence at mother's knee. The lines in their original form extend to twenty-eight verses.

> Gentle Jesus, meek and mild,
> Look upon a little child ;
> Pity my simplicity,
> Suffer me to come to Thee.

> Fain I would to Thee be brought ;
> Dearest God, forbid it not ;
> Give me, dearest God, a place
> In the kingdom of Thy grace.

> Put Thy hands upon my head,
> Let me in Thy arms be stayed ;
> Let me lean upon Thy breast,
> Lull me, lull me, Lord, to rest.

Hold me fast in Thy embrace,
Let me see Thy smiling face,
Give me, Lord, Thy blessing give ;
Pray for me, and I shall live.

I shall live the simple life,
Free from sin's uneasy strife,
Sweetly ignorant of ill,
Innocent and happy still.

Lamb of God, I look to Thee ;
Thou shalt my example be ;
Thou art gentle, meek, and mild,
Thou wast once a little child.

Fain I would be as Thou art ;
Give my Thy obedient heart.
Thou art pitiful and kind ;
Let me have Thy loving mind.

Loving Jesu, gentle Lamb,
In Thy gracious hands I am,
Make me, Saviour, what Thou art,
Live Thyself within my heart.

Blake (b. 1757) was a greater poet than Watts or Charles
Wesley, but he had not learned the art of hymn-writing (an
essential ingredient of which is straightforward lucidity) as
well as they. It has been conjectured that he was influenced
by Watts's modest hope, expressed in the Preface to the
Divine Songs, that some " condescending genius " would
undertake to " perform much better " his own slight work.[1]
Here is Blake's " Cradle Song " :—

Sleep, sleep, happy child !
All creation slept and smiled.
Sleep, sleep, happy sleep,
While o'er thee doth mother weep.

Sweet babe, in thy face
Holy image I can trace ;
Sweet babe, once like thee
Thy Master lay, and wept for me ;

---

[1] Professor Wallis's chapter on Blake in the *Cambridge History of English Literature*.

> Wept for me, for thee, for all,
> When He was an infant small.
> Thou His image ever see,
> Heavenly face that smiles on thee !

The ethereal beauty of the *Songs of Innocence* is perhaps unequalled in the whole range of children's religious verse. The poet,

> Piping down the valleys wild,
> Piping songs of pleasant glee,

becomes himself a little child.

> Little lamb, who made thee ?
> Dost thou know who made thee ?
> Gave thee life, and bade thee feed
> By the stream and o'er the mead ;
> Gave thee clothing of delight,
> Softest clothing, woolly, bright ;
> Gave thee such a tender voice,
> Making all the vales rejoice ?
> Little lamb, who made thee ?
> Dost thou know who made thee ?
>
> Little lamb, I'll tell thee ;
> Little lamb, I'll tell thee :
> He is callèd by thy name,
> For he calls Himself a Lamb.
> He is meek, and He is mild,
> He became a little child.
> I a child, and thou a lamb,
> We are callèd by His name.
> Little lamb, God bless thee !
> Little lamb, God bless thee !

If there is one poem worthy to be placed alongside that perfect gem, it surely is Francis Thompson's " Little Jesus, wast Thou shy ? " A marvellous man indeed was Thompson. The outcast of the Thames Embankment, innocent in the midst of guilt, he told little Monica Meynell that when she reached heaven she need not look for him among " the bearded counsellors of God," for she would be sure to find him in the nurseries of heaven. Let us set some of his lines by the side of Blake's :—

Thou canst not have forgotten all
That it feels like to be small :
And thou know'st I cannot pray
To thee in my father's way—
When thou wast so little, say,
Couldst thou talk thy Father's way ?—
So, a little child, come down
And hear a child's tongue like thy own :
Take me by the hand and walk
And listen to my baby-talk.
To thy Father show my prayer
(He will look, thou art so fair)
And say : " O Father, I, thy Son,
Bring the prayer of a little one.

Before the close of the eighteenth century, Mrs. Barbauld
produced her *Hymns of Prose for Children*. In the Preface
she questioned Watts's method of instruction. " It may be
doubted," she said, " whether poetry should be lowered to
the capacities of children, or whether they should not be
kept from reading verse till they are able to relish good verse " ;
and she proceeded to write twelve hymns in measured prose,
" nearly as agreeable to the ear as a more regular rhythmus."
The opening lines run :—

Come, let us praise God, for He is exceeding great : let us bless
God, for He is very good.
He made all things : the sun to rule by day, the moon to shine
by night :
He made the great whale, and the elephant ; and the little worm
that crawleth on the ground.
The little birds sing praises to God, when they warble sweetly
in the green shade :
The brooks and rivers praise God, when they murmur melodi-
ously amongst the smooth pebbles :
I will praise God with my voice ; for I may praise Him, though
I am but a little child.

In 1804 two sisters, Jane and Ann Taylor, published a
volume of Original Poems, followed rapidly by three supplementary books. Ann was then twenty-two years of age and
Jane twenty-one. Their father and their brother contributed
a few poems ; there was one by Barnard Barton, who was

just twenty ; a friend of the Taylors, Adelaide O'Keefe, who was some years older, was responsible for several ; but the great bulk of the work was by the two sisters. The book was an innovation. It followed to some extent the precedent set by Bunyan and Watts of using the phenomena of nature and the aid of rhyme to point a moral—the moral being only too obtrusive—but the plan was carried out on a much larger scale than ever before attempted.

E. V. Lucas's estimate of the work of the Taylors is that the book occupies a unique niche in literature. He cannot call to mind any other book written immediately for children by authors who from first to last wrote for children only. And these two sisters were themselves not far from childhood when their book was published, and had certainly preserved to a remarkable degree their appreciation of a child's mentality. Scott, Southey, Mrs. Browning, Dr. Arnold, and Swinburne are among those who have found their work worthy of praise. Indeed, it is questionable whether in its particular sphere it has ever been excelled. Charles Lamb, Robert Louis Stevenson, William Canton, and other well-known writers have charmed their adult readers with verses about children, but the Taylors, in their sweet simplicity, seem like children themselves. Jane has told us her secret. " My method," she says, " was to shut my eyes, and imagine the presence of some pretty little mortal, and then endeavour to catch, as it were, the very language it would use on the subject before me. If in any instances I have succeeded, to this little imaginary being I should attribute my success ; and I have failed so frequently because so frequently I was compelled to say, ' Now you may go, my dear ; I shall finish this hymn myself.' " Most writers bow the little dream-child out of the room too soon : some never invite her in at all.

It is difficult, from among so many attractive pieces, to choose examples that most worthily show the merit of these artless poems. Probably " Twinkle, twinkle, little star " and Ann's verses " My Mother " (obviously founded on

ANN AND JANE TAYLOR
(*By permission of National Portrait Gallery*)

Cowper's " My Mary ") are known to most readers. " The Violet " is regarded as showing Jane at her best :—

Down in a green and shady bed
 A modest violet grew,
Its stalk was bent, it hung its head,
 As if to hide from view.

And yet it was a lovely flower,
 Its colour bright and fair ;
It might have graced a rosy bower,
 Instead of hiding there.

Yet thus it was content to bloom,
 In modest tints arrayed ;
And there diffused a sweet perfume,
 Within the silent shade.

Then let me to the valley go
 This pretty flower to see ;
That I may also learn to grow
 In sweet humility.

An interesting comparison has been made between the poems on " The Cow " by the Taylors and by Stevenson. Here is a verse of each :—

The friendly cow, all red and white,
 I love with all my heart—
She gives me cream with all her might,
 To eat with apple tart.

(STEVENSON.)

Compare the above with :—

Thank you, pretty cow, that made
Pleasant milk to soak my bread,
Every day, and every night,
Warm, and fresh, and sweet, and white.

(J. and A. TAYLOR.)

Stevenson is charming, but his artistry is somewhat too obvious. Ainger wittily suggests that he had one eye on the child and the other on Andrew Lang.[1]

---

[1] Canon Ainger's lecture on " Children's Books."

Other pieces introduce us to a little girl who told a lie, a second who meddled with grandmamma's snuff-box, till

> Presently a mighty jerk
> The mighty mischief did ;

and to the good little sisters, Mary and Ann, who always ran to do any job papa wished done, and never quarrelled or wanted their own way. A positive superfluity of virtue oozes out of these pages. In the first of the *Hymns for Infant Minds*, " I thank the goodness and the grace," as in others that follow, the sisters fairly invite the criticism that " Charity here sits by the glowing hearth and comforts itself with the sophistries of Dr. Watts for the unequal distribution of faggots." [1] These girls gaze on the indigent children around them, and then soliloquize :—

> If I were so destitute, friendless and poor,
> How could I such hardship and suffering endure ?
> Then let me be thankful, and humbly adore
> My God, who has graciously given me more.

At their best, however, the " Hymns " are almost flawless children's lyrics, as, for instance, the verses based on the opening sentence of the Lord's Prayer, " Great God, and wilt Thou condescend," and these simple lines :—

> Lord, I would own Thy tender care,
>   And all Thy love to me :
> The food I eat, the clothes I wear,
>   Are all bestowed by Thee.

> 'Tis Thou preservest me from death
>   And dangers every hour :
> I cannot draw another breath
>   Unless Thou give me power.

> Kind angels guard me every night,
>   As round my bed they stay :
> Nor am I absent from Thy sight
>   In darkness or by day.

[1] Florence Barry in *A Century of Children's Books*.

My health, and friends, and parents dear,
　To me by God are given ;
I have not any blessing here
　But what is sent from heaven.

Such goodness, Lord, and constant care,
　A child can ne'er repay ;
But may it be my daily prayer,
　To love Thee and obey !

The work of Jane and Ann Taylor provoked a host of imitators. Two women Quakers, Priscilla Wakefield and Mary Elliott, sedulously undertook the improvement of the child mind. Their verses suffer by comparison with their model : they are goody-goody ; " only that and nothing more."

Mary Howitt, another Quaker, along with her husband, William Howitt, has a secure place among the minor literary figures of the early part of the nineteenth century. She translated some of Hans Andersen's stories, and is the author of the inimitable " ' Will you walk into my parlour ? ' said the spider to the fly." Her poem on " The Ministry of Flowers " contains the verse :—

God might have made the earth bring forth
　Enough for great and small,
The oak-tree and the cedar-tree,
　Without a flower at all.
He might have made enough—enough
　For every want of ours,
For food and medicine and toil,
　And yet have made no flowers.

To wade through the children's hymn books which sprang up with the growth of Sunday Schools is a tedious task. There is an " infinite deal of nothing," with death and hell the constantly recurring themes. The cult of death and hell for the benefit of the young is conspicuous in early hymnals. In 1702 we read of the author of a book for little children recommending the frequent study of treatises on death and judgment, and again in 1720 Janeway published his *Tokens for Children : being an exact account of the Conversion, Holy and Exemplary Lives, and Joyful Deaths, of several young Children.*[1]

Better days, however, slowly dawned. Mrs. Mayo, a worker in an infants' school in London, produced in 1838 a collection of hymns " for Infant Schools and Nurseries." In her preface Mrs. Mayo says it is difficult for children to attend school when once they begin work in factories (which at that time was at the age of nine). She explains that in her book she has not included any poems on arithmetic or geography, " as it is considered that the knowledge of such subjects can be much better imparted by direct lessons." Her collection contains several hymns and poems by Watts, Wesley, Cowper and the Taylors ; Dorothy Thrupp's " Poor and needy though I be " ; Anne Shepherd's " Around the throne of God in heaven," and John Henley's " Children of Jerusalem." There are also one or two action songs, among them being " This is the way we wash our hands," and a queer patriotic ditty, addressed to the Queen and set to " Auld Lang Syne " :—

> Victoria ! Victoria !
> We hail thy gentle rule ;
> Victoria ! the patroness
> Of every infant school.

Similar collections were making their appearance as the need was increasingly recognized, and here and there amid the chaff some wheat was found. In 1840 Jeanette Threlfall wrote " Hosanna, loud Hosanna," and this was followed shortly afterwards by Mary Duncan's " Jesus, tender Shepherd, hear me "—a little gem ; Jane Leeson's " Loving Shepherd of Thy sheep " ; Julia Carney's " Little drops of water," and Jemima Luke's " I think, when I read that sweet story of old."

In 1848 Mrs. Alexander issued her *Hymns for Little Children*, and it was at once recognized as a work of unusual importance. It is unequal in quality, " churchy," and at

[1] F. J. H. Darnton, in *The Cambridge History of English Literature.*

times a little patronizing in tone, but its influence has been
great. It contains forty hymns, mostly grouped round the
Creed, the Commandments and the Lord's Prayer. Keble,
in an introductory note, says that children, and those interested
in children, will feel at once whether it suits them or not.
He himself believed it would win a high place in the estimation
of all who knew how to value true poetry and primitive devotion.
The verdict of the children themselves has been unmistakable,
and millions have lifted their young voices to the strains of
" Once in royal David's city," " There is a green hill far
away," and " Every morning the red sun."

To quote from so well-known a book may seem superfluous,
but the following verses for evening, beautiful in their simplicity, are not to be found in many hymnals :—

> On the dark hill's western side
>   The last purple gleam has died,
> Twilight to one solemn hue
>   Changes all, both green and blue.
> In the fold and in the nest,
>   Birds and lambs are gone to rest,
> Labour's weary task is o'er,
>   Closely shut the cottage door.

> Saviour, ere in sweet repose
>   I my weary eyelids close,
> While my mother through the gloom
>   Singeth from the outer room ;
> While across the curtain white,
>   With a dim uncertain light,
> On the floor the faint stars shine,
>   Let my latest thought be Thine.

> 'Twas a starry night of old,
>   When rejoicing angels told
> The poor shepherds of Thy birth,
>   God become a child on earth.
> Soft and quiet is the bed,
>   Where I lay my little head ;
> Thou hadst but a manger bare,
>   Rugged straw for pillow fair.

Saviour, 'twas to win me grace,
Thou didst stoop to that poor place,
Loving with a perfect love,
Child, and man, and God above.
Hear me as alone I lie;
Plead for me with God on high;
All that stained my soul to-day,
Wash it in Thy blood away.

If my slumbers broken be,
Waking let me think of Thee:
Darkness cannot make me fear,
If I feel that Thou art near.
Happy now I turn to sleep;
Thou wilt watch around me keep;
Him no danger e'er can harm,
Who lies cradled on Thine arm.

Keble failed where Mrs. Alexander succeeded. His *Lyra Innocentium* has provided no really effective hymns for children's collections. It is redolent with the plaintive beauty we should expect from the author of *The Christian Year*, but it is beyond a child's reach. The following lines are taken from " The Lullaby " :—

A maiden rocks a babe to sleep,
And times the cradle to her song—
A simple strain, not high nor deep,
But awful thoughts to them belong,

* * * * *

Angels may read such words of power,
And infants feel them : we, the while,
But dimly guess, till in His love
We see the Lord's unclouded smile.

* * * * *

O awful touch of God made man!
We have no lack if Thou art there,
From Thee our infant joys began,
By Thee our wearier age we bear.

The part played by the Charity Schools of London in the development of hymn-singing should not be forgotten. These Schools, which included the Foundling and Lock Hospitals,

were founded largely as a result of the social conscience en-
kindled by the Methodist Revival. Hymn-singing was, from
almost the first, a marked feature in their curricula, and in
course of time annual singing services were held in St. Paul's,
where the sight of the four or five thousand children in their
quaint uniforms and the sound of their young voices
served to impress upon the minds of Church-people the
educational value of hymnody. Haydn attended one such
service, in 1792, and wrote in his diary, " I was more touched
by this innocent and reverent music than by any I ever heard
in my life." Handel, too, was much impressed. Musicians
of repute were glad to be associated with the Hospitals, and
to this circumstance we owe the popular hymn tunes " Morning Hymn " and " Horsley," still in wide use. The hymns
" Lead us, heavenly Father, lead us " and " Praise the Lord,
ye heavens adore Him," and others less known, were also
written for the orphan children.

The Whitsuntide Sunday School festivals which are so
popular in Lancashire and Yorkshire have usually produced
their own hymn sheets, which have contained a good deal of
original matter, Montgomery and Baring-Gould having been
among the contributors. It was for one such festival that
Baring-Gould wrote " Onward, Christian Soldiers " and " Now
the day is over."

Since the publication, in 1824, of a collection of hymns
for use at Rugby, many Public School hymn books have been
compiled. An enlarged Rugby book was issued during
Arnold's Mastership, and among its contents were two
good hymns by the Assistant Master, H. J. Buckoll, for the
beginning and end of term.

The Public School books are naturally suited to youth
rather than childhood : their literary standard is high, and it
is much to be desired that their contents, including the considerable number of hymns specially written for them, should
leaven our ordinary Sunday School hymnals.

It is impossible here to follow further the development of

children's hymnody. There is a great output of unsatisfactory matter, with a little, alike for infants and for youths, that is very good. It is pleasing to see, in our present-day collections, the names of such writers as Palgrave and Kipling and Canton. Here are three verses of Palgrave's " Little Child's Hymn " :—

> Thou that once, on Mother's knee,
> Wast a little one like me,
> When I wake or go to bed,
> Lay Thy hands upon my head ;
> Let me feel Thee very near,
> Jesus Christ, our Saviour dear.

> Once wast Thou in cradle laid,
> Baby bright in manger-shade,
> With the oxen and the cows,
> And the lambs outside the house :
> Now Thou art above the sky ;
> Canst Thou hear a baby cry ?

> Thou art nearer when we pray,
> Since Thou art so far away ;
> Thou my little hymn wilt hear,
> Jesus Christ, our Saviour dear,
> Thou that once, on Mother's knee
> Wast a little one like me.

The snatches of verse in William Canton's " Invisible Playmate " leave us wishing for more. How tender is that picture of " W. V.'s " bedtime, when the little one is nestling in her father's breast, repeating her evening prayer :—

> Dear Father, whom I cannot see,
> Smile down from heaven on little me.

> Let angels through the darkness spread
> Their holy wings about my bed ;

> And keep me safe, because I am
> The heavenly Shepherd's little lamb.

It will be gathered from what has here been written that a great clearance of existing children's collections, and their enrichment with finer hymns than are at the moment in common use, is urgently needed, and there are few tasks to which lovers of little children could more usefully devote themselves. Both words and music should be the best available for the special purpose they are to serve ; the basis should largely be Scriptural ; reality and honesty should be diligently sought after ; only such hymns should be admitted as the child can love and value all through life ; the child's capacity to dream, to soar, to give wings to his imagination should be fully recognized. In Anatole France's *My Friends' Book*, which is said to contain the story of his own childhood, we read how his governess once told him a story containing a large number of words he did not understand, and which he then heard for the first time. But the story—a tragic one—nevertheless appeared to him to be so sad, so beautiful, that it thrilled him to the depths. " The charm that belongs to melancholy was revealed to me," he says, " by thirty lines or so of verse whose literal meaning I should have been totally unable to explain." For, as Anatole France adds, a child finds pleasure in the undefinable. Simplicity, of course, has its appeal ; but doubtless it has often happened that a child, joining with his elders in the singing of Addison's " Spacious Firmament," has soared in young imagination into space and with innocent wonder probed its unfathomable expanses ; or as from the lips of the great congregation the sad words have quivered

> See, from His head, His hands, His feet,
> Sorrow and love flow mingled down,

a Rubens-like picture of the sufferings of Christ has risen before his young mind, and all the chords of his heart have been stirred to tender sympathy.

CHAPTER XV

HYMN TUNES

No less an authority than the Poet Laureate, Dr. Bridges, has expressed the opinion that the hymn tune is more important than the hymn itself. The enormous power of the tune to create a mood is, he thinks, "the one invaluable thing óf magnitude which overrules every other consideration."[1]

Even if we cannot go so far as the Poet Laureate, it will be generally conceded that the hymn tune, a mere miniature of the musicians' art though it may be, is an influential factor in worship. The power of music to educate and control, as well as to express, the emotions has been touched upon in an earlier chapter. If it has the spiritual power which so many claim for it, the leaders of our Church life cannot be indifferent to the musical content of their hymnals.

> Some to church repair
> Not for the doctrine, but the music there.

For good or ill, and whether it pleases the musical purist or perturbs him, the fortunes of a hymn book are largely determined by the "popularity" of its tunes. It is obvious that if a tune is not liked, the hymn itself, however helpful its words may be, is, so to speak, thrown overboard. It is pathetic to see how easily a good hymn drops clean out of use because it has been wedded to an "unpopular" tune. The tune may be a really good one, and yet be passed over because it is ahead of the musical taste of the people. Or it may be so bad that no one cares to sing it. But, whichever way it may be, a hymn that is never sung is, to most of us, as useless as if it had never been written.

[1] *About Hymns*, by Robert Bridges ; Church Music Society's "Occasional Papers."

The story of the development of the hymn tune is as worthy of study, and quite as fascinating, as that of the folk-song or the ballad. The beginnings of the story must be traced back to the worship-song in the Temple at Jerusalem. According to Josephus, no less than forty thousand harps and two hundred thousand silver trumpets formed a part of the musical outfit there. We know that these figures cannot be taken as accurate, but the very mention of them clearly shows that music occupied a prominent place in the Temple services. The Book of Psalms was the hymnal of the Jews, and it seems probable that some of the Psalms were set to song tunes. The heading in our modern Revised Bible to Psalm xxii, for instance, contains these words (see the marginal note) : " To the Chief Musician ; set to ' The Hind of the Morning.' " " The Hind of the Morning " is probably the title of a popular song.[1] The music of such songs, if judged by the modern ear, was no doubt crude and drone-like, a somewhat monotonous recitative.

A tradition survives that the " Tonus Peregrinus "—that is, the Foreign Tone—still in use in our English churches, was one of the Temple melodies. Some say that it was sung by Jesus and His disciples at the Last Supper, just before they went out to the Mount of Olives [2] :

The Church has continually " sanctified " popular tunes. What, then, is more likely than that this happened with pagan survivals ?

Little is known about the music of the early Church. Many of the primitive Christians must have been acquainted with the Temple worship, and we may safely conclude that they brought its music over with them into their meetings. It has been conjectured that Greek and Roman musical influences gradually crept in, probably following upon the adoption of

[1] Dr. Moffat's Translation gives the prefix to Ps. xiv as follows : " From the Choirmaster's Collection of Korahite Songs. To the tune of ' The Lilies.' An ode or love-song." [2] See p. 35.

classical measures by the hymn-writers. Musical instruments
were looked upon with disfavour. The pipe and tabret were
associated in the minds of the Christians with the licentious
revelries and cruel persecutions of Rome.[1]

From Pliny[2] we learn that the singing was sometimes
responsive in character. Basil, writing in 375, says that the
same custom was in vogue in his day. It was customary in
his church for one person to sing certain lines and for the
whole congregation to respond antiphonally : the people
found this method helped them to concentrate their attention
upon what they were singing.[3] Later, as we have seen,[4]
came more detailed organization. Choirs were introduced ;
song-schools were set up ; organs were installed, and official
attempts to control and direct the singing were elaborated ;
with the inevitable result that the congregation became more
and more silenced.

The first great figure in the long roll of Church musicians
is Ambrose, who was Bishop of Milan in the fourth century.
He made a collection of hymn tunes and antiphons, probably
based on the Temple music, on the Greek " modes," and on
popular airs, for use in his church. The Ambrosian music
is marked by the same simple strength as the Ambrosian
hymns. Here is a tune which Bede accepted as by Ambrose.
A copy, dating from the ninth century, is to be seen in the
Bodleian Library :—

The work begun by Ambrose was carried on in the sixth
century by Gregory,[5] whose musical tastes are said to have

[1] Duffield's *Latin Hymns* ; also Burney's *History of Music*.
[2] See p. 37.   [3] Burn's *Life of Niceta*.
[4] See p. 71.   [5] See p. 59.

been more severe than his predecessor's. The type of hymn tune for which these men stood is known as Plain Song. It is a kind of prose music. It has no time measures or bars ; sometimes it allows one note only to a syllable, and sometimes as many as a hundred. There are some people who still regard Plain Song as an ideal vehicle for worship. Curwen tells an amusing story of a clergyman who was so fond of it that he always used it when conversing with his wife ! It survives in a greatly modified form in the Anglican chant, where by the device of a double cadence the music is admirably suited to the parallelisms of Hebrew poetry ; and there is a marked tendency at the present time to reintroduce it into our hymnals.[1]

After the time of Gregory an uneventful period followed. The musical art developed slowly. Several centuries elapsed before any great advance was made. The outstanding fact is that through this important formative period the art developed in association with worship. It was nurtured through its adolescence within the protective walls of the monasteries, until at length it expanded into all the splendours of oratorio and opera, of anthem and of song. The policy of the priesthood, which has been traced in these pages, of precluding the people from their natural share in worship-song, had its inevitable reaction ; and through the medium of the carol, the miracle-play and the minstrelsy of the gleemen, many popular secular melodies were turned to religious use. An example of a carol so used has already been given.[2] " In dulci Jubilo " is another charming one.[3] Among the most celebrated song tunes was " L'homme Armé," which not only hit the popular taste, but was incorporated in the Mass music by Palestrina and other composers [4] ; whilst in England the same use was made of the melody of " Western Wynde."

[1] Several examples can be seen in *The English Hymnal*.
[2] See p. 106.
[3] Now usually set to " Good Christian men, rejoice."
[4] Greig's *Musical Educator*, vol. i ; also Grove's *Dictionary of Music*.

L'HOMME ARMÉ

The Donkey Festival tune " Orientis Partibus " [1] furnishes another interesting example. It, indeed, has sufficient virility to have ensured for itself a place in our present-day hymn books. Here is the air as it now appears [2] :—

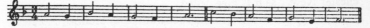

Hus and Luther both pursued the policy of utilizing song tunes. Luther from boyhood had been a passionate devotee of music. At Eisenach the vicar was a lover of poetry and music, and it was his custom to gather the musical young people of his parish around him. Young Luther sang in the church choir and earned for himself the nickname of " The Musician." When he came to compile his German hymn book he drew his melodies from three sources. Firstly, he himself composed some, including the famous " Ein Feste Burg," one of the most powerful hymn tunes ever written. Secondly, he by no 'means shared the Protestant prejudice against the old Latin tunes. It was the Romish words, " most vile and idolatrous " as he described them, that aroused his ire. The tunes he carried over into his book. " We have undressed these idolatrous, lifeless, crazy words," he

---

[1] See p. 99.
[2] *The English Hymnal*, No. 129. The tune is sometimes entitled *St. Martin*.

said, " stripping off the noble music and putting it upon the living and holy word of God." And thirdly, he commandeered a number of chorales, which are almost certainly, in their origin, nothing more or less than popular German folk-melodies. The chorale known as " Luther's Hymn " is not proved to be his workmanship, but he is believed to have noted it down from a wayfaring singer. " Innsbruck " was brought to his notice by a friend. It is one of a large class of farewell-songs which were sung to speed parting apprentices as they set out on their " Wander-year," and it emanates from the charming Tyrolese city after which it is named. Hassler's " Passion Chorale " was a love-song, but of such a timbre as to be exquisitely suited to the pathetic hymn of the Passion " O Sacred head, surrounded," to which it is now generally set. The fine chorale " Nun Danket " did not appear until the following century, simultaneously with and from the same source as " Cruger," to be followed a little later by " Winchester New," as it is now called.

Germany continued for many generations to produce chorales in great quantities—" a perfect sea of song." Their effect upon the populace, when first allied to the new hymns, was, we are told, as great as that created later in France by the " Marseillaise " or in England by " Lillibullero," which, with its strong martial air by Purcell, contributed not a little to the Revolution of 1688. Moreover, they have exerted their influence on musical art. Many of the great German musicians have delighted to embellish them with intricate and delicately wrought harmonies, and have incorporated them into their larger musical creations.[1]

To Bach their rugged grandeur made a special appeal. He is said to have collected two hundred and fifty of them for the enjoyment of his home circle.

It was a favourite diversion among German organists to play with them, improvising preludes, interludes, variations

[1] J. T. Lightwood's delightful volume *Hymn Tunes and their Story* should be consulted here, and indeed throughout this chapter.

and embellishments to suit their fancy. At this game Bach was a master-hand.[1] Hassler's Chorale he harmonized many times over, and introduced with dramatic effect into his Passion Music. Here is " Nun Danket " after it had passed through his hands. It will be seen that the tune, thus magnificently complicated, is no longer suitable for congregational use, but sung by trained voices it is indeed a thing of beauty :—

It will be remembered that an attempt was made, by both Coverdale and Wedderburn, to introduce the German chorales into this country,[2] but, owing to the conservative influence of Calvin, they failed at the time to secure a foothold. Nevertheless, the best of the Psalm tunes which reached us from

[1] Poole's *Life of Bach*, " Great Musicians " series.   [2] See p. 141 ff.

Geneva through Calvin's English and Scotch followers are, in their simplicity and rugged strength, equal to the best of the chorales. Several were collected, at Calvin's request, by a little group of French musicians, of whom Bourgeois was the chief, and they were sung in Protestant homes before being introduced to the churches,[1] and they must have ministered to the devotional life of many of our brave fellow-countrymen who had found in Geneva a refuge from tyranny before they were heard here. The first English congregation to hear them was that of St. Antholin's, London, in September, 1559, and soon thousands of people gathered together to sing them in St. Paul's Churchyard, and in course of time one provincial town after another followed the example of the capital.

Among the tunes included in *The Anglo-Genevan Psalter* which the refugees brought home with them was " The Old Hundredth," which they had heard the Huguenots singing to Psalm cxxxiv. Probably no tune is so universally sung and loved in this country. It is an imperishable devotional treasure.[2]

As successive Psalters appeared, the supply of Psalm tunes grew. " St. Flavian," once known as " the Old 132nd " (because it was first set to the Psalm of that number), appeared in an English Psalter in 1562. " St. Michael " was in the same collection. Este's Psalter of 1592 contained " Winchester Old," and from the early years of the following century we get " Dundee " and " London New." " York " was another early tune. Milton's father harmonized it, and it enjoyed a long run of popularity, " half the nurses of England," according to Hawkins, using it as a lullaby. Here it is :—

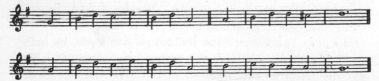

An examination of these tunes will reveal their distinctive character. They are strong and dignified ; there is no

---

[1] Hawkins's *History of Music*.   [2] See p. 146

ornamentation or show ; all is quiet and orderly. A flower, however, is not the less beautiful for being simple. All great art is simple.

In the sixteenth century a supplementary stream of song, independent of Calvinistic influences and native in its source, enriched our English tune books. The brilliant galaxy of musicians who arose in the time of Queen Elizabeth not only provided settings for the Church services, and anthem music of unsurpassed beauty, but also a few—would they had been more !—fine tunes for the metrical Psalms. Among them were such masters as Tallis and Byrd, Merbecke and Farrant, and Shakespeare's friend Thomas Morley. Some of these composers, before the Reformation in this country, had been Roman Catholics ; but they seem to have been artists first and sectaries afterwards, for (says Hawkins) " they fell in with that establishment which banished superstition and error from the Church, and became good and sincere Protestants." Byrd, perhaps now considered the ablest of them, has left on record a series of reasons why people should learn to sing :—

> The experience of singing is delightfull to nature and good to preserve the health of man. It doth strengthen all parts of the brest, and doth open the pipes. The better the voyce is, the meeter is it to honour and serve God therewith ; and the voyce of man is chiefly to be imployed to that ende.[1]

Tallis, who, quite as fittingly as Gibbons, may be described as the English Palestrina, still speaks with reverence to this generation through his Prayer Book " Responses," and through those two fine hymn tunes, " Tallis's Canon " and " Tallis's Ordinal." The former (now wedded to Ken's evening hymn " Glory to Thee, my God, this night ") is distinguished by a curious device musically known as a canon : the air is taken up by the tenor on the fifth note and follows the soprano right through.

[1] Hush's *Old Religious Ballads and Carols.*

TALLIS' CANON

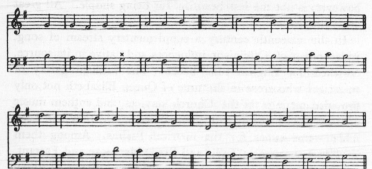

A hymn tune by Farrant, and bearing his name, which is still in wide use, has been adapted from one of his anthems.

The tunes contributed by Orlando Gibbons to Wither's *Hymns and Songs of the Church*[1] are of great beauty. Gibbons belongs in spirit to the great Tudor school of composers. His " Angels' Song " was first set to the " Gloria in Excelsis," Gibbons facetiously saying, " We ought to join with them in this song and sing it often, to praise God, and quicken faith and charity in ourselves." In Wither's book the air is repeated in several arrangements, always in two parts. This is the setting for the paraphrase of Luke ii. 13-14 :—

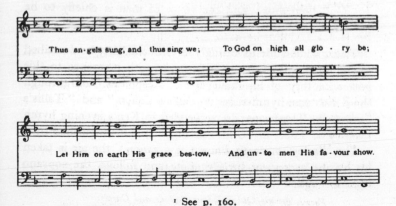

Thus an-gels sung, and thus sing we; To God on high all glo-ry be;

Let Him on earth His grace bes-tow, And un-to men His fa-vour show.

[1] See p. 160.

The contributions of this great school of musicians to the psalmody of their day, though very delightful, were but scanty, and when the early enthusiasm for Psalm-singing had exhausted itself, the churches settled down to a deadening somnolence, which reflected itself in the irreverence of the singing. The revival which Watts led had to some extent been anticipated, so far as the music was involved, by Croft, who, shortly before the appearance of Watts's first volume of hymns, made three additions to the scanty stock of hymn tunes—" St. Anne," " Hanover," and " St. Matthew." It is said that Croft found the first line of " St. Anne," and added the other three. What a pity more such finds cannot be made ! In its simplicity, dignity and strength, " St. Anne " is a perfect model of what a congregational hymn tune should be, and it has provided an altogether worthy setting to our noblest paraphrase " Our God, our help in ages past." The tune " Hanover " broke new ground, and pointed the way to the lighter order of tunes that subsequently came in with a rush. The " Easter Hymn," which appeared almost simultaneously with Croft's three, carried the new development a stage further.

The new departure provoked a good deal of criticism, especially when, as time went on, musical instruments were introduced into the churches. Mason, who was precentor of York Minster, regretted that the violin " presumed to mingle its heterogeneous tones with those of the organ " : for is not a violin, he asks, " naturally calculated to produce merriment and festivity ? " Croft's tunes he considered undignified, with their " frittering of one syllable into almost half a century of semiquavers." [1] But, in spite of protests, the florid tunes typified by the " Easter Hymn " and later by " Helmsley " have so far refused to be turned out of the sanctuary.

The Wesleys were on the side of restraint. Charles wrote his hymns in a great variety of metres, and new tunes were urgently called for. Their first tune book, the famous

[1] *Essays on English Church Music,* by Wm. Mason, 1795.

" Foundery " collection, contained fourteen of German
origin, two of the Croft tunes already noticed, and a few
entirely new ones. Among the German chorales was " Winchester New," one of several which John had learned from
the Moravian Brethren, whose singing had so profoundly
impressed him.[1]   The " Easter " tune also found a place in
the book, set to Charles's festival hymn " Christ the Lord is
risen to-day." The Wesleys secured as contributors to their
successive tune books Handel and his satellites Lampe and
Madan, the latter of whom first gave publicity to the fine
tune " Moscow." John Wesley was not above admitting
a good song tune into his hymn books. The extent to which
this has since been done may surprise some who have
never taken the trouble to examine present-day collections.
Mendelssohn's adaptation to which we sing " Hark ! the
herald angels sing " is a song in honour of Gutenberg the
printer ; the tune of " When Mothers of Salem " is the
German drinking-song " Crambambuli " ; " There is a
happy land " is said to be an Indian melody ; " Stella " is a
love-song; " Innocents " was once set to a North Country
song to the sun, beginning " Who am I with smiling face ? "
" Rule, Britannia " has even found its way into a hymn book,
and there are snatches of the " Marseillaise " in Sankey's
collection.[2] Similar examples could be multiplied. There
is, indeed, a pronounced tendency at the present time to draw
on the treasures of old English folk-melodies for hymnic
purposes. Whether the tendency will become permanent,
whether it will prove possible or desirable to wrest a whole
literature of sound from the purpose for which it was created
and use it to express a different set of emotional ideas, time
alone will show.

After the death of the Wesleys the demand for hymn tunes
grew apace, and particularly for those of a light and popular
order. And so we come to what are generally known as the
" Old Methodist Tunes," which enjoyed so long a run of

[1] See p. 215.   [2] See the hymn entitled " At the Cross."

popularity in Methodist circles, and have produced as a by-product a whole host of stories, apocryphal and otherwise. Their characteristic device, by which the closing words are repeated over and over again, is a very old one, and is to be found many times in the poetry of the Old Testament.[1] The great masters of music, too, are fond of introducing and re-introducing the " motif," which gains in impressiveness as the composition proceeds. It is the same law that makes the little child keep saying " Do it again, do it again." Dr. Frere quotes a verse which was subjected, somewhat violently, to this treatment :—

> And ever in this calm abode
> May Thy pure Spirit be—rit be,
> And guide us in the narrow road
> That terminates—minates in Thee ![2]

It sounds dangerously like Gilbert and Sullivan ! But, in spite of an occasional *faux pas*, the " repeat " tunes proved of real value. " Diadem " and " Nativity," " Bethlehem's Plain " and " Justification " may not satisfy the musical savant, but they undoubtedly touched the heart of the multitude. John Wesley almost certainly would not have liked them. He was not a skilled musician, like Luther, but his rules for Methodist singers nevertheless are worth summarizing :—

1. Learn the tunes.
2. Sing them as printed.
3. Sing all. " If it is a Cross to you, take it up and you will find a Blessing."
4. Sing lustily and with a good courage.
5. Sing modestly. Do not bawl.
6. Sing in time. Do not run before or stay behind.
7. Above all, sing spiritually. Have an eye to God in every word you sing. Aim at pleasing Him more

---

[1] See, for instance, Psalm xlix and Isaiah ix. 8 to x. 4.
[2] Historical Introduction to *Hymns Ancient and Modern*.

than yourself, or any other Creature. In order to
do this, attend strictly to the sense of what you
sing, and see that your *heart* is not carried away
with the sound, but offered to God continually.

It was not unusual, in the early days of organized Methodism,
for a " scratch " string band to lead the singing. Often, in
a village chapel, the little group of amateur musicians would
sit together in the gallery, sometimes, with refreshing verve
and abandon, playing in their shirtsleeves, led by the clarionet
and the bassoon ! It is easy to smile at these simple proceedings, but much happy human fellowship must have been
experienced, and doubtless, though artistry may sometimes
have been wanting, the players' hearts were lifted up with
thankful joy as

> Diminished chords that quiver with desire,
> And major chords that glow with perfect peace

brought release to their worshipping hearts.

It is surprising to learn, from so high an authority as J. T.
Lightwood, that of the many hundreds of tunes composed
during the eighteenth century—the century of Watts and
Wesley—only about forty are now in common use. Those
forty, however, are among the gems of congregational music.
Besides those already noted, they include " Wareham " and
" Stockport," " Abridge," " Miles Lane," " Warrington,"
" Rockingham," and " Praise." Lightwood considers " Ware-
ham " to be one of the best congregational tunes ever written.
The same may surely be said of " Warrington."

To attempt (within the limits here imposed) to enumerate
those who, since that time, have enriched our psalmody would
necessitate the marshalling of a long catalogue of names.
Conspicuous among them are such well-known musicians as
Gauntlett, Steggall, Monk, Dykes, S. S. Wesley, Barnby,
Goss, Stainer, Hopkins, and Sullivan. The work of these and
kindred men forms the general groundwork of our modern

tune books. Alongside it stand some precious legacies bequeathed to us by the Latin Church ; a solid body of the old Genevan Psalm tunes and of the equally impressive German chorales ; a few noble Welsh tunes, such as " Hyfrydol " and " Aberystwyth " ; and the best of the lighter and more florid tunes of the eighteenth century. It is the fashion nowadays to speak contemptuously of the Victorians, and to assume that they created next to nothing worth preserving. But there was some grain among the chaff. The weakness of the modern school is generally agreed to consist in a certain relaxing of reverent restraint. Sullivan, for instance, has quite fairly been criticized as being " too much at ease in Zion." [1] Sir H. Walford Davies—a musician of unerring good taste—speaks of the " superabundant melodiousness " of much of our modern religious music. The chief offences, he says, are of the " pretty " order.[2] There is a falling off in dignity and reserve ; the element of massiveness has gone ; the Norman architecture has given place to the Flamboyant. Happily with the twentieth century there are signs of a return to simplicity and restrained reverence.

In bringing to a close this brief story of the development of the hymn tune, some few general considerations may perhaps with advantage be submitted for consideration. The issues are important, and it is encouraging to know that they are receiving careful thought on the part of the leaders of our Churches.[3]

It should always be remembered that we are dealing with a special type of music, which has to be used for a distinct and restricted purpose, and that consequently the judgment we bring to bear on music in general must be modified to suit the needs of the case. We are not here concerned with the

[1] *Music as an Element in Worship*, by Sir Henry Hadow.
[2] *Music and Christian Worship*, by Sir H. Walford Davies ; Church Music Society.
[3] The Archbishops' Committee's Report on " Music in Worship," etc.

listener to a song, or anthem, or oratorio, but with a congregation's self-expression in a common act of worship ; and congregations, as a rule, contain but a small proportion of people with trained voices or a knowledge of musical rules. The tunes should therefore be of a simple order. Unison singing meets the need better than harmonized singing, not only because it is easier, but because it " enhances the feeling of fellowship in common worship."[1] The innate-conservatism of the average congregation which makes them want to keep singing the old familiar tunes is a pitfall. That the familiar strain of a dearly loved piece of music can enhance the value of a hymn none can doubt, but experience shows that it is easy to go on singing the same tune for years until the act becomes one merely of physical pleasure, and worship is reduced to the gramophone level. If our forefathers had never deviated into the realm of novelty we should still be singing the drone-like chants which Augustine brought to Canterbury thirteen hundred years ago, and nothing else. Each age needs to express its life in its own way and not always in the way that satisfied its ancestors : and if this need is not met, worship becomes unreal.

The final issue, overshadowing all others, is a moral one. It may be urged that there is no fissure between art and morals, and that an inartistic creation is necessarily immoral. Let it be freely admitted that, for our own souls' welfare, we should do all that we can to raise the level of our understanding and appreciation of the artistically beautiful. In the meantime few would suggest silencing the congregation until all can sing with artistic perfection, for to do so would be to fasten upon the worshippers a burden too grievous to be borne. We ought to demand from the musician a type of music that will evoke what is noblest and purest in the spirit of the worshipper ; and it is profoundly regretful that we have not done so, but have sometimes been content with the veriest rubbish. Meantime

---

[1] The quotation is from G. T. Fleming's *The Music of the Congregation,* as are some of the thoughts in this paragraph.

one test is clear. Though the tune be imperfect and the voice artless, our singing must be sincere. For no other song, however perfect the notes, will reach Heaven.

> Childlike though the voices be,
> And untunable the parts,
> Thou wilt own the minstrelsy
> If it flow from childlike hearts.

CHAPTER XVI

CONCLUSION

MUCH thought has been given during recent years to the alleged failure of the Churches. It is said that the habit of attending places of worship is dying out among large sections of the people, and that institutional religion, as we know it, has had its day. Christian people are charged with a lack of courage in applying the principles which they profess to the practical affairs of everyday life. Our church services are frowned upon as unreal and insincere, a mere mouthing of ancient shibboleths and conventional phrases ; and our creeds, our sermons and our hymns are almost regarded with indifference or contempt.[1]

Now it must be admitted that so far as current hymnody is concerned there is justification for such criticism. Some of the hymns sung in our churches do not ring true. Read almost any standard collection right through from cover to cover : an honest analysis will discover an admixture of unhealthy sentiment and downright unreality. One of the most urgent needs in the religious life of our nation to-day is a thorough overhauling of our hymnals and the sacrifice of those hymns and hymn tunes that do not minister to true worship and to real spiritual experiences and needs.

But there is another aspect of the situation which demands our thought. It may be that the defection is not so much in the editors of our hymnals as in ourselves. We have, in this busy age, largely lost the spirit of devotion ; and it is hard for us to soar where the poet-saints have soared. Cowper and Wesley and Faber—to name three writers in whose hymns the

[1] Among much literature, the Archbishops' Report on " The Teaching Office of the Church " and the Reports of the " C.O.P.E.C." Conference deal with this situation.

personal note is conspicuous—lived and moved upon a higher
spiritual level than the average church-goer of to-day.

The difficulty we are considering is accentuated where
personal hymns are concerned. Many such hymns "go
beyond anything which the average human being can truth-
fully say."[1] Some of them enter into an elaborate description
of their author's individual experiences, and we seem to be
watching an operation in self-dissection on a public stage.

> Jesus, I my cross have taken,
> All to leave and follow Thee,
> Destitute, despised, forsaken,
> Thou from hence my all shalt be.
> Perish every fond ambition,
> All I've sought and hoped and known ;
> Yet how rich is my condition !
> God and heaven are still my own.

It may be that so fervent an utterance reflected the sensitive
and saintly spirit of the author of " Abide with me," but it
obviously is not suitable for ordinary congregational singing.

Yet few would suggest the complete elimination of personal
hymns. It would be difficult to find a hymn that exactly
suits everyone's condition ; and if it could be found it would
not necessarily be worth singing. When men unite together
in worship they are seeking after something that transcends
experience. Montgomery held that worship-song should be
expressive of sentiments or dispositions which *we ought to
possess*. It should be shot through, that is to say, with
imagination, and should uplift us to heights where we may
catch a vision of the immediately unattainable, and may

> Send hope before to grasp it,
> Till hope be lost in sight.

A rigid insistence upon the cutting out of all personal hymns
from public worship would mean that such classics as " Jesu,
Lover of my soul " and " Lead, kindly Light " would have

[1] *As Tommy Sees Us*, by A. Herbert Gray, chap. ix.

to go. Such hymns have, however, abundantly proved their
power to kindle our devotion and steady our faith ; and to
dispense with them would mean a needless impoverishment
of our spiritual life.

A further criticism which is often advanced may perhaps
be illustrated by a quotation from *Modern Painters*. When
Ruskin was revelling in the " almost unearthly beauty " of
Bellinzona, he says that he never seemed to tire of hearing the
peasants sing their Madonna hymns, but he had " a woful
feeling " that it never did them any good, for he noticed that
they quarrelled with much louder voices than they sang.[1]
Has our church-going become a mere form, our ritual a mere
pageant, our worship-song a mere emotional pleasure ?
Psychologists tell us that emotion which does not become
active does more harm than good. Church music and congregational singing act as powerful external stimuli upon our
emotions ; but if those emotions do not find an outlet in
behaviour, a weakening of the moral nature inevitably follows.
A recent writer claims that when a person goes to church and
hears the ninetieth Psalm beautifully sung, or the closing
verses of the seventh chapter of Revelation beautifully read, it
increases " the intensity of his awareness both of the shortness
and sadness of human life and of the eternal and overcoming
peace of God." [2] But the crucial question is, does this en-
hanced " awareness " make us better men ? Or does it
evaporate in merely a pleasurable pious feeling ? The value
of religious emotion must be measured in terms of conduct.
History bears abundant testimony to the fact that Christian
hymnody has helped countless men and women to " fight the
good fight " and to live in closer touch with God ; but constant
watchfulness is needed lest our acts of public worship fail to
fulfil themselves in righteousness of life.

One of the most ominous dangers to public worship to-day
is the commercialization of our contemporary hymnody. The

[1] *Modern Painters*, vol. v, Introduction.
[2] *Reality in Worship*, by W. L. Sperry.

publication of hymn books and hymn sheets and their accompanying music has become a highly lucrative business. A " popular " hymn by an eminent living author, and still more a popular tune by an eminent living musician, carries with it a considerable copyright value : and the " cornering " of copyrights consequently proceeds apace. It is scarcely necessary to say that the more reputable publishing houses try to fulfil the responsibilities which this situation imposes upon them with public spirit ; but in other cases there is a dangerous tendency to flood the " market " with " bestsellers." We have indeed travelled a long way from the simplicity of the singing in the Early Church ! The heavy cost involved in the purchase of copyrights and the printing and " marketing " of a hymn book lead to this unfortunate result—that the content of a denomination's worship-song is fixed for a lengthy period, during which the people have no access to any notable new hymns that may be written. The " life " of a modern collection may roughly be estimated at twenty-five years. This means that the hymnody of each branch of the Church is standardized for a whole generation. The Wesleys produced book after book in bewildering succession, and their hymns, as we have seen, constituted a living commentary upon actual passing events and experiences. That note of immediacy is now lacking. Business exigencies have so decreed it. The natural consequence is that sense of remoteness from life's actual experience upon which the critics fasten their attention.

Yet, after all has been said, it is not altogether to be regretted that a new hymn should be compelled to bide its time before coming into common use. The great hymns of the past that are still to be found in our hymnals have survived because of their intrinsic power to help successive generations of men and women. There is an air of " everlastingness " about them. They deal with themes which never grow old ; the majesty and love of God, the mysteries of the Incarnation and redemption, the need of pardon and of grace, the warfare and ultimate triumph of those who follow Christ. There is, no doubt, a tendency to hold on to some of them too long, as if there were some special virtue in stale bread. The wise policy is thankfully to sing them as long as they really minister to life, and then to sing them no longer. By all means let us gratefully accept all the good that our forefathers have bequeathed to us—and that they have bequeathed us rich treasures of devotion these pages have abundantly shown—but God is our God as well as theirs, and the fountain of love and praise that is to refresh our pilgrimage must well up in our own songs of praise, and not merely in echoes across the gulf of time.

> Their joy unto their Lord we bring;
> Their song to us descendeth;
> The Spirit who in them did sing
> To us His music lendeth.
> His song in them, in us, is one;
> We raise it high, we send it on—
> The song that never endeth!

Thus one generation after another is bound together by a golden chain of praise. At every stage of its journey humanity marches to the sound of a solemn music. It began when the foundations of the earth were laid and the morning stars sang together and all the sons of God shouted for joy; and it will grow in volume and in sweetness until at last the voices of the angels shall blend with the voices of every creature which is in heaven, and on the earth, and under the earth, and such as are in the sea, saying, Blessing, and honour, and glory, and power, be unto Him that sitteth upon the throne, and unto the Lamb for ever and ever.

INDEXES

I. GENERAL INDEX

U

II. FIRST LINES AND TITLES OF HYMNS, ETC.